1991

Ancient
Memories

Ancient Memories

RONALD WAY

Edited by Cork Millner

MasterWorks Publishing
Santa Ynez • California

MasterWorks
PUBLISHING

P.O. Box 1858
Santa Ynez, California 93460

First published in 1991 by MasterWorks Publishing

Edited by Cork Millner
Cover by Mathew Caine

Library of Congress Catalog Card Number: 91-62007
Way, Ronald, 1943–
Ancient Memories: Travel Back 2000 Years to Walk with the Son of
Man – Jesus / Ronald Way. –
p. cm.
ISBN 1-880004-05-4

1. Jesus Christ–Biography–Miscellanea.
2. Visions.
I. Title

BT304.96   232
QBI91-1163
MARC

Printed in the United States of America on Acid-Free Paper
First Edition

1 2 3 4 5 6 7 8 9 10

For my wife, Trudy, who believed, and brought me love.
For my children
Marnee, Katrine, Heidi, Lisa, and Nick,
who suffered for their dad's *vision*.

𝒴𝟫𝒲𝟫

The symbol used on the cover is one of the oldest known Hebrew renditions of the name of Jesus. It was found carved on an ancient ossuary, a container holding the remains of the dead.

Except for one instance, all bible quotations at the beginning of each chapter are from *The Living Bible*, Paraphrased, Wheaton, Illinois, Tyndale House Publishers, 1971, Distributed to the general book trade by Doubleday & Company, Inc. One quote was taken from *The Revised Standard Version of The Holy Bible*, New York, Thomas Neson and Sons, 1957

Awakening

Jesus felt genuine love for this man as he looked at him. "You lack only one thing," he told him; "go and sell all you have and give the money to the poor — and you shall have treasure in heaven — and come, follow me."

Then the man's face fell, and he went sadly away, for he was very rich.

Mark 10:21-22

What would you have done on that ancient day in Judea, had you faced the man of Galilee? Standing there, unable to avoid his piercing eyes as he silently stared into your soul, what would you have said or done? Would you have rushed home to sell everything you owned, or would you have tarried too long and lost the opportunity?

What would you do *today*, if, like Paul on the road to Damascus, you were struck by a *blinding light* and then told to give *everything* away.

Tell me: If he touched you, just what would you do?

✳✳✳✳✳✳✳✳✳✳

Bright billowy clouds arched their way across the ocean, as the sun played shafts of light across the sky. As we walked along the beach, the shimmering heat reflected from the water warming our faces and bodies. A pair of dogs barked and snapped at the foaming waves crashing on the sand. Children laughed, danced and sang in the surf. I glanced at my family, and friends who had come to visit for the weekend, as we left our footprints among the others in the moist sand on the edge of forever. I remember thinking how all record of our passing would soon be wiped from existence when once again the earth turned, and the tides cleansed the earth.

The beauty of the southern California day was complete, or so we all thought. Little did I know that the peacefulness of the moment was soon to be shattered, and my life was to take a different path – forever.

Far down the beach, perhaps a half mile away, I saw it, a fast moving, brilliant point of light. It was shapeless, more like the glint of the sun on an automobile windshield – and it was rapidly coming straight toward me. The flash of light screamed down the beach about twenty feet above the sand, growing larger and larger. I was directly in its path. There was no getting away... It hit me with great force. I felt as if I had been knocked off my feet; my mind reeled from the stunning blow, too numb to think. Then the light engulfed me in its radiance.

A figure formed out of the shimmering glow.

A man. Not tall, not handsome. He wore a robe of off-white coarsely woven cloth without decoration. It was his eyes that captured me. Yes, *it was his eyes*. I could feel them penetrate deep into my soul.

There could be no mistake. The figure that had appeared in my path was my Master of old, the one I had sought with such earnestness throughout my life, since my earliest memory. My heart leapt in spellbound, breathless wonder.

Standing before me was Jehoshua ben Joseph – Jesus of Galilee.

I followed his gaze as he slowly looked down. Between us stood a low wooden table made of three hand-hewn planks pegged one to another. There was one object on the table, a dull silver goblet, the hammer marks of the craftsman visible on its sides. I could see a small amount of red wine in the bottom. He motioned with his arm – the long sleeve of his robe flowing in the light – for me to take a seat. He sat down cross-legged, with an easy youthful grace. We were sitting on a hard floor, made of what, I cannot say.

Wordlessly, he reached out and took the goblet, swirled the contents lightly, then stared silently into the wine for a long time. Then, as if finishing a silent prayer, he lifted the chalice, extended it to me, and asked me to share the *Mystery* with him as I had done before, long, long ago.

At that moment, the memories of another time and another place, memories that lay just below the surface of my conscious struggled to burst full born into my being. It was as if some long-past experience was there for me to grasp – if I but knew how. I did not hold the key and thus the images remained just out of my reach, a whisper of a thought in the corner of my mind.

I sipped the wine, and handed back the cup. In a

wonderfully deep, resonant voice that exploded in my mind, he told me that I had the ability to share with all his people a part of him that was locked within *me* – if I was ready to give up much to share. He told me I could give his people the new life he had breathed into the world two-thousand years before.

Then he said, "To do this, you must follow my words – and write the story about your past with me."

In my mind, I screamed, "Yes, yes, my Lord."

There, at a simple wooden table, somewhere between the surf and eternity, totally oblivious to anything beyond what I was experiencing, he told me what I must do *before* I could commit to this task.

"If you will share the memories I promise to awaken within you," he continued, "you must be willing to let go of everything you know – *everything* – and trust in me."

"*Everything?*" I wondered. Was this true? I had to give up my family, my friends, my business, my home, my place in the community, my newly-won advance-ment to Commander in the Navy Reserve attained with twenty years work? And – as stupid as it may seem, this was the first thing that came to my mind – "*even my new Porsche?*" Would I truly have to give up all the things I held close and dear to follow this man who now sat silently before me, watching and waiting for my answer?

My mind flashed to the story in the Gospels of a time long ago, when the rich young man asked Jesus what he must do to follow him. I sensed somewhere deep inside me that my life was about to change dramatically. I didn't know how or when, but I *knew* with nothing further said between us, save the look in his eyes, that in order for me to tell this story as he wished, I would be required to live totally on faith. I would have to give up everything in pursuit of this goal.

At that moment, my senses began to pull me back into my world. It wasn't as if Jesus faded into a mist; no, I felt myself being jolted back and forth from vision to "reality." One instant there was the ocean. *Pow!* The next instant I was sitting at the wooden table. *Pow!* Back to the ocean. *Pow!* The table. I crashed back and forth, frame to frame, like a surrealistic movie. A terrible burning sensation filled my mouth and nose. I felt my body tumbling, thrown about in the water, and realized the tide had come in and I was being buffeted about by the surf.

Aware now of my surroundings, I reached out for something to steady myself – and was totally engulfed by the next incoming wave. Coughing and sputtering from the salt water burning in my nose and throat, I staggered toward dry sand. There, in front of me were my family and friends, sitting on the beach staring at me, as were a number of other on-lookers. They must have thought I was having some kind of spasm or fit. Seeing that I couldn't stand on my own, my friends helped me to where they had spread several towels on the sand. I collapsed in a daze.

I lay there quietly for some time. No one spoke or asked me anything, but I could *feel* their questions bombarding me, and I knew I couldn't handle them as yet.

I learned later that my companions had walked a few paces down the beach before they noticed that I was no longer with them. When they turned they saw me standing with my arms spread in supplication, palms up, eyes closed. They watched as I sank to my knees at the edge of the surf. I had been known to meditate often in the past, so no one disturbed me. They said that they just *felt* like something very special was happening to me. So, they spread their towels on the beach, sat down – and waited. One of my friends confided later that I had had an incredible look of peace on my face, and a radiance about me that made them want to honor my space and protect me.

Now, with salt water still stinging my nose, and the sound of surf pounding unbearably in my ears, I lay on the towel and buried my head in my arms. I wanted to be alone to cry. The experience was too real: I had been so deeply touched by this man of my *vision* that I couldn't speak of it to anyone. Not yet. My wife started to talk about some problem we had with our camping trailer parked at the beach. "The couple parked next to us..." Her voice was terribly loud, and seemed totally out of context, as did the innocent conversation of my friends, the giggles and laughter of children playing on the beach, the teenage sound of rock and roll. All were now permeating my mind with an intense sharp-edged cacophony that set my raw nerves on fire. I felt like I was inside an amplifier at a rock concert.

When I could stand it no longer I got up, still without saying a word to anyone, and hurried back to the trailer.

There, away from the people and noise, I cried for hours, wondering what had happened to me.

I kept going over and over it in my mind. Jesus had touched me in a special way, then asked me to leave everything I had been taught to hold dear to follow him to the end. To the end of what? During the vision I was told that I had one year to end everything – to give up all my worldly belongings. "Are you willing to give up everything?" he had asked. Once I had done that, I was to write the story about *my past with him.* How? I did not know. I assumed the memory would come in his time – not mine.

To carry out my part I had to place my faith totally in him, like Abraham, who was asked to kill his own son, or Noah, who was told to build a boat on dry land. Could I, like Noah and Abraham, let go of everything and lay myself open to ridicule, and possibly shame my family before our friends and neighbors, all for something so nebulous as a vision?

In my heart of hearts I already knew the answer – I had answered Jesus by saying simply, "I will."

I returned home in a few days eager to tell the world of my miraculous vision, only to be greeted with sarcastic, condescending words:

"Really, a vision from God, you say? I'm sure you *thought* it was real."

Then disturbed reactions:

"What do you mean you are going to leave California? What about your businesses? How are you going to live?"

And finally – anger:

"You're a liar! Christ doesn't speak to people like you. You're from Satan!"

Most of my friends and business associates could no longer tolerate my company. They could not understand a person who would give up everything to follow a call he had heard from *within*. Nor could they fathom anyone who would give up their future to chase a mystical vision of some long-lost past. As for becoming *One* with Jesus, and believing that he had asked me to leave everything to follow him – nonsense. In fact it was *blasphemy*.

Strange and angry sessions ensued with my friends, most of whom refused to accept that I merely wanted to follow the path laid out for me, wherever it might lead. I never understood the anger from these well-meaning people. Why did there have to be hate? People would walk across the street to avoid me. My children were mocked at school with chants, or were ostracized by whispering knots of kids who heard bizarre stories from their parents.

I had hurt none of these people. Yet, I appeared to be a threat, a threat to everything they thought was permanent and true. As for me, however, I had no choice. I had given my word. I would either write the story as he led me to find it, and prove (to myself at least) that the vision was true, or if no memories came to me from within, then I'd know that they were in the end right – I was quite mad.

In less than a year most of my lifetime friends were gone. My partners in business chose Christmas Eve to tell me that I was being thrown out of the companies that I had founded. I had been threatened by the president-elect of the Rotary Club, and asked by the board of directors to resign, as I was an embarrassment to the organization. A truck load of manure was dumped in my driveway. I retired from the navy, as I knew

I must. And finally, but not bitterly, my marriage of almost eighteen years ended in divorce. I felt like I was desperately clinging to a rocky shore, torn by winds and tides that I no longer controlled.

I wanted to scream to the heavens, "Okay, God, I don't know what you have in mind, but everything's gone wrong. What I didn't "give up" you took away: my business, my position in the community, my home, my *Porsche*. The only thing left is the vision." Had I been wrong?

Then it began to dawn on me. I had tried to *sell* my interest in my businesses, but he had asked, "Are you willing to *give up everything* if I awaken a memory within you?" Maybe he didn't mean sell my business, or any of those things, he meant exactly what he had said – *give them up*. Well, whether I wanted to or not, it was done. At that moment, I simply let go and trusted the voice that was within me, for everything else was gone. And my world began to slowly change.

The one wonderful thing that happened to me in that year was Trudy. Trudy was present that day of the vision, and never doubted the reality of it one moment. She was my strength during the days of the dismantling of my world. We became constant companions, and in April, 1982, ten months after the vision, we were married.

On the 4th of July, one year after Jesus had appeared before me on the sand, I took my new wife, Trudy, her son and daughter, as well as my own three lovely daughters, and headed east to an unknown future in the northern woods of Michigan, near the little town of Gaylord. I knew that I had to get away from the life I had left behind, so I selected Gaylord, a peaceful place in the north woods that I knew from having attended past business meetings nearby. I thought that this would be a peaceful place to wait for the story to unfold. I knew not how, or when, but I was sure the words that I had been directed to write would come to me there.

We took what was left of the money I had salvaged from my businesses and marriage, added what Trudy had, and started across country with a house trailer, enjoying whatever sights we happened to encounter. A week or so out, we stopped at Bryce Canyon National Park in southwest Utah. I wandered off to meditate alone, as was my custom, and sat by the meandering river. The canyon rimrocks were turning dark purple and crimson, alive with fire in the twilight.

Suddenly – and this is the toughest thing to explain – a feeling overwhelmed me. Something began to bubble inside, reaching for the surface. There was an incredible pressure within me like a feeling of great pride. Buried within this welling up of feeling I could hear his voice again. And I knew what I was to do.

Excited, I went back to Trudy and the kids. "It's going to happen," I said. "I know it." I held my wife tightly. "And Trudy, it's going to happen in the Holy Land."

She looked stunned. "How can we go to the Holy Land?" she asked. "We hardly have the savings to last a year."

She was right, there was so little money, and the children had to go to school. To travel to the Holy Land would be very expensive. Yes, it would have to wait. Maybe I was wrong, perhaps there was some other meaning. It's funny how the "logical mind" can so easily override the inner world of *faith*. And fear, of course, overrides all.

We continued traveling east and found a tiny summer

cabin just outside of Gaylord, Michigan and set up house-keeping. We passed the time pleasantly enough, for it was a beautiful land and we learned to love it. Trudy, the children, and I played in the lake, walked through the woods, and acquainted ourselves with the town's people. Each night we returned to the cabin – and waited.

There we stayed throughout the long summer, and into the early months of fall – without a single word put on paper in fulfillment of the vision that was now almost a year and a half old. Time after time I sat down to write, but nothing came. Slowly the thought of failure insidiously edged its way into the hidden recesses of my mind.

"Are you mad?" a voice screamed at me from deep inside. "You have followed a false prophet. Your friends are right, *there will be no book*." Over and over the hideous voice leapt at me, crying, "Go back. Go back where you belong before it is too late. You fool."

Several times I forced myself to start writing something – *anything* – in hope that my Master would speak to me once again. But it was useless. The book was not going to come from *my* mind. I would just have to wait, and trust, and pray that before our savings were completely depleted, my faith, and in turn my family's faith in me, was not woefully ill-placed. In all too human a fashion, as each day passed, the doubts and fears began to eat away at the fortress of my mind, for the *vision* that was once so clear was now, with the coming of the autumn chill, growing cold.

As the colors painted their way across the wooded land, I chopped trees and split firewood, stacking twenty-two cords of wood upon the porch. Winter was coming, and with it...

what?

Finally, I could wait no longer. It was late September, the children were in school and we had someone to care for them. I decided that if God would not come to me, then Trudy and I would go to Him. We would go to where I had been told it would happen, no matter what it cost. I had to *know*. We would use what money we had and go to where the memories lay – Israel.

✢✢✢✢✢✢✢✢✢

From the moment we arrived in Israel on the last plane of the day, at sunset on Sabbath eve, at Ben Gurion airport, Trudy and I knew that we had returned "home." It began the moment we walked out of the door of the giant 747. The pilot, standing there on the gang-way, wishing everyone goodbye as they left, gently grabbed my arm as we started down the ladder, and said, "Look, I want to show you something." We followed his wistful gaze as he pointed toward the mountains in the east. While the rest of the unnoticing passengers hurriedly passed by, the three of us stood transfixed. A majestic shaft of light split the backdrop of the rain-darkened storm clouds in the west. There, illuminated on top of the mountain, gleaming in its golden glory like a jewel against the rapidly darkening purple evening sky, was *my* city, the city of David.

The Holy City of Jerusalem.

I didn't know why I called it *my* city at the time. All I knew was that I felt as if I were coming home.

Trudy and I were blessed with a sensitive and knowledgeable guide who led us to the spots every tourist visits:

Bethlehem, the Jordan River, Galilee, Nazareth, and also to places that escape most who tour the ancient city: the Arab quarter, and the Hasidic quarter where I celebrated the Sabbath even though I wasn't Jewish. With each new vista, each historical sight we saw, I felt I was filling in missing scenes in my mind, places I had not yet *seen* from within. Ancient memories were growing, but I couldn't quite grasp them as yet. In a strange way, I felt like they were always just beyond the reach of my consciousness. I would see a sight, watch a person move, hear a sound that would *almost* trigger a memory, but then fade again just before I could grab hold and examine it for what it was.

On our last day in Israel, while Trudy waited in our room for the bellman to pick up our bags, I went down to the hotel lobby to pay our bill. I also wanted to check on the final arrangements for our planned Nile river trip to the Aswan Dam in Egypt. With my mind occupied by these details, I sat down at a lobby desk to write a thank you note to our guide.

After writing a bit, I stopped. Oddly, I hadn't been paying any attention to the message as I wrote on the paper. It was like reading a book late at night, and reaching the bottom of the page, only to realize that your mind had been elsewhere. I can't tell you how it felt, it was almost like writing from memory – what memory I knew not – yet I was totally blank as to what words I had just put to the page.

I reread the thoughts I had just written. It appeared I had quoted some passage from the Bible, but I couldn't remember where the verses came from. In fact, I doubted that the Gospels were their source at all. For, although I was not (nor am I now) well versed in the Old Testament – I had read the

New Testament several times over the years, but never the Old Testament, it never interested me – I felt that nothing I had written this day had come from either of these traditional sources. I looked at the paper again. Why would I write phrases like, "and God sayeth," and use such words as, "thee," and "thou" in a thank you note to the guide?

Just then Trudy showed up with the bellman and our bags. I let it pass.

After arriving in Cairo, we made our way south to a point just north of the Aswan Dam where we boarded a boat to float down the timeless Nile. For a week we saw nothing more modern than camels burdened with commerce on the river banks heading north with us. Just before dawn, on the second day on board, I climbed the ladder to the topmost deck, to be alone, and to meditate. It was there that Jesus came to me once again saying, "You have done all that I have asked. Now it is all to begin."

Suddenly, I felt the shock of falling, falling through a tunnel of light. Falling... Then, as the first rays of light danced upon the river Nile, the sights and sounds of the ancient past surrounded me. I landed with a "thud" – that's the only way I can describe it – and I was in another body, another time, and another place altogether. It lasted only ten or fifteen minutes at most, then, exhausted, I felt myself being pulled back again to the present. I took a deep breath. I was totally exhausted, but exhilarated beyond what I can describe. I began to write. The book had begun.

Each day for the next week, I would get up before dawn and find a quiet space on the boat, meditate, feel myself falling, then join a different world and a different time. I wrote what I saw, what I smelled, what I felt, what I thought and what I experienced. I wrote it all. I started by writing in a journal and later switched to my computer to record what was happening every day. In the beginning I could hold onto the vision for only a few minutes, ending totally exhausted.

Several weeks later, after our return to the cabin in Michigan, it continued. I would rise well before dawn, build a roaring fire, then settle into a comfortable chair to meditate, and fall two thousand years. As the days passed into months, I found that I could write for six hours in a day. I simply opened myself to the memory, and wrote as fast as I could, describing what was happening to me. Through this awakening, I wrote the story of an old man who had walked the path with one greater than he called Jehoshua ben Joseph – Jesus of Galilee.

So now, I put this story before you, hoping that you have the ears to hear, and the eyes to see. For it is the story of a wise and devoted man who loved his teacher, Jesus, more than life itself, a man who stored within his soul the memory of things his Lord had said and done during those wondrous years so long ago.

Ronald Way
Santa Barbara, California

My dear loving friend,

J would ask you to sit very quietly now, to still your soul. Before you read these words, J beseech you to open your heart and mind. J need you to see. J need you to hear, J need you to walk on a path with me back in time and space. Jt is a long journey, yet to me, it is only a day.

J need you to open every sense of awareness, longing, and understanding that you have. Jf you are to have ears to hear, then you must immerse yourself in the sights and sounds that were a part of me. You must know my world, you must hear the sounds, you must see the sights as J saw them, you must touch the rough ground, you must know the hope, you must feel the fear and pain of my people. You must truly under-stand them, if you wish to understand me.

You must touch inside of me, you must know me, you must become ONE with me.

The story that follows, J have given to my disciple, Asher ben Ammi. Jt is my gift to you.

ישוע

Chapter 1

*But you shall receive power when the Holy Spirit
has come upon you; and you shall be my witnesses
in Jerusalem and in all Judea and Samar'ia and to
the end of the earth.*

Acts 1:8

My name is Asher ben Ammi, father of John, beloved disciple, whom you all know. This is the story of our Teacher, Jesus, the Messiah.

I first knew of Jesus early in his teaching, at the time of his first trip to Jerusalem during the holy Feast of Tabernacles in the autumn. He had spoken in the Temple to the large groups of people who had come to worship God during the holiday. Many who were there at this time were young priests, such as my son, John, and Jesus caught not a few ears and hearts as he spoke of a new and loving covenant with our God.

The courts of the Temple at festival time were filled with peoples from all over the world who streamed into Jerusalem during these special times. The atmosphere was noisy and boisterous, and the holy grounds teemed with money changers, sellers of birds and goats, teachers and prophets alike. Milling throngs came to offer a sacrifice, or to listen to the teachers, who gathered knots of people around them wherever they were speaking. One such teacher this year was Jesus.

Although I did not happen to see him then, I soon heard from my son, and many others, that there had appeared a Rabbi from the north who taught like no other they had ever heard. When he spoke, it was with the authority (and the sometime acrid tongue) of the prophets. Yet, with but a change of breath, he could mourn the cry of the poor and the lame. He spoke of the Law with a power ungranted by the priests, as if it were *his* Law to give. Within a few days he had attracted the attention of most of those who count, including myself.

John, my son, instantly became a follower of this strange man. Our home was filled each evening with tales of miracles, of healings of both the sick and the lame. The younger priests, such as my son, were clamoring to hear him, and talk with him. The crowds were growing about him each day. The older priests, such as I, were cautious and wary and distrustful of miracle workers; the land was full of them, we had seen our plenty, and needed no more. We discussed this new young Rabbi, and decided that he bore mild attention if he stayed. However, we felt that after the holidays and the crowds stopped coming, he would just fade away into the countryside as did so many before him, no more than a wisp of smoke in the morning haze.

Yet, a haunting thought began to pull at the corner of my mind: what if the things my son said of Jesus proved true? It was then that I knew that I had to seek this new teacher out, for I was over sixty, and had dreamed from the days of my youth that the Anointed One would come, and I would know him before I died. You might think that I'd simply wander out into the court and listen to him at will, but I could not. I could not because of who I was. I was respected, a Pharisee, a member of the ruling body Sanhedrim, and I could not let myself be seen trampling with the masses after some uneducated preacher – a miracle worker – a common tradesman – a Galilean!

I have learned much from our beloved teacher, but in the beginning I was a terrible hypocrite, and stern judge of all who fell below my station. So, when I sought him out, it was in the shadows of the early evening, at a private home where I felt that I would not be known. I had ferreted out the time and place from my son at the noon meal. I then waited until John left that evening to see Jesus, donned my hood, then proceeded toward the gathering where I knew he would be found. I walked freely into the courtyard of the home: the doors were left open for visitors to come and go. I felt no threat. I was too powerful and self-confident for that, but I was nervous, for I did not want to be recognized by anyone who could report me back to the Temple, and thus I came in stealth.

My memory of that fateful evening was seared into my mind. I lowered my head to keep within my own shadow as I made my way through the crowd, trying to get close enough to Jesus to hear what he was saying. But, as I thus quietly approached, he suddenly turned, and through the circle of men standing around him, saw me coming, naked and exposed. He met my eyes, and the impossible happened. My mind stopped functioning – went totally blank. Such a thing had never occured before. I stood transfixed, as his power exploded in my mind.

This happened in an instant; in the meeting of two men's eyes, and in that moment he knew me. He knew me to the very depth of my soul. And I realized truly, he was the special One, the One for whom we had waited. I know not how long I stood there; a year, a second, it matters not, nothing else was important from that moment on – I was his. It was as impossible to explain then as it is now. So in my frustration, I can but write down everything that he said and did, and that I heard. By doing so, perhaps I can explain the mystery to myself first, then should I be so lucky, to those who are to follow.

In the following words, I have tried to tell the stories that he told to us, as they came from his mouth, in his words, and as I have heard with my ears, and seen with my eyes. The remaining is from my own knowledge, and in the words of his disciples as they told their stories to me. I speak as one counted in his one hundred and twenty, and from one who is closer in his secret ways than even the twelve.

This then is my story, the honest tale of an old man who lived long ago, and had the privilege of knowing another, far greater than he, who walked the earth as you and I, yet came like no other before him. A man who gave us the example of his life for us to emulate throughout all the centuries yet to come.

I welcome you to join me in my memories of an ancient time, long ago.

Chapter 2

Behold, a young woman shall conceive and bear a son...

Isaiah 7:14

Our home is situated in what is referred to as the upper part of the city, for Jerusalem is a city that lies in the cool high hills of Judea, built and added to over the centuries, and divided into several parts, separated by protective walls, one more ancient than the other. Since the earliest times, the Temple grounds have occupied and dominated the ridge to the east, surrounded as it is on one side by the Kidron Valley and on the other by the Tyropoean. The Temple grounds pervade the high point of the ridge, where it broods over the rock where Abraham once prepared to sacrifice his son in his own test of faith.

During the time of the Maccabees the walls were extended to enclose several other hills and valleys. And, finally in my own time, Herod completed our division by building his palace close to our home, further separating the large and wealthy from the "lower city," housing the tradesmen and the poor.

Our home sits directly upon the street that runs south from the palace, and although it is not on the scale of a Roman country villa, it is yet not small. The home is built of local stone from the nearby quarries, and is cool even during the warmest months. The walls themselves enclose the living quarters for my family and the families of my servants; a beautiful garden from which our vegetables, flowers and greens come; the warehouse; and the stables where my horses are kept. It is most comfortable indeed, for an old man like myself.

It is here, in the early dawn, sitting at my writing table on the roof above the family quarters, high above the resting city spread out before me to the east, that I begin my story, the story of my Lord, Jesus, as I know it. I have tried to piece together what I have learned from my Lord himself, his dear mother, his disciples, his relatives and friends. So, together, let us begin.

To start the journey, I wish to take you back before his birth. Herod is the undisputed king, and rules from Idumea in the south, to Galilee in the north, with no authority save Rome, to tell him right from wrong. The little town of Nazareth lies then, well within his grasp, as do a dozen or so other villages, no different than it, in the rich land of Galilee.

Nazareth is situated right in the middle of Galilee, and is separated from Judea by Samaria, which is also ruled by Herod. It lies in the wooded hills in the far north of our land. Here, from its airy loft, it gazes down upon the fertile valleys below, valleys that have contributed their share of manpower and pain in Herod's rise to power and wealth. But, Herod is not in the minds of the people this day, for as I begin this story of my Master's birth, it is summer, the busiest time of the year, and work is everywhere to be done.

It had been a wonderful, lovely, warm day in this hilltop village. The young girl had gone about her chores with an easy grace, and a light, lithesome step that could not help but reveal the happiness and contentment she felt inside. She was betrothed to a gentle man, a man with a trade, a man she could love and care for, and who would provide for the children that were sure to come. Yes, this girl was happy in her heart as she lay her head down in the cool of the evening, this special night that was to change the world. This special early summer evening, that was to tell her of his coming.

Slowly, the village sounds faded into the quiet of the night, as the nearly full moon crept over the eastern horizon. The fertile valley stretched out for a million miles below the village, and the cool moist air rose to send the breeze into the silver evening light. Softly, easily, she drifted into a dreamless sleep.

Suddenly, her breath quickened, then seemed to stop altogether, as her eyes fluttered open to look about the empty room. The room was strangely light. She looked about to see that she was alone in the shimmering, moonlit room. Joseph was not with her, but she felt no fear. A strange calmness and lightness came over her, and a feeling of peace descended upon her. As she sat transfixed in quiet wonder, she knew that she was somehow different, that this night was different from any other night she had known.

Then it came. It came in such a gentling way that there was no fear, only a feeling that her heart was suddenly growing, and filling with love. It felt as if it was going to overflow in the overpowering grace that was all about her now, and that could never be explained in human words.

"Mary," came the deep soothing voice from somewhere within her mind. "Mary, my handmaiden, I have come." Mary was absolutely still, then she sat up in bed, every nerve feeling more alive than she had ever known. Her eyes drifted upward as the beautiful presence took her within, and she began to see and hear of a time that was yet to come, a time that was yet to be. The scenes were within her, and of her, and love and lightness filled her to overflowing. It was impossible for her to tell when the voice was with her, and when the visions were just unfolding without the need to communicate, but flow they did, and she watched, and the future was in her.

She saw the birth that was to be, and it was beautiful and sweet. She saw the son who was to come, she saw him teaching, and she saw him as one with the One whose name she could not speak. Then she was told of John, the baptist to be. But it wasn't in words she heard. She saw it as now. She saw him in the wilderness, half crazy, destined to cry his life away for the repentance of his people. She saw him tell them of the One to come.

All these things she saw, and when the visions ended, she heard again the rapturous voice within her saying: "Go to Elizabeth. Tell her of her son, and tell her too, of your son, the one who will light the way. Go and tell her everything, everything that you have seen, that she may know, and bear witness to you that all of this is to come."

Then, as softly as it had come, the presence was gone. Mary sat in the silence of the empty room, her senses awake in every cell of her being. She still felt as light as a feather, and in some strange and wonderful way, she knew that she had been changed by what had happened to her that special night. She knew that no matter what life brought her in the future, she would never again be quite the same.

Quietly, almost afraid to break the spell, she lay back upon the bed to stare at the ceiling, and wonder in those quiet dark hours of the morning, how she could be the one chosen to bear the child, the child who would show the world a new way.

Silently, sometime before dawn, this gentle child drifted into sleep, thinking, "I must watch him when he comes. I must watch my child for a sign."

As Mary slept that night, another event was taking place far to the east, at Sippar in Babylonia. There, on the rooftop observatory the royal astrologers saw something unusual taking place in the early morning sky that filled them with exceeding wonder, excitement, and awe. For nearly two hours they watched as Jupiter and Saturn met in brilliant conjunction (as if a single start) in Pisces. The importance of the event was breathtaking in its magnitude, for it meant the end of an age, and the beginning of a new age in its place. Pisces was the sign of the land to the west, of Israel, and to these men of learning, it meant the coming of the one for whom the Jews had been waiting since the time of David. The King had been conceived, the Messiah was to be born.

That same night, plans were drawn to begin a journey to reach the land to the west nine months from that day; and in their records they wrote, "We have seen his star appear in the first rays of dawn. To its source we shall journey. He has come!"

Mary raised herself early the morning after the dream and did what the Lord had commanded of her. She told her mother what had happened, told her of the child, and said that she had been commanded to go to Elizabeth. Mary was happy and excited. She couldn't wait for Joseph to return, she wanted him to know of the impending birth. She wanted everyone to know.

But, instead of the happiness she thought she would find in sharing with her mother, a cloud came over the older woman's face. As Mary told the wonderful news, that she, a lowly young woman in this insignificant mountain village, was to bear the child that all of Israel prayed for, that she was to give birth to the savior of their country, the Anointed One, the Messiah, her mother stood still as a statue, her face turning an ashen gray.

As Mary finished her story, her mother's hands raised to cover her face, and she gave one long anguished wail. What was wrong? Mary was ecstatic. She wanted to tell everyone, she wanted to tell the world: "I'm with child! I am going to give you, oh Israel, a child – the child you have been waiting for." But, her mother's hands remained over her face. The wailing grew, as her mother sank to her knees and began to rock back and forth as if Mary had announced her own death – not life. Mary felt an uncontrollable chill. This was not the greeting that she had expected to receive. What had she said that was so wrong? What was going awry?

Slowly she backed away from the woman bending low to the floor before her, then numbly turned and left the house. Her mind was seized by panic. She began to run – and run – and run. She didn't know where she was going. Tears streamed down her face as she raced through the narrow streets, past the mud brick and stone houses that crowded in on either side. She was out of control! Totally out of her mind with rage, fear and dread.

Down she went, down the path that led to the woods. She wanted to be alone. What had gone so terribly wrong? Where was Joseph? Where was he when she needed him? Surely, the Lord would make it right for him. If her own mother did not understand, though, would Joseph? He couldn't deny her could he? He couldn't deny their first child could he? "Could he?" her mind screamed!

There, in the sun, among the trees, she fell to her knees, and prayed, prayed as if her young heart would break.

This was only the first disappointment for Mary. For, instead of understanding and joy in the miracle, she was soon to be met with anger, rejection and disbelief from her closest friends, and loved ones too.

It is said that God has many ways to test a soul, to make one strong, and rejection is the loneliest way of all. And so the handmaiden of God, so young, now dry-eyed and drained, finally stood up, squared her shoulders, took a deep breath, and headed out along the trail back to the village – back to Joseph's home – ready to face her fate alone.

After Mary ran from the house, Mary's mother gathered herself up and went straight away to Joseph's home to await his return. Joseph returned home to find this old woman on her knees before him, sobbing and wailing, pleading her case before him. She begged him not to expose Mary, begged him to keep her in spite of her condition. He didn't know quite how to react when she first delivered the news, shrieking and wailing and pleading, all the while on her knees before him, clinging to his cloak.

As he heard the horrible news, Joseph pulled away from the woman and slumped back against the wall, then slowly sunk to the floor with his face buried in his hands as he tried to think. "Maybe it was someone else," his mind cried. "No, who am I fooling? She really loves me," his mind countered, "this marriage wasn't just arranged by her family – *she* wanted it. No. Another young woman maybe, but not Mary. She is more jealous of the Law than any other of her age whom I know. You fool, Joseph, you fool!" he said to himself over, and over again.

A thousand things crowded the mind of this simple carpenter, who had never been confronted with more than the span of a beam, or the width of a door. His status in the village, though meager, was very important to him. It was all he had.

Although the conception of a child during an engagement was not strictly forbidden, it was certainly frowned upon in this small conservative village, and he would be scoffed at, at the very least, for his lack of control. And, of course, the innuendoes, the whispers (never spoken to his face to be sure), would always be there. "Is he *positive* the child is his?" Or, "I heard that Joseph..." "I saw Mary talking to..." He would be forced to defend his honor over and over against the unseen enemy of the tongue, for which there is no defense, save the truth, which they care little to hear.

He was a good man to be sure, an honest man, and he tried his best to keep the Law, which was clear on simple things. But this, this was totally beyond him. How should he react? What was expected of him? What did the Law say? Why did she have to get pregnant? Why? This marriage was late, and perhaps he was too old anyway, he thought, trying to extricate himself from the problem that had been forced upon him.

Then, Joseph made up his mind. He was not an unkind man, so he would simply visit the Rabbi, and see if he could quietly dissolve the marriage contract.

When he talked to the Rabbi, Joseph told him nothing of Mary's condition. He carefully worded his probing of the Law, going over *every* aspect of the Law with regard to marriage so as not to raise any hint that he was just interested in pregnancy. The Law was clear. He could obtain a secret Bill of Divorce, a "git", witnessed privately, and never filed. It was the only way. No one would know, they would just think that he had tired of her, and Mary would be free to marry again immediately. So this was his solution, really his decree, for it needed no approval from anyone, least of all the woman. How could he be faulted? He had done the decent thing hadn't he? He hadn't made a public display of her. And, best of all, it followed every jot of the Law, right down to the smallest detail. He returned home to await Mary.

Walking through the entry of Joseph's home, exhausted, and empty of any more emotion, Mary looked up at her betrothed standing with his hands placed squarely on his hips, his face dark with rage. Her mother, she noted, was already there ahead of her, and was now hiding pitifully in the corner of the room, her cloak drawn up around her small huddled frame. Spitting out the words, Joseph told her he was dissolving the marriage contract.

If Mary could have felt anything, it would have been disgust, for she had done nothing wrong. She had done nothing to deserve the trial she was about to be put through. But, these were not her thoughts, for she was dazed beyond feeling at that moment, and could only vaguely understand what was going on around her; to her, this felt like some horrible dream.

So it came to pass, that what Mary thought would be the happiest day of her life, turned into a day of numbness that was beyond understanding.

No matter how he tried to justify the decision, all was not well with Joseph either, for he was ashamed, and sick inside. He knew the truth, and it troubled him greatly. There was no dealing with him that day. He threw the leg of a chair that he had badly cut clear across the workshop, cursing in a way that was most untypical of this gentle man. It narrowly missed one of the two apprentices working with him, who had already had two run-ins with him earlier in the afternoon.

They didn't say a word; just bowed their heads, avoiding his furious looks, and worked with renewed vigor, in hopes of getting through the day without further mishap. The Rabbi came later with words of counsel, and a set of harmless, but deviously designed questions, all aimed at finding out what terrible secret Joseph had refused to divulge. But Joseph was in no mood to field his questions, and threw the old man out, most unceremoniously, which added further to the burning fire of shame and guilt that was now welling up within him.

He ate nothing that evening. Sick and confused, Joseph strode out the door, slamming it so hard it would wobble for months before he would fix it again. As Mary had run through the streets earlier that morning, so Joseph walked aimlessly, not knowing where he was going, not caring. Out of the town he walked, as in the sleep of death, neither looking right nor left, nor answering calls of greetings from those he knew along the way.

A good hour had passed before he sat down, exhausted and empty, on a mountainside in the woods, not knowing that it was exactly here that his betrothed had cried herself into emptiness on that same bright and shiny morning – the morning of her glory – and shame.

Joseph unconsciously drew his cloak about him as the cool moist breeze drifted up from the valley below. Shuddering, he pulled his legs up close and huddled himself into a ball. There, miserable and alone, he sunk into a sleep, a sleep such as he would never know again – and it was then that he heard the voice. "Joseph. Joseph, wake yourself."

Slowly, ever so slowly, he raised his head. Evening had drifted into night. The moon had risen full round over the eastern mountains, and the peaceful valley stretched into blackness miles away. Looking around, seeing nothing, hearing only now the soft whispering wind through the pines, he pulled his cloak about him even tighter. Another shiver went up his back, as a prickle of fear entered his awareness. He could not see the source of the strange voice which had spoken to him, but he was sure he had been awakened by someone.

Then it came again... "Joseph, you have done wrong!" Now, his eyes were wide with fear as the voice continued: "The girl you will marry is my handmaiden; blessed is she, I find no blame in her. She carries a child in her womb, a very special child, a child who belongs to the world – a child who belongs to me. Your child, Joseph. Your child to watch over, to teach, to see grow – a child born to die.

"Go this night, find your betrothed, take her unto you, take her this night as your wife, and know that she is good."

Joseph sat still for a moment in the dark, waiting, listening, not knowing if the voice within his being was finished, not daring to move. The soft whispering of the wind in the pines and the cold seeping into his body finally roused him to sit upright again, then pick himself up and stand. His muscles ached from the rock upon which he had lain. His foot tingled with the pain of a thousand needles as his dead and sleeping legs began once again to come back to life.

There was no question of what he must do. He must see Mary. He began to walk back to the village from whence he had flown.

Then something in the wind, or was it the darkness, began to grip his being. It was that voice! Fear filled him; it coursed through his body in uncontrollable waves. His walk became hurried. Then, without warning, terror took complete charge. It took him by the hand as he flew over the ground, the rocks, and past the trees. His wild mind had frozen, locked in terror of the unknown. Nothing could save him from the voice – except Mary. As he ran, his feet found their own way in the darkened streets, his robes went flying behind him, and his mind screamed, "Oh, Mary, Mary, I am so sorry. I am so sorry. Please forgive me, Mary. Take the voice away from me... *please!*"

The sudden crashing sound of a fist striking the wooden door so startled the occupants of the small mud and stone house, that for a moment there was no sound, no movement at all from within. Then the sound of Joseph's hoarse voice pleading at the entry roused Mary's mother from the frozen position that she held, mending clothes by the fluttering, yellow firelight. She shuffled to the door and timidly opened it.

Joseph lunged through the door, closing it rapidly behind him. A dozen eyes from neighboring homes withdrew from their windows, as people began to whisper in their beds at the strange goings on between the betrothed pair. As Joseph raised himself from the floor where he had prostrated himself, Mary's mother stood silently at the door. Her hands trembling as she clutched a veil over her wrinkled face. Mary, sitting on a ledge at the far side of the room, calmly lowered the sewing she was working on by the light of a small oil lamp, and stared at the blank wall in front of her. Drained of any emotion by now, Mary simply stared, refusing to acknowledge Joseph at all. Her face was like that of a statue, carved in exquisite alabaster, flickering now in the dancing flame of the lamp, still buffeted by the sudden rush of night air. She heard, but nothing showed across her unblemished, young face, a face now strangely at peace.

Joseph was pleading now, "Mary, please Mary, forgive me, let us leave this place. Come with me, come to me, please, Mary, please!" Mary raised herself, slowly turned, and walked silently, elegantly, over to Joseph. Her voice was quiet, controlled, and carried a cutting edge, touched in ice, and born of a new knowledge and strength that she had not known before.

"Do you want me in marriage, Joseph? Are you sure you

want me in marriage?"

"Yes, Mary, yes – in marriage. I want you. Please forgive me, I take you just as you are."

"Tell my mother who is the father of my child, Joseph. Tell my mother!" She spit out the words with a vengeance now.

Silence fell like a leaden weight, but lasted only a second, as Joseph cried out, "I am. I am!" and his head bowed, and he cast his eyes to the floor. "I admit it to you, and to your mother. Mary, what do you want from me?" His voice was husky, as he spoke in a lowering, warning tone.

But, Mary was not a coward. She had not finished with him as yet, and continued in the same icy tone that bespoke her new-found strength, "Why are you here, Joseph? Why in the middle of the night? Why now, when this morning you threw me away?"

"I came because I felt I had done an injustice to you, Mary." His control had broken again. He sobbed, " I could not live with myself... that is all."

Mary suddenly turned to face him squarely, with such force, and such a frigid stare, that he felt she had seen everything within him, clear through to his soul. "I heard a voice," he said. "A voice, and it told me you were the handmaiden of God. It said that the fruit of your womb was blessed, that our child is to be special. Oh, Mary, please forgive me. I have wronged you, I know it now. Please forgive me. Come with me this night; stay with me, be my wife."

Mary would wonder later, at the source of the courage she possessed to act as she did that night. Had God spoken through her? Or, was it just that she had nothing left to lose?

What had caused her to act with such authority toward the man she loved more than any other? Yet, with all of this, she was not through with Joseph as yet, not until she had dictated the rest of her demands.

"I will not go with you this night, Joseph. Go. Go to your home alone. Tomorrow you will make arrangements for the wedding. It will occur in ten days. Until that time you will not see me alone. Tomorrow my mother will bring you a list of things that you must do.

"And, Joseph," she added, as he raised himself to leave, "remember this night. God has spoken to you, as he spoke to me. What is to come is holy. If you wish peace, never forget this night, and what has transpired here."

Days, months, and years later, as Joseph worked in his shop, or wandered the dusty road, he would wonder at this night. He would wonder if he had been a fool, if his conscience had gotten the better of him. He would wonder a thousand times whether he had really heard that voice, or had he not? Had he dreamed it, or had he not? It had seemed so real.

Each time the voice of doubt came into him, as it must to every man who has *"seen,"* it was followed by something sweeter, something far sweeter than any nectar of the vine. Each time he felt the pain of doubt and fear, he would shut his eyes, calm himself, and experience the lightness and joy that would flood his being, bringing with it a certainty that he had been witness to a very special happening. And with this experience, also came a certainty that this child of theirs would be special – very special indeed.

Since that night last June, almost nine months had

passed. It had been a very difficult time for Mary. She had told one or two of her closest friends the good news, with an admonition not to tell a soul of the impending birth, but as things went, the news had a way of seeping out, and this only added to the speculation, and added fire to the flames of Joseph's enigmatic trip to, and subsequent stormy visit in return by the Rabbi. And, of course, there was the most unusual late entry into Mary's home that night, that night of Joseph's vision. Even now, nine months later, there were still whispers, but the worst had passed. There were better items of gossip to occupy the towns people, now that the months had worn on, and Mary and Joseph both seemed to be content in this marriage that had started in such agony – and bliss. Most of the uproar only served to strengthen Mary in her resolve, and to deepen her love for this special child soon to come forth from her womb; but the vicious gossip still hurt, and would not soon be forgotten.

During this time Senator Sulpicius Quirinius (later to be known as Governor, Legate to Syria) had come to Syria, to defeat the enemies of Caesar. It was in the days of the Procounsul Saturninus, and he had come at the will of Caesar Augustus. He brought with him at this time a decree: to insure that taxes were fully paid by all the people of our land – to the north, to the south, to the east, and to the west as far as the sea and his army would allow. To accomplish this task, he employed the offices of his Idumean tool, Herod by name, who decreed that each and every person should go into his own city, and present himself, and give count, and pay a tax according to his means.

So Joseph took with him a donkey, and borrowed yet

another, for Mary's term was near. And from the hilltop village of Nazareth they ventured forth, setting their sights south to the ancient city of David – Beth-lehem – a short walk from the Holy City itself.

Slowly, they descended the wooded path from the hills of Nazareth, to the large spreading valley of Esdraelon below. The valley was rich with the coming of grain, now sprouting green in the late winter's "spring." The soil was rich and moist from the rains just past, and smelled wonderful. The newness of the countryside, and the coolness of the air lightened their hearts as they ventured south on this, their first journey together as man and wife. Mary's heart was full of song, as she walked with the pride of youth along the path beside her husband. She resisted Joseph's urgings to ride the donkey he had brought for her; after all, she was young, and took pride in walking beside her new husband. Besides, she thought, the walk was good for her child. Her child, her very special child.

After staying the night at the town of Esdraelon, Mary and Joseph departed early the next morning to join the teeming crowds on the busy road leading north and south. They continued past the city of Scythopolis, to cross the Jordan, and camp the next night at the hot springs, close to the town of Pella.

Joseph had planned to stay the night at the hot springs, as many did, and travel south again early the next day. They arrived late in the afternoon, and set up their small camp before heading for the two sections of the springs – one for the men and another for the women. Just as Mary began to step into the women's pool, however, she felt a strange tingling, a tingling that began to hurt, all over her body. She was so affected by this strange sensation, and even more so by a powerful foreboding, that she withdrew immediately and sent for Joseph, saying that she wanted to be away from this place, that it was not safe for the baby. Joseph had looked forward to this popular stop, and tried to talk Mary out of, what seemed to him, an unnecessary and ridiculous objection. But Mary would hear none of it and pleaded with him to take her this night to the nearby village of Pella, just a few minutes walk from the pools. Although Joseph disagreed, and spoke to her of logic, he too was none too anxious to take any chances with his young bride, and his first child within her womb.

The next day brought warm bright sun. Light fluffy clouds drifted by in the deep blue sky. It was early in the year, and the weather was cool and fine. Refreshed with a good night's rest, Mary and Joseph set off again with renewed energy and in good spirits for the day. Because of the tax being levied upon the people, there were many travelers along the way, and there was much to talk about, many stories to tell, and many interesting people with whom to share. Thus, the trip went rapidly. They followed the Jordan River as it meandered south through beautiful farms and groves of date palms that lined the banks. The expectant mother hardly realized the toll that all the riding and walking was taking on her body, and the child. The fifth day had been the longest, and her body ached when they finally reached Jericho to spend the night with family friends.

They started out early the next morning thinking they could reach Beth-lehem by nightfall. But as they traveled, Joseph became more and more concerned with Mary's condition. By mid-morning she was beginning to show signs of pain, and would sometimes turn an ashen white, her eyes tightly clenched, as she held her swollen belly and moaned. Joseph slowed their pace slightly to give Mary a chance to rest, as this leg of the journey was the most difficult. From the low Jordan Valley, and the town of Jericho, they had a continuous climb up the hills leading to Beth-lehem, and Jerusalem, not much farther to the north. By early afternoon he knew they would be still another day away from their goal, and worry engulfed Joseph as he sought a refuge for the night. He was sure of it now. She was going to give birth to the child early. He only hoped that by going slow he could reach the town before her time came.

Joseph saw that Mary's face was strained and worried. The jostling of the donkey didn't help and Joseph was frantic that he would have to deliver the child himself. This was his first child, and he had no idea of what to do, should the baby start to come. He did the only thing that he knew; he tried to comfort Mary with words of caring and love. He told her that it was just a little further, just over the next hill, and he asked her to hold on just a little longer. All the while he was talking to her, his eyes scanned the rounded hillocks and small, rocky cliffs for any sign of a village or a wandering tribe with whom he might seek refuge for the night. "Why didn't I take the well-traveled road up to Jerusalem, then cut over to Beth-lehem? Just to save an hour of time, I put us in this rarely used valley without another soul around," he moaned to himself as he hurried the donkeys along.

The new grass was light yellow-green in the afternoon sun as they crested a high rounded hill. Joseph gasped with joy. There, just a short distance ahead on the next hill, were shepherds, their flocks feeding peacefully on the new shoots of grass. The grass was young and tender, and the green rolling hills were everywhere. Happiness overcame Joseph as he headed toward the men, pointing to show Mary, now rejoicing too, that there would soon be help for her. Down the next hill they plodded. Then, as they rose to the other side, they saw in front of them a rocky cliff, about three men high. Above the cliff the sheep grazed contentedly, and at the base of the cliff lay a flat area that served as a camp. It was then that they saw the families of the shepherds he had seen on the hills above. He could count ten or fifteen women and old men, plus a large group of noisy running children racing up the far hill, playing a game of tag.

It was late afternoon. The cooking fires were smoking, and the smell of food hung low in the valley, bringing warmth and joy to Joseph as he hurried up the hill leading the donkeys. Mary held on to the rope reins with the last bit of strength she possessed.

As they approached, an old woman who had delivered many a child in her sixty-plus years, stood up from her chores and squinted at the approaching couple. Before Joseph had even entered the camp circle, she was issuing orders to her two daughters-in-law to ready one of four caves, for she could see the condition of the young woman coming up the road. As Joseph walked into the camp, the old woman motioned to him to follow her.

"Come, my dear," she said, with a voice as old and as dry as the stone itself. "Lift her into the cave; she will be all right there. Don't you worry, it's dry and warm in here. Just lay her down on the robes. She will be fine. I've brought more babies than I care to count into this world. Now go, shoo! Go out by the fire. Eat something. I will call you if you are needed." Sensing that she was finally in capable hands, Mary relaxed. Joseph squatted by the fire – and worried, almost unto death.

Twilight had come. The men called the boys up to the hill, while they came down to take their evening meal. They knew strangers had arrived, and a baby was to be born in their little camp, and they were all anxious to see for themselves. They had just arrived at the base of the cliff when they heard the cry, the unmistakable cry of a newborn child; but indeed, none of them knew as yet how special this child was to be.

A sweet, beautiful, natural stillness fell about the shepherds as they noiselessly entered the cave. Hushed by the peaceful quietness within, the sight of the flickering, warming firelight, and the sleeping young child, they became aware of a rapturous presence that descended in their midst, which wrapped about them, and nurtured them there. Each unto himself felt the beauty, the sweet and gentle presence of a soul such as they had never known. That night they knew was a special night. It was like no other night they had ever known. It was a night they would long remember, when each, without exception, felt the presence of their Father God within the special child, and within themselves. Without a word, one by one, the shepherds came forward to silently kneel, and reach out brown, work-hardened hands to touch the baby, lying so peacefully against his mother's breast. Then, each again in turn, filed out to stare silently at the evening fire, and watch the stars. The stars that had months before foretold of His coming, and now held his future in their reading.

The next day, Mary rested and nursed the child. It would be a few days before they would resume their journey to Bethlehem, and she and the baby were the center of attention in this little cave just outside of town. Mary's needs were tended to by the women, and the simple men with their flocks were just beginning to relate their experiences of the night before to one another. It was such a natural thing, this birth of a child in their midst, but... But somehow, something was different. Each in turn told how he felt the glow that seemed to radiate from the child. Reluctant at first to speak aloud of their feelings, the gentle shepherds, one by one, recounted the strong, extraordinary sensations they had felt within themselves. One said, that it seemed as though an angel had spoken to him. Another said, that as he entered into the strange quietness of the cave, it appeared that the cave was glowing and shimmering with an iridescence that seemed to fill his whole body with a newly felt love for the whole world, and everyone in it. "Even the Romans?" one shepherd chided, while the others nervously chuckled. There was a long pause, then he answered, "Yes, even the Romans." There was no further response by anyone, for each was deep in his own secret thoughts.

The children saw it first. They were well on their way to the hill below the cave as the small, but very richly adorned caravan came winding its way up the road from the valley below. Upon hearing the shouts from the children, the shepherds shielded their eyes from the low morning sun, and strained to identify the new strangers coming their way. From the trappings, and the dress, they could tell these were wealthy men indeed, and they wondered at them taking this road, away from the more well known travel routes just north and west of them, leading from Jerusalem.

At that moment, in the caravan below, there was a man, a very unique man to be sure. This man was very wealthy, but not in his own right, for he came as a gift of a king. He had powers beyond any of his land, for he could *see*, and he was the king's most valued possession. A mystic, a seer, a wise man without question – and an astrologer. He was the one, who nine months earlier had gone to his liege with the story of a special one in the land of Judea who was about to be born. He was the one who told his king the story of one who would rise greater than himself, one without peer in the land of Judea. And so his king had sent him out to find this *special one*, with the admonition that he send word when he found him, and he would send his twin sons to witness the event for all time.

The seer had set off, in the direction of the stars when they appeared for the second time in the western sky. He followed them to the land of Judea, to the Holy City itself, where he stayed without notice, awaiting the last sign.

It came on a cold night in December, from the roof of his Jerusalem home; he saw it, he saw what he had been waiting for – the last conjunction of the stars. They lay just before him to the south. It fit. That was it! Less than two hours walk to the south lay Beth-lehem. "Beth-lehem, that is where he will be born!" he rejoiced with great jubilation.

Knowing the scriptures, this strange wise old man from a country far to the east, danced on the roof-top under his stars, and as he danced, he recited Micah to himself. Hardly able to contain himself, he recounted, "O Beth-lehem Ephratah, you are but a small Judean village, yet you will be the birthplace of my King who is alive from everlasting ages past."

His joy knew no bounds. Silently, that night, he sent word, through his servant to his king: "Send the twins, I will await them in the little town of Bethany in three months time, from there I will lead them to Him."

So this was how he, and his royal companions came to be traveling up this little used road leading to Beth-lehem, heading straight for the cave. He had met his royal twins the night before, and now, using his senses, he was leading them toward their goal. One of the twins would be king one day, and it was fitting that they should know that there was one born – one far greater than they.

He had been feeling it now for days, as he waited impatiently for the small royal train to arrive from Babylonia. Now, he knew they were close to their goal; he couldn't explain it, he could just *feel* it! Then, without a word, he pulled his camel to a halt in front of a row of rock-hewn caves. He sat absolutely still for a second, as if listening intently for something no one else could hear, then silently, he slipped to the ground.

The gentle spring breeze murmured its way over the rocks, that pushed their way through the lush green grass on the hills. Everything was still, and seemed to be watching, as this deeply touched, and spiritual man gazed at the opening to one of the caves. Through tears of joy welling up from within, and with gratitude to God surrounding his being, he headed up the hill toward the cave with a slow purpose and grace – a beatific smile had fallen across his face. He could feel the specialness, he could see the glow within, as he effortlessly glided toward the light within the cave.

The awed and dumb-struck shepherds, their families and children alike, stared in disbelief as next they watched two identical young princes likewise alight from their steeds, and without a word, follow this singular old man into the cave.

Mary looked up from the child as the wise man entered. For a second the old man stood there unmoving, watching the mother and child, their faces bathed in the morning light, shining like nothing he had ever seen. Then he moved within, bowing as he went, ending on his knees. A look from the old man toward the two silhouettes at the entrance, and a welcoming smile from the mother, brought the two young princes within. There, they too bowed low, and with the practiced grace that announced their position, they set before the child two identical boxes. Each box, wrapped in gold, and beset with jewels, contained the rarest of incense, brought from India to please the senses of the new king.

Then as the man of wisdom bent low to see the face of the child, the child looked up at him. The man pulled back with a start, for the eyes he saw were not those of a child, but of a gentle soul, fully conscious, aware and as probing as he. Jesus held the old man's eyes with his, and at the corner of his little rose-bud lips, the barest hint of a knowing smile. The wise man had found himself looking into the depth of the baby's soul, and the child into his, and in that instant the old man knew, he had found the Messiah. He had come! "Oh Lord, the Messiah has come!"

And in the darkening quiet of the cave, as they sat to watch the babe, the old man looked deeply within, and there he found *them*. First one, then another – two men like himself, astrologers, seekers of knowledge. He felt them searching, heading this way, as the star and their intuition guided them, as he had been guided before. He saw too, an enraged king, and disaster, pain, and fear. And thus, he made ready to leave.

The wise man rose, and went to the opening of the cave where Joseph was standing, pressed against the rock. Joseph had been staring in wonder. Awe and fear of these men of obvious power, wealth, and learning showed on his face. Mary's story of this child's birth, and the *voice* that had haunted him to this day, were hard in his ears: "She carries a child, a very special child who belongs to the world – a child who belongs to *me*."

The wise man bowed slightly to the child's father, then leaned near to whisper in his ear. "Go, go far away," he said in a voice rasping old with age, and wise beyond its years – a voice with the timeless quality of fathomless understanding. "Go, take this special child, flee into Egypt, where you will be safe. A great disaster will befall you and your little family if you stay. The king will follow you to the edges of his kingdom, and your child will be killed if you do not flee by Sabbath, next. Heed my words, Joseph, I know of what I speak. Take the jewels and precious gifts, for which you have no need, and sell them. Use the money to flee this land of mad Herod's greed."

It was that night that the *voice* came again to Joseph, and roused him, trembling from his sleep. It was that night that the *voice* also admonished Joseph to leave for the land of the Pharaohs, to flee before the beast.

Chapter 3

After they were gone, an angel of the Lord appeared to Joseph in a dream. "Get up and flee to Egypt with the baby and his mother," the angel said, "and stay there until I tell you to return, for King Herod is going to try to kill the child." That same night he left for Egypt with Mary and the baby, and stayed there until King Herod's death.

Matthew 2:13–15 5

S lowly, the incredible consciousness of the soul called Jesus was being absorbed into the child's being, and he became, much as any child, only vaguely aware of his unique difference. But differences there were, for his mind, limited only by his undeveloped body and brain, was already working, loving, searching, probing. If you had known him, if you could have looked into the depth of his blue-gray eyes, you would understand. In our home, sitting by our fire one cold, wet night the Master told us of his first memories, and of his sojourn into the land of the Nile.

"My first memory is of being so tightly bound to my

mother, I could barely move my arms or legs. I was wrapped in a carrying scarf, and from my position, tied close to her, all I could see was the bobbing head of the donkey – up, down, up, down – all day long. The unending rhythm made me very sleepy, and I would doze off, wake, nurse, watch the bobbing head, feel the gentle swaying, and sleep again – day after day.

"I can remember the campfires at night, however. I remember because I could understand everything the people said, but it did me little good because I couldn't speak a word. I was confused and anxious at first, trying to understand this new world that had been thrust upon me. But, slowly as time and world held sway, I lost my memory in the everyday life of my people. I was absorbed, as we all are, in the world of sound and sight, of the woman next door fighting with her husband, the donkey braying, the children screaming and playing, the heat of the sun, the dust of midday, and the loving of my parents in the same room where I lay. In these events I found my humanness, my love for my parents, my love for my Father, and most of all, love for my people.

"We settled in the village of the Israelites, north of Heliopolis. There, father purchased a house made of mud brick, roughly twelve cubits on a side, with an enclosed yard of about the same size which he used for his work. Father had taken the wise man's advice and sold all the gifts, save one, for our use on the journey. The coinage he received from the gifts helped to get us by, along with the income father brought in from his wood–working.

"Father was used to the plentiful soft woods of Galilee, but in Egypt he found that wood was a precious commodity, not used lightly for construction or large deeds. It took him almost half a year before he received his first commission, and that was for a beautiful chest, not for house or beam. When a man is used to working in rough wood, it takes time to learn the economy of precious woods. It also takes time to learn the new tools that are used to work the precious hardwoods, tools that were little used in the town of Nazareth. It takes a special patience to feel the grain, to take the most economical cut, to waste the least. It takes a special learning to understand the delicate jointing and joining of wood, the sanding and rubbing, the lacquers, stains and paints. These things my father learned, but an artisan's soul is also needed to develop the patience and resolve for working on the delicate and small, and my father's heart still yearned for the bulky and the large. His work, in candor, was adequate, but lacked the life that makes inanimate objects sing.

"I was too young to remember much, but there are things that linger in my memory, special times for me, of little meaning to others, but real and important to a young lad.

"On the way to Egypt, we had stopped for the night amongst the date trees in an oasis. I remember the camp fire blazing in the dark, sparks rising high into the air, only to disappear into the star spattered sky. Supper was through, and everyone was taking their ease. My mother held me playfully as I watched the fire, which always made me feel so very safe and special. The fire danced its yellow light amongst the people and flung shadows on the surrounding trees. I was fascinated by these dancing shadows and the patterns of light and dark that were cast upon the faces and clothing of those who sat around to talk, and to listen the night away. The night was cool and clear. The black sky above was a sea of shimmering stars, in a heaven I knew most intimately. I could hear the people's words, but most of all, I could *feel* their thoughts as if they themselves had been spoken out loud.

"The next day, before dawn, I knew we would start our journey again. However, one of the camels was sick, and they didn't think that he would be able to make another day. That was bad for our little caravan, for he carried one of the heaviest loads. They didn't want to leave him there, for he was too young and valuable, but they didn't know what else to do.

"Listening to the men, I also learned that there had been robbers in this area. The men decided that they had better post a watch all night. There were seventeen that could fight if need be, but I knew to a man, that they hoped they would not be tested. Lots were drawn for the evening watches.

"The men talked of the next oasis, and its water, which they thought was just a day or two away. Fears were expressed about reaching the water with the few animals that were left. They talked of the water as a practical thing, but their thoughts, ah, that was a different matter. Their thoughts flew from one thing to another, through association, as rapidly as the twinkling of an eye – first one thing – then another. One minute the man across from me was following the conversation, the next he was thinking of a waterfall, and a pool, and a beautiful girl without clothes. We all have random thoughts that roll on and on, but for me it was different. During this period in my life, my world was filled with a cacophony of thoughts that danced merrily within my mind. They amazed me, and played with me when I had the time. For me, it was a time to absorb; to watch, to hear, and to learn the ways, and the feelings of my people. This was a passive time for me, a time in which I could feel their hurts, their fears, their hopes, their desires, their jealousies, their loves and losses. These early years of my watching I will never forget, for they are burned within my mind.

"There was one other event while we were in Egypt, that made a lasting impression on my young consciousness, an experience that will stay with me until my last breath.

"We were living in upper Egypt, not very far from the city of Thebes, where there was a large Jewish population, and my father had been employed by a nobleman to prepare some items of furniture for a tomb. If my father wanted the work, he had to work there, and no place other. So he packed what little things he thought we needed, and my mother, my father, my brother James and I traveled with our donkeys by foot and by boat up the beautiful Nile to Thebes, there to be assigned our places across the river on a hill near the Valley of the Kings. The land there is only a short distance from the lush, fertile Nile, yet there isn't a single living tree, bush, blade of grass, or shrub in the rugged hills. The sun is a vicious companion there; it is relentless to noblemen, and lowly slaves alike. Except, the nobleman can take his rest in the shade of his tent, sipping a cooled drink. But for one who has no shelter, the sun is a constant enemy, tormenting him, and driving him, until his will to survive can no longer urge him on – and it is precisely then that the slavemaster's whip holds sway.

"I believe I was about three years old when father took us to this valley. I judge my age from what I remember of the looks of the other boys there who were about my age. We lived along the top of a hot, barren wind-swept ridge, looking down upon a narrow valley, which ran down to the flat land below. The valley was the working ground for the slaves employed by the nobleman to dig the cave, and on the hill were the living quarters, the tents set up for the craftsmen and freemen employed by him. Our tent was really quite large, and housed our small family, and all our goods, with plenty of room to spare. Those who had employed father had set up a canopy and provided him with beautiful hardwood from Africa. Here it was that father worked from early morning, until the sun dropped below the burning, barren hills. Toward the end, he even worked by lamp light, to finish the furniture on time.

"I have so many memories of this time! I remember one morning standing by the corner of the tent when the nobleman himself came to view the progress of father's work. The nobleman was not at all pleased, as father wasn't working fast enough for what he had promised to do. I remember my father being as polite to him as he could, while all the time the man yelled at him, and pounded on the work table before him. I remember the dirt and the stink of that hot day. I remember the terror that gripped my father, the sweat that poured from his body, for he needed the job, and we needed the money to live. I wondered at the difference between my poor father, doing his best, which wasn't good enough, and the poor slaves down in the valley working under the eye of the slavemaster, and the threat of the whip. Father had been whipped as surely as if the straps had felt his back.

"That was the first time and only time in my life I saw my father work on a Sabbath. He worked out of fear; fear for his little family, fear for himself, and fear for who he was. The Sabbath is *never* broken by a Jew! Only mother and I knew what that did to him inside – no one knew what it did to me. I watched as the other Jews who worked on the tomb turned their backs on father from that day on, and I felt the pain and sickness my father felt deep inside. His smiles stopped, and his laughter ceased from that day on. I saw my father age ten years in the next three.

"On that sabbath day, I knew, that someday I would set them free. Not just the poor slaves in the valley, but also my people, who were just as surely slaves to the Law, as any slave I knew, or could see.

"That was a turning point in my young life; that was the time I found that I was different from the rest. I would play with others of my age sometimes, but those times became rare, and this caused my father much concern. `Go play,' he would say to me. `Go play with the other boys. Kick dirt, throw sticks, wrestle!' When one of them hit me he would say to me; `Hit them back, boy. Don't let them do that to you!' But I couldn't, I could never hit back. They were mean because I was different. They made fun of me, and taunted me because I wanted to be alone – which drove me even more into myself.

"I found the silence and peace I sought when I could get away from them, and it was in this silence that I first heard the *voice*. It came as soft as a gentle whisper – so alive, I turned my head to see from whence it came – but there was no one there. It was in the desert in the land of the Pharaohs, that I found my Abba, my true Father, my beloved Guide within. A voice, a vision, a light, a knowing, a presence. Yes, that was it, it was a *presence* that came about me, and when it had left, I had a special *knowing*; I was changed!

"I was still a child though, and I thought as a child. I remember thinking, `If only I were grown, then it would be different. No one will make fun of me then. Someday they will see how different I am. In the meantime I'll play the game. I'll go play with the children. What a bore!' I would think, `I'd rather be with my Abba, my dear Father within.' I loved Him so, even then.

"When I listened to my father, and the other men talking among themselves, I heard them recite passages from the Law. The Law, which has been all–important to us since the time of Moses, rules every aspect of our lives. Yet, somewhere deep within I knew there was more. I knew there was something infinitely more ordered, more compassionate, more loving, more understanding than any of the laws I heard repeated over, and over again. The Law was used as their justification, their comfort, their excuse, but none of them talked about that *feeling*, that *voice*, that *something* that spoke to me. That *something* lay within me – it was part of me. It was a natural beauty.

"I remember thinking that if they would just stop talking long enough, and find a silent place, they could hear Him too. I thought that if they just tried to listen, they would find that the pains and pleasures they held so close were nothing. If they could but turn within, there they would find our Abba, waiting with open arms for them.

"I tried to tell my father about the *voice* once, at the supper table, but his mind was on his work, and our struggle to live. So it was with some feeling of sufferance that he kindly brushed me aside with a hint of ridicule, and insufferable, mocked gravity. He gave my mother a wink, and said that if I didn't want to play like other boys, then I should do something constructive, such as helping my mother clean. With that he let out a hardy laugh and tweaked me on the cheek. I was sitting across from him at the time, and my mother was behind him at the cooking fire. I looked behind him to my mother, a pout growing on my face the minute I caught her eye. In her eyes I saw the hurt, the hurt for my feelings, and in her eyes I also saw the question, `Who are you, little one, who are you?'

"But, who in any family listens to a little boy, save his mother? She would hold me by the hand, or tightly in her arms, and I would feel so very close to her. I loved her so.

"There was a strange thing between my mother and me. She knew when I was deep in thought; she above all others honored my time alone, but her deep eyes were always probing, and asking, `Who are you?' From my earliest memories, I can remember her holding me in her arms tightly and hearing her whisper, `Are you? Are you, little one? *Are you?*'

"Often were the times that I would find a quiet place in the shade, where the boys couldn't find me, but she did. With her eyes, those probing eyes, she would always ask the same question, `Are you?' I can remember thinking, `Abba, help me. Abba, help me to know. Who am I? Look at her, she's watching me for some reason. Father doesn't do that, he's busy, always busy working, trying to please someone, but she does. I wonder if all fathers are like that? Yes, mother, I am different, I feel it, but why... why? Oh, Abba, teach me. I'm just a little boy, teach me. Why am I the only little boy who wants to sit and watch everything, learn everything? I have an insatiable thirst to know everything about this earth, and beyond. There is more than just Egypt, I know there is!'

"This would be my cry over and over. I can also recall thinking, `I know something they don't know. If only I had an older body, I could find out what that is. I have the feeling I must wait, and wait, and wait. I was born to do something, but what?' `Abba... Abba... Abba,' I would wail. In fact, Abba, the name I had for the *voice* within (meaning father or daddy), became a wonderful chant for me. I would chant it over and over again, rocking back and forth, eyes closed, until He came."

When Jesus was in his second year, word was received that the terrible King Herod was dead, but Joseph hastened not to return to Judea, for fear still gripped his loins. To understand why Joseph, and so many others still feared to return to our country you must understand the tyrant and king called Herod. Words cannot describe how terrible this hated man was. To slaughter all the young male children in a village was nothing to him; after all, he had had his mercenaries butcher entire villages before him. What did it matter if he killed a few dirty children – especially if it meant safeguarding his kingdom from a rumored new "king" – however slight the possibility might be that the rumor was true?

Herod could find no one of Israel to serve him as a soldier. There was no one he could have trusted with his life, anyway. He relied on mercenaries: Germans, Gauls, Africans and Thracians did his bitter bidding. His sick and fetid body was a just dessert for a life spent spreading horror and pain to every household, in every corner of his kingdom. On many an occasion, if a man incurred his wrath, Herod would order the entire family annihilated – butchered; this included the youngest child (the "furthest branch"), to the most distant relative ("the deepest root").

His own family, friends, and loved ones were spared nothing, in his insatiable lust for life and power. He killed two husbands of his sister Salome, whom he loved; the only wife he truly loved, Mariamne, whose death haunted him to his grave; two sons, namely Alexander, Aristobulus; and five days before his death, his eldest son Antipater; also, his brother–in–law, and his mother–in–law; and, who really knows how many more.

He erected the golden eagle of Rome over the entrance to the holy Temple itself, and when a learned scholar and his students pulled it down, he burned three of them alive, like human torches, in front of all the people. The remaining thirty or forty he had hacked to small pieces by his men. It was said truly that he "ruled like a wild beast," and was hated by all who came under his foot.

Because of these misdeeds, God visited upon Herod every manner of horror and pain known to inhabit the body. His once lean, hard body had become obese to the point where he could hardly haul its sickness about on legs and feet swollen beyond recognition. His genitals had rotted, and worms lived in the mortified flesh, as part of his member had fallen off, and he lived in constant pain. He gained an incredible appetite, which only fed the pains in his bowel and stomach. Immediate cramping, convulsions seized him for the better part of an hour after each intake of food. Even after the cramping stopped, the burning fire within never gave him a moment's peace. As he spoke, waves of putrid stench emanated from his interior, so that only the hardiest of souls could control themselves, and keep from retching while close at hand. Even as this is terrible to contemplate, there was more, for he had living sores that continually oozed and caked upon this grotesque, living beast.

Thus, just weeks before his demise, this mad creature, not done with his people even unto death, caused all the leaders of the entire nation to gather in Jerusalem, and there be shut up in the hippodrome under guard. He ordered that, upon his death, the soldiers slaughter each and every one of the leaders, sparing none. Thus the death of Herod was to be grieved throughout the nation Israel and beyond, wherever Jews did reside. Fortunately, before the king's death was made known, Herod's sister and her husband, dismissed those shut up in the hippodrome. But knowledge of the plot did not escape the people, and their fear of the Herodian line grew mighty.

Now, in the land of Egypt, the news of the events transpiring in Israel did not go unnoticed. Daily, the caravans were met with trepidation and excitement to hear the news. Herod was dead! It was certain now, his evilness was gone. But what of his stead? Herod's will had been read, and Archelaus was to be king. All Jews held their breath, waiting to see whether Rome would uphold his will, and what kind of a king Archelaus would be.

Without the approval of Caesar Augustus, Herod's will was in doubt, for Herod had ruled at the whim of Rome; and because Archelaus wished to consolidate his rule before going to Rome, he tarried for more than a year before going to

Caesar for approval. In the meantime, without a formal king, sedition and war spread throughout the land. Many there were who set themselves up like kings, gathered an army (some containing thousands of men), and made war on the armies of Herod and Rome.

But, these things were happening away from Jerusalem. In and around the city, Archelaus was busy trying to consolidate his power. This was not as easy as it may seem. It is true that Herod's armies pledged their loyalty to Archelaus in Jericho immediately after his fathers death, but he desired to win the Jews' favor at this time without force – for he wished to proceed to Caesar with the leaders of his country behind him, acclaiming him as a true and just man. He needed this because of questions about his father's will, raised by others in his family. Some of the people believed him, and were willing to curry his favor in hopes that the favors would be returned when he was king. However, more remembered his father, and looked upon any Herod with deep hate. Seeing that Archelaus' position was not sure, they sought to bring him down in any way they could.

Toward the end of the first year after Herod's death, as Archelaus tarried, the sedition became worse. At last he could allow no more. Fearing for himself and his kingdom, on the occasion of Passover, he sent a regiment of a thousand men to control the throngs of people (numbering in the hundreds of thousands), who were gathering to celebrate the Feast of Unleavened Bread. Before the trouble had been quelled, Archelaus turned his army upon the people in and near the temple. The foot soldiers killed those they found in the Temple, and his horsemen who followed, killed those who had escaped, and those in tents around the Temple area who thought themselves safe. The horsemen alone killed over three thousand. Thus the reign of Herod's terror continued even unto his son, and the people of the land lived in constant fear.

Sedition became even worse as Archelaus and his relatives left for Rome to plead their case. Rebellion spread throughout the length and breadth of our land, and before Varus, the Roman governor of Syria, could stop the trouble there had been no less than ten thousand battles, ending in Jerusalem itself, where Varus set up crosses along the road, and thereby crucified two thousand of our people who had opposed him.

Thus the people ended their fight against Herod and his kind; some lived in fear, and some in their hate, but all waited for the promised one – the Messiah – to come.

"I was now four at the time father finished his work on the furniture for the tomb. I remember it as if it were yesterday. Father was packing up the donkeys. He was done with his work, and we were all glad to be going back to our home. Father had been paid that morning, but the nobleman was still far from happy. Father had done his best, but it just wasn't good enough. I remember looking at him as he received his pay, and for the first time thought that he looked so old to me that morning, as he silently bowed his head and took the verbal abuse. I loved him then, his skin dark from the sun, and his wrinkled brow, that gave him an air of dignity I had not remembered in the past.

"After the men of Egypt left, he stood silently for a moment staring out over the sand, across the Nile to the east, and his vacant eyes spoke to me of our beloved homeland, our Israel. Then he shook himself with a great sigh, and bending toward me, a splendid smile came over his face. The wrinkles at the corner of his eyes deepened as he picked me up, threw me about in the air with a great shout, then he hugged me to his breast with his great arms wrapped about me. My mother's eyes lit up with relief and delight at the sight, as she watched, my baby brother in her arms. Never had I seen my mother looking so young and pretty, and never had I felt such warmth, joy and love from my father. I was overjoyed as my father set me upon the donkey's back, and we were off to join the caravan, the slow caravan heading north to the lush Delta region of the Nile. I wondered then, for the first time, when, if ever, we were going *home*.

"We headed north to our residence near the House of Onias, and father's shop that awaited us. I knew now that this place where I had spent my early years wasn't *home*, for I had *seen* father's vision of what we had left behind. But it was the warmth and safety of friends such as Lazarus, the only friend I had who understood me, who awaited my return with as much delight as I felt for them. Lazarus' family, like ourselves, were just one of many displaced by Herod, who awaited their return to the Promised Land.

"We then had the occasion to cross paths with two men, strange men, whose stories changed both my family's, and my life. As we traveled north, my father's thoughts were of going home, from whence we had fled four years before. After all, Herod was dead, wasn't he, thanks be to God. And we could afford to go now. Father had worked for the Egyptian just less than a year, under terrible conditions, in the desert, but the pay was exceptional, so we had the ability to make the long trip back. We would have gone then too, had it not been for the two strange men that I mentioned.

"Just after we had finished supper the seventh night out, a man appeared out of the darkness, dressed all in rags, but of blond hair and light skin, so as to make him altogether a strange and unusual sight. As he entered, stumbling into the flickering light that the campfire cast, the men rose as if one to protect the families there. But the strange man raised his hand, and in perfect Greek, stayed them with his words. When the men knew there was no harm intended, and that this man was a slave to the hated Romans, and that he had news of happenings in Israel, they made him exceedingly welcome, feeding and clothing him as best they could at that hour of the evening.

"When he had supped, and thanked everyone for their kindness, he told a tale of our homeland so horrible, that not one Jew of our camp that night could find a moment of untormented sleep. As he spoke, he relived the horror of it, and his words fell within my soul and moved me to my core.

"It seemed that the stories we had heard of the thousands dying at the hand of Archelaus the year before were all true, but they were not the end of the terror that had befallen our land. The Greek told us that after the slaughter at the temple gates, Archelaus, his brother Antipas, his mother, sister, and most of Herod's family and high placed friends went to Rome to plead in favor of, or against, Archelaus and the last will that his father had left. This had taken the better part of the past year, and while he was gone, with only Romans about, and no leader to guide the kingdom, the kingdom in turn rocked with revolt.

"Finally, in an expedition meant to wipe out the last of the rebels, Varus, governor of Syria, sent his legions to crush the rebellion, which had captured Jerusalem itself, and had laid siege to the last stronghold that the Romans still held.

"I could feel from this sensitive Greek the horror he now relived in his mad mind, amongst tears and wails for those who lay dead at his feet. The Greek, although a slave, had been treated as a member of the Varus household. He carried with him the privilege of that family's rank, and was sent by Varus to see the happenings in Israel as they transpired, and to write back his account, which often was at variance with Varus' commanders in the field.

"This battle he told us about was not like the skirmishes he had seen before: a battle between trained soldiers braced against each other, each giving no quarter, nor asking any in return. This battle had no glory in it. The Romans came upon an unsuspecting camp of rebels and took them completely by surprise; their women, their children and the rebels themselves – all were butchered alike. What was done to them, you wouldn't want to see. Although they fought bravely, ten thousand fell, yet but only one hundred Romans did they slay.

"At this point the Greek began to lose touch with reality," Jesus said, tears welling up in his eyes and glistening in the firelight. "He was walking among the dead again, in that valley of death. In his mind he was back where he had walked all night, and now the dawn was coming... `You have to be careful where you walk!' he cried. 'Yea, though I walk through the valley of the shadow of death, I shall see no evil. How can I say that? I am the conqueror! How can I let myself be used! I am worse than any of them. They know no better, the swine – the barbarian pigs! By the gods, at least they're dead and free, I, however, must serve my master still. If only we Greeks had a general, if only Alexander were alive again.'

"His eyes were glazed. There was no sanity left in this poor devil as he continued his grim tale. `Death hangs like a storm under the lightened blue sky. Smoke rises on the far horizon. The moans of the dead and the dying hang heavy in the gathering gloom. There's no poetry in this thing. The stench and pain are beyond human understanding. Ten thousand dead, and those who did still cling to life, were slaughtered like cattle, without a care.

"`Do you know what the Romans are doing now, just on the other side of the hill?' he asked the wide eyed and silently growing crowd, some of whom were now weeping, and rocking back and forth in mourning for their fallen brethren. Delirium seized the man reliving the horrible scene, for the thousandth time, as it appeared before his eyes – each time more real than the people listening could imagine. `Their tents are alive with light! They drink their wine, they sing their songs, and this poor Greek here wanders among the dead. Strangling, more dead than alive, I walk the night and wish that I could be one of those who walk the muted past.

"`No place to sit, no place to rest my head. I stumbled into the officers tent, exhausted, numb, out of my mind with hatred. They were still there, celebrating their *victory*, as dawn's light broke the crest of death's hill. They wish me to speak of wisdom, poetry, and mirth, yet around me I see only death in their glory. Glory! Yet what shatters me inside, is that I don't have the courage to stand up and die for what I believe. I am not brave enough to end my life. I remain a *slave* in the truest sense of the word, for I am a slave to my mind. I despise myself, and bemoan my fate.

"'And you, poor bastard Jews,' he spit, looking about him at the crowd, `your puny power deludes you, and your God won't save you. You fanatics! Nothing can stand against Rome. The world crumbles at her feet. You challenge her, she dissects you, then crushes you under foot – you are no more important to them than an insect. The world despises you – laughs at you for trying.'

"With this last lament upon our nation, he seemed to come out of the trance," Jesus continued. "There was a long pause, then the Greek apologized for what he had said, and finished his tale quickly. `The last I remember was running from the camp. Mercifully, a ground fog came to hide the evidence of this vile deed that lay all about me. The next I knew, I was on a hill overlooking the Mediterranean Sea; it was dawn of the next day. I had wandered many miles, and as you can see, I had many miles yet to go before you came to find me. I thank you friends, I wish you well. I will not impose my presence upon you any further.'

"That was the last I ever saw of him, but his impact lingers yet. Somehow, although I could not understand it at the time, it was different for me than the others that listened that night. While the others imagined the terror, I truly *knew* his torment, and I prayed someday God would grant him peace. As for our little traveling band, it was much sobered with the news of terror loose in our land, and once again father seemed heavier, more withdrawn – and mother – she kept looking at me as if she expected something of me; what, I could not fathom as yet.

"Then it happened! We met a man the following night, while I was still filled with the memory of the experience from the day before. I had remained silent most of the day, as had the rest. We were coming close to the water's edge, where we were going to spend the night, just as the cool of the evening approached. I remember it so vividly. I even remember what I was wearing – a white tunic and a stripped robe of many colors, with a cap to match. It was here then, as we passed close by the water's edge, that I saw him. He was a man of about forty, a Jew by the looks of his dress, of no import – but to me. I was riding the donkey when we passed. I turned to look at him, he was no more than three paces away... I looked into his eyes, and he held my stare for what seemed like an eternity; and in that moment, it happened! I *touched* his mind like I had done so many times before with others, without a single mishap – but, this time was to be different, and I learned a lesson I never forgot.

"My mind burst into flame! I screamed so loud, and with such horror, they later said, that the animals all stopped in their tracks, the hair up on their backs, and refused to go another step. I had probed his mind – and found death! For the first time in my life I had tasted the bitter pain of death. It was not just any death, but the most painful death of all – crucifixion.

"There was a twisted smile upon his face, as he held my eyes, and terror passed from his demented mind into mine. The smile turned to a mix of anger and fear as the men grabbed him. His eyes bulged from his head, as they slammed him against the tree. They killed him there, when they saw and heard what he had done to me. They killed him for being a sorcerer, for giving the evil eye. It was actually the most blessed thing that they could have done for him, for in death, I knew they had given him peace.

"Although he was now dead, there was no way to stop the scene that unfolded within my brain. It rushed at me with a force I could not comprehend. I cried for my mother, saying, `I know it's coming. I don't want to go, I'm scared, mother, I'm so scared.' My mother raced to my side and grabbed me, but it was too late. There was no power on earth that could have stayed me from tumbling into the thoughts and visions within his head. `There are people. There are people dying!' I cried. `Oh God, they're dying!'

"`Come back, my baby, come back!' my mother wailed.

"`You don't see them,' I moaned, `I am there! Oh, it's so hard, so hard. Oh, it's so hard to watch those people die, dying so hard, how can they do that to them? How? Abba, Abba, please help me!' I pleaded.

"I was watching from the man's eyes, watching from behind the rocks, below the place where they were crucifying them – two thousand of them in a line as long as I could see – and the one in front of him was his brother!

"My voice changed, and became as deep as it could be, my throat tearing to speak, wailing its lament, `It's so unnecessary! Oh, Lord, they said he was the Messiah. *He* said he was the Messiah! Oh, Lord God, we followed him, we believed in him and in his signs, and this is what has come of it. All Israel see what has happened. We followed him and they are all dead. Not a single Roman died – not one – but I have two brothers hanging from crosses crucified!'

"Suddenly, all I could see was the soldier standing between me, I mean him, and his brother. 'I drew my sword and crept up behind the Roman...'

"There was no end to the terror! *I was now inside the Roman.* All the hate for them I still felt, but now I was him! They were so cruel, so tough, and I was one of them. I was crucifying them, and I didn't care, I didn't care. I just wanted to get rid of these rebels. I mean, they were a nuisance, that was all they meant to me. The purpose of their death was just to get rid of them, so I didn't have to do this troublesome work any more. I felt absolutely nothing in my heart. They were wailing and crying. I just wanted to get them dead so that they would stop that noise, and then I could get back to Syria. The rebels stretched for as far as I could see. We tied them to the crosses for all who passed to view, as a lesson to the Jews, to let them know that their `Messiah' was *never* to be!

"Then I felt the sword enter my back, and come out the front. That was the end. How merciful.

"`At least one Roman will die for this deed!' I screamed in the horrible pain–racked voice of the man now lying dead against the tree. I grabbed for my back, as my eyes opened and began to clear. I could still feel the sword as clearly and painfully as if the wound was truly in me. Slowly, ever so slowly, my mind cleared, and I knew my mother held me, and that my father was at my side. The entire caravan stood around me, with worried looks on their faces, not so much for my well being, although they cared, but more for their own fear – they were afraid of everything they didn't understand – afraid of evil they couldn't see.

"For weeks after that incident, I never left my parents'

side. I was so afraid. Even after we returned to our friendly home, familiar surroundings, and our friends, the vision of the crosses, the memory of pain and suffering of those men I had seen, stayed with me. They haunt me day and night now, in these days just before my time. The thought of the cross is with me even today."

With this frightening tale told, Jesus stared into the warmth of our fire for a long time. We were barely breathing, feeling the incredible sadness, almost feeling ourselves the pain that was so much apart of him these days. Our Master had helped so many, had relieved so many of their afflictions and their pains. How we wished we, too, could now reach out and help that man who sat across from us. How we wished we could reach out and take away his pain!

Then with a mighty sigh, and a sheepish grin, he relaxed, and back we went with him in time. Within seconds we were lost again within the sounds, and words of childhood.

"We stayed in Egypt for almost two more years after we returned from the tomb work on the upper Nile. The terror we experienced from the mad man and the Greek were borne out by tales from others who were traveling through, or sought refuge within our communities between the great cities of Alexandria and Memphis, along the mighty Nile. Many there were living here in exile, afraid for one reason or another to return to the land of their fathers, Israel.

"We found during that time of our continuing stay that the emperor Augustus had finally decided to divide Herod's kingdom into three parts. The hated Archelaus was appointed ethnarch over Judea, Idumea, and Samaria. His land stretched from the border with Egypt on the south, to the border of

Galilee on the north; from the Jordan River on the east, to Mere Nostrum in the west. Father and mother's home in Nazareth was spared the rule of this beast of prey, and was granted, along with all of Galilee and the land east of the Jordan, to Herod Antipas. Although Antipas would not tolerate the least threat to his portion of the kingdom, at least he did not turn to the slaughter of innocents as a means of control. The last son to outlive their monster father, Philip, was given the newly settled lands of Batanaea, north and east of Galilee, which was sparse of man or beast, and certainly of Jew.

"Finally, after nearly three years of riot and war, we heard that a tense peace had settled over the country, and once again thoughts of home entered the people's minds."

As Jesus spoke, I mused that be it ever so short lived, these years since Herod have provided a rich medium for us all to learn, and to grow. Unique in all of history, God has taken Rome, the unchallenged, cruel master of the world (with her imperial talons in the flesh of every man, woman and child of her kingdom) and banded her to an oppressed people, totally, inexorably, dedicated to God's will, and holding to a messianic fervor never before seen to such a degree in all the history of the world. He located them both at the same place, at the same time in history, at the crossroads of the civilized world – and there He sent a son. One who would do His will without question, would bear Him humiliation, and hate, yet teach His people about Him, and about His love.

Jesus continued: "To this day, the earth has had a peace administered through fear, hate, hope and waiting; but now," his eyes met mine, "now dear, Asher ben Ammi, *now* is the time, that one time in history when all things come to pass. The heavens have opened to humanity – no man can hold it back. There will be no other time such as this for eons. We must leap with joy at the opportunity our Lord has given us. It is now! Do you understand? This is the good news I have been trying to get them to see – the time of heaven has come. *Now*. Don't look for some time in the future. It is *now*. This is what I have been trying so hard for all of you to understand. Take it now, within your heart, never let it go. This is the peace that surpasses all understanding. This is a peace administered by love, joy, sweetness, and compassion. The kingdom of heaven is here dear, Asher." His eyes moved to my young wife. "And you, Miriamme, do you understand? Go within, dear ones, go within – open your hearts. In the silence that follows, he will speak to you – he will love you so."

By now our hearts were tearing, and tears of devotion for our beloved teacher moistened our faces. My dear wife, Miriamme, left her place to sit on the floor at his feet. There she placed her head on his lap. He stroked her head, stared again into the fire, and continued again.

"Yet, though a degree of sanity had returned to our land, so great was the mistrust of its leaders, and so great was their fear, that it was over another year before father finally felt that it was safe enough for us to return. In actual fact, father knew my mother's heart, and how it yearned for the companionship of her family, her friends, and the village she left behind. I think this was what finally drove him to decide. He used to watch her at night, as did I, and see the yearning in her eyes. Although she never said a word to him, never complained, just supported and honored him in every way; he knew, he knew her most secret desire. And so the day came to pass, when father could stay her heart no more from the land she loved, the peaceful hills, the tall trees, the rocky meadowland, and the people, the people who made it home. And so we made ready for the long trek back to our homeland – Galilee."

Chapter 4

When Herod died, an angel of the Lord appeared in a dream to Joseph in Egypt, and told him, "Get up and take the baby and his mother back to Israel, for those who were trying to kill the child are dead.

Matthew 2:19–20

T he story of our Master's youth that I have just told I heard during the last year before his death, but there are many more stories beginning early in his ministry that I must relate.

Shortly after I met Jesus, I had an occasion to travel to Jericho with my son John. After my first encounter with Jesus, I knew in my heart that he was unquestionably from God, but I hadn't as yet let anyone know my true feelings, so stubborn was I in the ways of my peers.

I did know, however, that I had to see him again. I had to learn more about this man, who, by all my standards, was nothing but an illiterate, itinerant carpenter from, of all places – Galilee. But, even though I thought him to be illiterate, and beneath my station at that time – see him I must. So, unknown to anyone, I made the trip a necessity. I knew that Jesus was at the house of a man called Jonathan, and I would be welcome there. My son knew of him being there too, but as is usual with fathers and sons, being *men*, we let not each other know our true feelings. And so, in separate worlds, we traveled the very same path, on our way to see (as Peter oft called him), the great fisherman.

As we rode along, side by side, I glanced over to catch a glimpse of the young man I loved, and of whom I was so proud. His name was now John, a Greek name, a name Jesus had given him some months before, but to me, he was just my son.

As we cantered down the dusty road together, against the flow of the holiday throngs streaming to Jerusalem, I wished with all my heart, that I could share what had happened inside me, inside my heart, with my son. But, of course, my lofty male pride, the thirty–two years that had passed between us since his birth, and my social standing had worked their subtle ways, and made this father's feelings inaccessible. Later, Jesus would break down all the barriers and rules I held so dear; but that is about me, and I wish to tell you of my Master, my Lord. I tell this story now, because it was here, under the fruited trees, that I heard him first tell of his growing years.

He was seated upon a garden bench, within the vine covered garden walls of Jonathan's home in Jericho. There were perhaps fifteen or twenty others, spread out around him, sitting on the ground. Jonathan was a genial host, and his wife, Ruth, kept us well supplied with fruit and drink as the day wore on. I remember thinking, "I have never felt so welcome, so surrounded with love, as I do here." This was my first real meeting with him, and I fought tears, and emotions the entire day as I sat at his feet to listen. I didn't want to speak. I didn't want to eat. I didn't want to do anything that would take my eyes or my ears from him. By the end of the day, my head was reeling as if from drink, and that night, as my son slept, I wrote. I wrote everything that I remembered.

Jesus was speaking casually, answering questions, joking lightly with his friends when my son and I entered. Then someone in the group said, "Master, tell us of your youth, tell us of your growing up in Galilee."

Jesus grew silent, as I have seen him do on so many occasions since, when he is about to tell of himself, and then with a soft, gentle look in his eyes, he began.

"We traveled in a caravan from Egypt, until we reached Joppa. There, the caravan broke away from the coast, to head south and east, up the foothills to Jerusalem. Father dared not go there, for although Herod was dead, his sons lived on, and this was the land of Archelaus, who turned out to be the most vicious of all those who came from Herod's loins, from that day until now.

"From Joppa, we also headed east, but by the route that also heads north through Samaria. I had heard nothing good about the Samaritans from my own people, because, I was told, they broke from the true religion of our fathers. But I tell you, I remember nothing but kindness from these gentle people; kindness to us, to my mother, my father and me, my brother, James, and to the babe, Joseph, my second brother born shortly before we left. I loved them for that. They did not turn us away, as our own village had done to my mother so many years before, but took us in and treated us as their own."

Later, I was to hear Jesus tell a story about a good and noble Samaritan, to chastise one of our own, who forsook the helping of a man in need along the road, because it was the Sabbath. When I heard this story, I remembered his feelings this day for our neighbors to the north. Enough digression, I have my notes of that day, let our Master's story continue.

"The closer we got to our home, the more excited we all became; all of us except mother, that is. For me, there was so much to see and hear. I had never seen anything except palms, green fields, the river Nile, sand, and rocks. But here in Israel, was the beautiful sea, the rolling fertile hills, real trees that I had heard so much about – not palm trees, but trees with small delicate leaves, and others with long needles. You can't believe what joy there was in every step along the way for this wide-eyed boy.

"I will never forget the day before we reached Joppa. We made camp overlooking the sea. A band of heavy gray rain clouds rolled over the western sky. My father stopped me along the road. He said nothing, but just held onto my arm and looked to the east. As my eyes followed his gaze, the setting sun, colored a molten gold, in all its rain–cleansed radiance broke from under the clouds, and I saw a sight I will never forget. There, atop the deepening, purple hills shone a brilliant golden jewel. Shimmering, and glowing in the heavenly beam was the most radiant sight man will ever see, the Holy City itself, Jerusalem!"

Here Jesus stopped for a moment. I am sure he was still recalling in his mind the sight that had so impressed him, lo those many years ago. He painted such beautiful pictures for us when he would tell us stories, that in no time at all we were also seeing them in our minds at the time of their telling. So when he paused, we too saw the scene and were lost in the same warm reverie of his past that he felt, and was experiencing.

After a moment, a little sigh escaped him. I learned to expect this little wistful sigh, and then a quick sheepish grin, whenever he paused in a story, and then started up again. I loved this special part of him, that only those close to him ever saw. And so, with the delightful grin the tale of his journey home resumed.

"I mentioned that we were all becoming more and more excited as we neared the north and our home; all that is, except mother. Father had long forgotten the foul, vicious gossip that accompanied their wedding, but mother had not. No one in Egypt had known her, or the strange events accompanying my birth, but she *knew* that the village wouldn't forget. She alone could watch my growth and wonder, but Nazareth, that was a different story, indeed. The little village thrived on gossip. The seven years since the uppity carpenter and his pregnant wife left without a word of good-by had not gone unnoticed. Oh yes, they had heard the stories of kings and wise-men who came from countries far away and left expensive gifts for Mary and Joseph's son... but really, Joseph, the carpenter? Who would expect anyone to believe that! And, what was that about a star? They hadn't seen any special star, and even if they had, what did that prove?"

With these candid revelations, Jesus had us completely within his grasp. He was leaning toward us now, his blue-gray eyes flashed back and forth with mocked earnestness and hurt, and wide with pretended alarm (his hand to the corner of his mouth as if someone outside our group might overhear). Then, he whispered the most damning revelation of all, "some said that my mother had a *bastard* son!"

The whole group gasped! This was too much! For if it were true, all in attendance knew that the Law stated, "*A bastard may not enter the sanctuary, nor any of his descendants for ten generations.*" We were aghast at the idea that anyone would think that our Lord was a *bastard*! The people rose as one, anger flashing in their eyes, their faces growing crimson as their blood rose rapidly to a boil. They demanded of him to tell who had said such a thing.

Jesus, a master of the moment, held the hurt look for a moment, just enough time to hear us rise to the bait. Then, unable to contain himself any longer, he rolled back upon the bench, and doubled-up with laughter. As we stood there, dumbly looking at each other, and wondering what had happened, he roared with delight.

When we realized that he had been purposely playing on our sensitivities and emotions, teasing us to be sure, the group broke into nervous laughter, still feeling a bit unsure, sheepish and self–conscious. Jesus looked at us again, then continued to laugh uproariously. As his mirth infected us (and how could it help do otherwise?), real, joyous laughter, the likes of which I hadn't heard for years, poured from us too. It was useless to go on with his story after that, so with a promise that he would continue soon, we followed our hosts into a supper they had prepared in their Master's honor, a supper like no other I had ever had. There was such joy in these simple people, a joy I had never experienced! I couldn't say why I felt so good, I just did, whenever I was in his presence.

That was the first experience I had with Jesus' wry humor, but it wouldn't be my last. He could tell stories on himself that would embarrass us terribly, then laugh at his own absurdity and stupidity. I didn't understand then how our beautiful teacher could ridicule himself so in front of us, and more importantly, in front of strangers, brought by us to be shown his divinity. I didn't understand how this man of God could show us his weakness one moment, then his unique, singular gifts from God the next. It took me a long time, but with his help, I did understand, and in time, loved him all the more for it.

Jesus taught in so many ways. Once, after a time such as this, I brought a Pharisee, such as myself, to see him. He was an old friend, a man of great learning and importance, a man I wished Jesus to impress with his unequaled knowledge of the Law. I impressed upon my friend ahead of time to expect a finesse in the interpretation of the Law, the likes of which he had never witnessed.

This was to prove a day of lessons for me, however, not for my friend. For my comrade stayed only long enough to hear my Master confess one story. I held my breath, for as Jesus spoke his first words, I immediately sensed my mistake. Jesus was not speaking with the refinement of manner and tone of which he was capable, but rather, he portrayed the heavy, guttural accent of the north, and I knew this would not set well with my Judean friend. Not well at all.

The story Jesus chose to tell, showed himself up to be an unlearned soul, and additionally, fell hard about a certain unnamed man of the Law, a Pharisee. His moral struck far too close to home, and my friend bolted in a rage. "What a waste of time!" he snorted, as he pushed his way through the mostly illiterate and poorly dressed crowd. Looking back, he wagged his finger at me, and sputtered, "Bring me not again to hear your Galilean friends, Asher. Spare me the effort, bring me not again."

Nothing escaped Master's eye, and thus, after he had finished teaching, (and there were well over a hundred there), he came over to me, put his strong arms around me and hugged me. Knowing the hurt and embarrassment within me at that moment, he held me at arm's length to look into my eyes. It was just as he had done the very first time I had seen him. There was magic in those eyes. He said, "Asher ben Ammi, I love you." He said it with such feeling, that I couldn't help the lump from forming within my throat.

"Do you believe in me, Asher?" "Yes Lord!" I said, surprised at the question.

"Then do you think I would embarrass you without a reason?" He knew I couldn't answer. "No, you know I wouldn't. Then why did I send your friend away, and hurt you? I did it for a reason. I did it to teach you, and all of them here, that we cannot judge. We cannot judge anyone. First, your friend came to judge me, then after he left, *you* judged me. Dear Asher, only God knows another man's heart. Neither you, nor I, can presume that we have that knowledge of another.

"Why do I tell stories on myself, Asher? Why? I do it to let you see that the least shall inherit the earth, Asher, not the greatest. For in my Father's eyes, the least is first, and the greatest is least. Don't you see? The great have already reaped their reward on earth, they need nothing of Him. But, Asher, there are so many poor souls in this world, who give nothing but love. They give everything they have... and receive so little. These are *my* people, Asher, these are mine. For them I feel. For them heaven will be opened. There is nothing I do that the least among them cannot do, I am no better or no worse than they, and it is by example only that I must show them this. Lofty words will not do. They feel humble and unworthy of me, Asher. I must show them it is I who is humbled. It is I who is honored to be in their presence."

How I learned from him that day. He spoke with such feeling, love, and pain in his eyes, that I wanted to slink away. I was so ashamed. I was wealthy beyond measure, and in my life I had given so little, and had humbled myself before none. The pain in my chest was overwhelming. It was true that my friend came not with an open heart, but to pick my Lord apart, and to show him as a fool. And I, I was worse. I brought him here knowing he came to judge. I brought him here to show Jesus off. Woe unto me, for I was judging worse than any. How dare I presume to judge this man of God by being embarrassed by him – for him! This man, who for our sakes, makes himself the lowest among us. Oh, how this man could touch that something special deep inside me. Oh, how this man could teach!

It wasn't for another year again, at passover, with the city full to the brim with people, that Jesus took time to rest awhile with us, and tell us more of the story of his youth. Although I heard more details later, while with others of his disciples, this night was special, and I want to keep its telling apart. It was at supper, and we were lying about on couches, in the manner of the Greeks. Though the dining room is large enough for a sizeable party, this night only my son, John and his wife, Jesus, Miriamme, and I were there. He came alone, without any of his twelve, as he often did here. This night it was in answer to my dear Miriamme that he picked up the thread from where it had lain that lovely day in Jericho, and continued telling the story of his youth.

"First, my dear Asher, I ask you to understand that our worlds were far apart. You, all of you, are Judeans, and I am a Galilean. We are not the same. You were raised with the holy city all about you. You are the most educated, the most honored of the Jewish line. Coming from a small town in Galilee, however, one is not favored with such luxury. Here, you profit by association with the Temple; in Galilee we feel only the sting of its taxes, and the priests' contempt for our very existence. Here you coexist with the Romans in an uneasy peace; in Galilee, we suffer with whip and chain the slightest whim of the lowest Roman or Greek. For you, a good year is measured on a tally sheet of profits and losses. For us, a good year is measured by whether we had food enough to spread on the table each night to eat.

"I say these things not to be cruel, not to make you feel better or worse than me, but to help you understand my story, and my people, the people who surrounded me as I grew. I tell you so that you understand *all* people in the future, as they come to you for help – and they surely will. When I am gone, your home will become a refuge, a gathering place for those who are seeking after me, and are lost. Each of you in this room is special to me, so special, I wish you only knew. Each of you lies cradled securely within my heart, and in our

Father's mansion, there I shall reserve room for you."

Jesus had a way of filling our hearts to breaking. He taught us lessons, (and some of those were very hard to take), and then he filled us with the love that passes all understanding; and in his love, somehow, the medicine became not quite so bitter, and our resolve to meet his expectations became, as he intended, a burning desire within. He saw us as shining beings, and that was what we wanted to be. We wanted to be to others, as our Master had been to us; and even if we fell short, as we often did, we made the effort, which was more than we had done before. And Jesus, as a mirror of his loving and gentle Father, showed us in his own gentle ways and in his deep forgiving eyes, that we were special, that we too could attain the heights of love he demanded of us.

And, now it is your turn to forgive, for I have rambled on with my comments, and left our Master far behind. Please let me go back to our teacher's story, the story of his growing, as he told it that night.

"While in Egypt, mother had heard from friends that the stories about her and father had grown while we were gone. And sweet as she was, she felt anger and fear inside, for the gossip had been mean. Our welcome, however, was exciting and wonderful for me. The whole village turned out to see us as we arrived. They hugged mother and father, then turned their attention to my brothers and me. My mother was so proud of us. I looked up at her, and adored her so. My father was the biggest surprise of all, however. He was smiling, and for the first time that I can remember, I noticed he had lost some of his teeth. It makes me laugh now, to think that this is one of the things that I remember most clearly about that important day so long ago.

"As the day wore on, I came out from behind my mother's legs and began to watch the people, some of them gathering into small groups, thinking that no one was watching, or could hear. It was then that I understood my mother's fears, for the welcome from many was a false one. Now, there would be more stories for them to spread. And who picks up mean stories faster than anyone? Why, the children, of course. So my life in the village started with taunts, and name calling once again, and as it had done in Egypt, and did again here, it drove me more and more within myself, where I found and explored my difference.

"Our home was just as mother had pictured it to me in her stories while we were away. It was one of many mud, brick and stone houses that lined the streets. The house was built right to the edge of the dirt pavement, which was wider than some of the streets in town, and proved most helpful when my father brought lumber into the yard. The house itself, was one story, up against the side of a small hill, which, by digging, had been made into a vertical cliff. The house was of one room only, which was of fairly good size. However, on the side of the house built into the cliff, a wide bench had been carved. The bench ran along the full length of the house. It was here father placed two wooden partitions, centering them, to separate the two platforms on either side for the children's sleeping spaces. Mother and father then used the small space remaining in the middle for themselves. I loved these cozy little rooms, for the partition, which was at the foot of my bed, was made of the most beautiful wood, finished in the way father had learned in Egypt, and had the most magnificent shine. On the side of their enclosure, that faced the rest of the room, mother had hung a curtain for their privacy. To my way of seeing, our house was the most wondrous in all the world.

"The rest of the room contained a large wooden table with two benches on either side, and two chairs at either end. It was here that the family lived, ate, and entertained our guests. At the back of the house, against the other stone wall was the fire pit that mother cooked in, and which heated the house. The oven was in the work yard, outside. Because the house was very dark, father built a glorious wooden louver wall between the house and his work area adjacent to the house. At just the right time of day, the light would flood through the slats, and cascade through the air to land at my feet. My brother, Joses, would play in the light and shadows as if they were real. To my mother's distress, he would kick up all the dust he could, so as to make the shafts of sunlight into solid bars of light.

"The work area outside the house was backed against the hill on one side, the house on another, and a low wall surrounded the last two. Over the entire work area was a cloth canopy, held up by vertical and horizontal poles. In later years, although I never wished to make for myself the life of a carpenter, I did come to love this cool, light, breezy work area most of all.

"With his small family settled, father turned his energy to his carpentry, and to my education. He took me to the little synagogue in the village, a large square building, hardly distinguishable from any other house along the street. Here he entrusted my education to the old rabbi, who had a face etched with deep rivers of time, and a long unruly white beard that was sprinkled with just a touch of black around his chin, and five thousand years of our history lost in the corners of his mind.

"The only thing I can remember of this holy place was the darkness, which spread into every corner of the room, and which to a young lad, was very mysterious indeed. The only light came from a square hole in the roof, where a brilliant shaft of light streamed into the room. It provided enough light for the seven or eight of us studying to see and read the Torah, which is why we came. I used to love to listen to the old rabbi tell us the stories of our people. By the time I was ten, I knew them all by heart, and most of the Torah too. He was a Pharisee, and believed with all his heart that the Messiah would soon be coming to save his nation Israel from the Herods, and the oppressing Roman conquerors. Those prophecies he could find in the Torah that told of the Messiah's coming. He would read to us with tears streaming down his face, a far away look of longing in his eyes.

"It was in that small, dark room, listening to the old man drone on, that the thoughts of my special being first entered my mind. It is so hard to explain now, so many years later, but it was like having an idea flit on the edge of your consciousness, or like seeing a figure in the mist coming off the lake. There is something so familiar about the image. The way they walk, or hold their head, perhaps. You hail them, but there is no response, and a great uneasiness descends upon you.

"I knew I was different. From my earliest memories I knew things that others didn't, but even to myself it was incomprehensible. It was an awareness just beyond my consciousness, something unsettling and uneasy, something just out of my grasp, something I *had* to know! But what, I did not know.

"It wasn't just dreaming of becoming the Anointed One, for every young boy in the village had at one time or another dreamed that he would grow to be the Messiah, and save his people from the tyrant Rome. Every young lad also thought that he would become the long awaited warrior–king. But for me it was different. I did not play at being a warrior–king, for there was something inside me that said that they were wrong. Somehow I *knew*, and that knowing is so hard to explain. I just *knew* that when the Messiah came he would save his people with love and grace, not with pain and war.

"The Father that I found within, was the Father of *all* people, and he had given nothing to me but love, compassion and grace. So when the boys took turns playing at being king, I would turn away. I would go to my quietness when work was done, I would go to my mountainside, and here I would watch the animals, the flowers and the trees; here I would still myself, and *know* that my Abba and I were One. It was a very special time, my youth. In solitude I found my Godness, and that is where I was, and what I was. It was here that I began to understand that the slaves I had known in Egypt were no different from the people of my land, nor from you, today. Freedom comes from within, and when one finds freedom there, no Roman, no Herod, no king can ever take your freedom again.

"My day started early. While father ate his morning meal, I straightened up the work shop, swept up the wood chips, scraps and shavings, and saved them for my mother's fire. After I finished, I would come inside for fruit and bread before I ran off to my lessons with the old rabbi in the synagogue. When my lessons were through, about midday, I'd return home, where my mother would have a bowl of porridge and goat's milk waiting. Then while I ate, she would busy herself at the cook stove, for she had to cook for my father's workmen too. My new baby sister – my third brother, Simeon, had been born a year earlier – would be slung to her breast nursing, yet she never missed a step. I remember sitting there at the great wooden table watching her, and wishing wistfully that she would look at me like she used to do before the other children came. That was when she had more time, when her eyes would ask me, `Are you son, are you?' And I felt so special! But those days were gone forever, lost in the busyness of everyday life. How important to grant oneself time away from this, to find the quiet place, to still the harried soul, to just be still, to find His healing peace within.

"When I finished my meal, I would once again go out to the work area and clean up whatever mess there was, and put away any tools that were left about. This chore I did as rapidly as possible, for if I finished cleaning before my father took the noon–day break, he would sometimes let me walk to the synagogue with him, where the men gathered to talk and debate. I always found a spot were I could see and hear without being in the way, for the men didn't like playful little boys who raced through the dusty street and were full of endless noise. On fine warm days they would gather in front of the synagogue in the open, or under the shade of the broad, spreading trees where my grandfather had placed benches for the old men so long ago. There was no other diversion in our village, except the news of the day, and of course, our religion which they loved to debate endlessly. It was here that I sat quietly, never moving a muscle for fear the men wouldn't let me stay, just listening and watching. It was here I learned of the hope, the desires, and the pain that lived within the soul of the people Israel.

"Our village lay close to a military road from the north, and although it was not used with great frequency, the legions and troops from Rome and Antipas would sometimes storm through the town. I learned early, as did every other man, woman, and child in the land, to stay out of their way if possible, and do their bidding rapidly and well when you could find no escape. They took what they wished, and feared no law save their own. After they had taken what they wanted, they passed on with a great flurry of bravado and grit. It was then that I would race to the synagogue, for it was here that the men of the town would invariably gather to scream their vengeance and lament their lot. It was in watching the incredible force of the imperial eagle that I realized that a new way to freedom must be found, and somehow I knew that its new form was within me, waiting only for the right time to be born.

"Rome may have conquered the world, but not in the mind of a Jew. For in the minds of our people, we were the chosen of God, we were the center of the universe. Our people were converting the world with our religion. In Cyrenaica, Syria, Asia, Galatia, Macedonia, and even in Italia people were circumcising and becoming Jews. We may have been the poorest of nations at home in our own country, but we were spreading our finest throughout the empire – it was the time and place for a Jew. I was a Jew, and as a child

I absorbed the consciousness of our people. We were special, we were God's chosen, and God said, `From my body Israel must come a child, and that child shall become the savior of the world. He shall spread my word and spread my name.'

"Thoughts such as these raged within my soul. There was a hunger there that needed to be fed. No, there was fire, and the more I fed it the more it raged. And I was pent up, and yet could speak of this to no man, no woman, nor with any other that I knew could I share what was held within me. And so, before I came to man, I had been prepared, and when the time did come, I could do *nothing* but follow the path laid out for me. I cried out to my Father, `God, oh please, tell me when it is time, show me a sign!' And He showed me a sign, and the sign was my cousin, the Baptist, John by name. He reached forth from the river Jordan to touch my forehead, and my skull exploded in wonder and ecstasy – *my God had finally come!*"

It was here that Jesus stopped, for I think my mouth was agape with astonishment. I had never heard the story of his awakening, and it was all a bit too much for me to comprehend. I know he was reading my mind, which had filled with a dozen questions all at once, for he said, "Why the look of surprise, Asher? What is it that you cannot understand, what is it you find so unusual?" *Unusual!!* Unusual wasn't the word, for I was speechless. My Lord had revealed himself in such a touching way, so intimately, that I could do nothing but sit in dumb silence while my eyes filled with tears, and I experienced the most intense loving I could ever feel.

It was in the early morning hours, while the household slept, that my Lord took me apart, and taught me the mysteries – the mysteries that even now wait for you.

Chapter 5

When Jesus was twelve years old he accompanied his parents to Jerusalem for the annual Passover Festival, which they attended each year. After the celebration was over they started home to Nazareth, but Jesus stayed behind in Jerusalem.

Luke 2:41-43

B y now the hour was late, so we left our repose at the dinner table and adjourned to the large living room with the fire, for I knew the servants were ready for their beds, and yet had to wait to clean up the dining room from our supper. I, too, would normally have been trying to adjourn, lest I offend our guests by yawning in their faces – but not this night. This night was special, more special than I knew at that time, and I was awake with an alert eagerness I hadn't known since my youth, quite a few years ago.

How rare it was to have our Lord alone and all to ourselves without the ever present crowds about him. Without the threat of spies from the Temple, from Rome, and from Herod. Jesus could relax. He didn't have to guard every word that came from his lips. How rare, indeed, that he could speak in plainness and understanding, and not in parables.

Jesus, too, seemed caught up in the telling of his youth, and made no attempt to end the evening as long as we seemed eager to listen. The dining room lies between the kitchen and the living area, so, after rising from the table, it was but a few steps through the small door at the rear of the room, into the large comfortable room beyond.

There had been a cold northern wind blowing all that day, and the warmth of the blazing fire was welcome against the howling intruder outside. I guided Jesus to the couch nearest the fire, and we all relaxed, hoping that he would continue from where he last left off. Jesus leaned against the couch, and let out an easy sigh as he sat staring at the orange flames dancing in the fireplace before him. His eyes drifted into the past as we watched the reflected flames dance in his eyes. The fire cast long shadows along the weathered lines of his sun-darkened face. Once settled, he leaned back comfortably and took up the story where he left off.

"In the afternoons, if there was no work for me to do, or no errands for me to run, I would often times go away, up into the hills to be alone. Mother didn't have much time to spend with me now, as she had the other children to care for, so my focus tended to turn within, rather than develop a dependency on her.

"We had an old woman living with us at this time to help mother, but that never stopped her from working as hard as ever; she tied my sister to her as she had done with my brothers and me before her, and continued her tedious tasks. My time was generally taken up with watching and listening at the synagogue, or being alone in the vastness of my Father's land.

"As I sat on the hill I could feel the warmth of the earth beneath me, the grasses, the flowers, the plants, the blue sky above, the drifting formless clouds that showed every color of my moods. And it was here that I knew I was One with my Abba. I would sit silently, looking out over the rolling hills to the north, and the vast valley to the south, feeling the gentle breezes in my upturned face. I would smell the air, and a feeling of exhilaration would course through my veins. When I was alone in this way, I felt my specialness with Him who was somehow my life, and my searching. Alone, I could talk to my Abba, and although there was no voice in answer, somehow I knew he was with me, and everything was all right. I felt so calm and sure. I had a *knowing* that my time was coming, if I could only wait. I could feel His presence as I slowly, silently walked backed to the village in the evening's deepening shadows, cast by the last rays of the rapidly sinking sun. My time was coming.

"How can I describe the feeling that was growing in my breast? How can I say in words the aimless anticipation that surrounded me? All these things I kept in my heart as I worked through the days, waiting, always waiting. At times I was overwhelmed with the feelings that flooded my being when I looked into a person and knew compassion for them beyond understanding, for at that second *I truly was that person!* How I struggled with these feelings when I found myself helpless to express them in this body of a small lad, not yet of age. The frustration was swelling each day. I felt like a volcano, as the pressure of my youth met the germinating awareness of the spiritual being who was developing within me at the very same time.

"I was twelve years old, and unbeknownst to me, my life was about to change in a way I could never have foreseen."

My attention sharpened here, for I had met our Master's mother several times before, and had heard the stories of his youth from her. Now, hearing from our Master how he saw himself during these formative years, I was enchanted. His mother described him as a strong, silent lad, with a consuming need to have his time alone. Sometimes he seemed a moody young boy who didn't get along very well with his peers, unless they were of his ilk. He could be raised to passion by incompetence or slowness in others, and in a fit of temper he could lash out at them with little warning, so that he was not well liked at all. He was far above the understanding of others his age, or any in their town for that matter, and his frustration knew no bounds. Time and age were his enemies then, although it seemed in listening to him, that as a lad, he knew not why.

As I talked to his mother I found that his greatest struggle came when presented with man's injustice to man. Galilee is, and always has been, the core of rebellion within our land. It was here he was raised, and heard his countrymen cry out against the injustices perpetrated against them by Herod, Rome, and we Judeans alike. Since the time of his earliest memories in Egypt, he had been determined that the downtrodden of the world be lifted up, and he, in his youthful ways, was impatient for the righting to begin. His mother, Mary, wished, as I suppose all mothers wish, that she had had more time with this youth, to counsel him in patience, softness and understanding, but her young household was growing, and all of her brood needed their mother's touch as much as he. As it turned out, however, our Master became the softest, most understanding man I have ever known.

Asked about his schooling, she said that where the other children studied by rote, Jesus absorbed, analyzed, and critically understood the Law that made his people the nation Israel. So it was, that the old Rabbi in the town filled with pride when he heard that his student was to visit the Temple in Jerusalem. He sent with Jesus a letter that he was to keep unto himself, introducing him to a bright, young, ambitious priest, Nicodemus by name, who would take care of him and look after him for the next few years.

As I would find, it was far more difficult than I could ever imagine for this special man, this special soul, trapped in a body of a boy, locked in the little town of Galilee (the people of which were known by all Judeans as 'am ha-arez,' a denigrating term connoting an uneducated peasant). I was constantly amazed as I watched Jesus rise to prominence, as he gained the respect of all those who would bypass their prejudices long enough to hear his words.

"Passover was approaching," Jesus continued, "and my parents were making ready to go south to Jerusalem as they had so many times before, but this journey was to be different from any they had taken, for this time my father had told mother and me that I too was to accompany them to the Holy City, where I had yearned to go. I was a man now, father said, and it was time I visited the Temple and made myself clean through my first sacrifice – an unblemished lamb.

"This wonderful news brought great joy to me, and I ran to the synagogue to tell the old Rabbi. It was here that I felt for the first time the full impact of this great man's caring; he who had been so tolerant of me during my years of growing. I will never forget it. He sat me down, and with tears forming in his eyes he handed me a note, written on skin, with instructions to present this to a certain priest of the Temple proper – none other would do. Then he hugged me, swore me to silence, even to my father, and after assuring himself I had stowed the missive properly, and understood my directions rightly, he showed me to the door.

"Jerusalem was beautiful! It was a city such as I had never seen. There were people by the tens of thousands; so many, I could not grasp the immensity of it all. The sights and colors, the smells of animals and spice, the sounds of voices and the horn of the ram erupted and mingled into a dumbfounding dream-like state within my mind. The days of preparation ran one into another, with only patches of clarity to mark their passing.

"When we arrived, we took up residence within a tent of sorts. Our tent was one of thousands like it that had been set up around the Pool of Bethsaida to the northeast, and within a few steps of the great Temple itself. The closeness and color of the tents and lean-tos that surrounded us with their multitude of occupants, astonished me, for I had never in my life seen anything like it. But if I was astounded by this, it was nothing compared to what was waiting for me within the Temple walls themselves.

"The following day we stumbled our way through the circuitous path shared by both man and beast in the haphazard placement of this city within the City, until at last we found ourselves walking directly under the very fortress that housed our powerful captors. It was in this tent city that Herod

Archelaus, not so many years before, let loose his dreaded horsemen upon the people. From these mighty walls over-looking the Temple, built by Archelaus' father, with stones larger than I, the Romans watched everything and everyone that came and went into the confines of the Temple itself.

"We entered through what was called by many, `Death's Gate,' for it was through this passage Archelaus' soldiers rode to attack this same camp of pilgrims.

"An audible gasp issued from my throat. I grabbed for my father's hand as my knees buckled, and the awesomeness of it all brought fear rushing at me. My mind made a vain attempt to sort out and catalog the scene, but it was useless. We picked our way through people of every kind; small and tall, dark and light, wealthy and poor, ignorant and bright, those with golden tongues and those who were dumb. All whom I saw seemed to be crowding and aimlessly milling about in a totally incomprehensible manner – or at least so it seemed to this country lad of twelve. At the south end of the Court of the Gentiles, father exchanged our Roman coin and bought an unblemished lamb for sacrifice. I was amazed and confounded at the noise and clamor from the vendors, each vying for our coin so that we could be about our Father's business. If you could have seen me, you would have seen a boy's eyes wide with wonder, surprise, fear, and absolute delight.

"Why, Asher, I might even have seen *you* there that day!" I blushed, aware of our Master's well-known feelings toward those Sadducees, and Pharisees (such as I), who profit at the well of the Temple gates. Although, I hasten to add, I make my living as an honest tradesman, and not as a moneychanger or profiteer, I cannot deny that my well-paid connections have served me well. My Master, always ready to teach those who were willing, and knowing all there is to be known about me, could not help delivering the painful jibe with a sly grin and a twinkle in his eye. And the result was exactly to his liking, as my wife Miriamme began to snicker, and my son and his wife met my embarrassment with outright laughter. At first my blood ran hot, as my pride rose to defend my lost honor, but moments later we were all laughing uncontrollably, as I threw up my hands in total surrender.

As we somewhat belatedly controlled our mirth, and threw more wood on the fire to keep the chill from the evening, we assured our Lord in the most forceful tones that we wished him to continue. His eyes sparkled in the dancing light as he looked my way and asked if I was recording everything. I assured him I would write everything on the morrow so as not to forget anything that he had said. Thus, seemingly satisfied, he continued with his memories of this, his first trip to Jerusalem.

"For the next two days leading up to Passover eve, father and I cleansed ourselves daily in the pool, and walked the Temple grounds, stopping here and there to listen to one rabbi, priest, lawyer, or teacher of one persuasion or another share his knowledge of the holy books. I found that father, like most of those from our town, loved to point out a weakness or add a point to an argument whenever he felt that he could contribute anything meaningful to the discussion. However, to be a Galilean, I was to quickly learn, meant many things, not the least of which was that we had heavy accents, and those of Judean background would stare at us or give us surly looks. They even mocked my father openly on more than one occasion. Because of this, I began to listen very carefully, and found that our language, the language of Galilee, was quite imprecise, as it had lost many of the subtle sounds that made the language so rich here in the south.

"I remembered back when father was buying the lamb for my first sacrifice. My father asked to purchase a lamb. Instead, the Temple merchant sneered at him and said, `You stupid Galilean, do you want something to ride on? Or something to drink? Or something for clothing? Or something for a sacrifice?' My father blanched, realizing his lack of education. His embarrassment was made all the more painful because of his son's presence. He could only point at the small lamb to make himself clear. He wanted me to be proud of him, and he had been belittled because of something he couldn't help, because of the way he was raised. I suppose he couldn't know it then, but I tried to show in my eyes that I adored him, and was more proud of him there, standing in front of all those people, than I had ever been before, for he was doing this for *me*."

Jesus affected me on so many levels – he moved me so. All he had to do was caress a memory, and remembrances of my own welled up within me – and within each of us who heard him. Every father who has ever lived knew of the father/son relationship of which he spoke, and knew the burning pain of shame at being shown up in front of your son, being made to look less than you so desperately wished to be for him. And each of us in the room with him knew the language difficulty that faced our brothers from the north. To a Galilean, the subtle differences of intonation in the word 'lamb,' were meaningless; but to us, the way he pronounced the word it could have meant 'wool,' 'wine,' or even 'donkey.'

Jesus turned from the fire to look at us with eyes that seemed to say a thousand things, that seemed to be looking at all of us, and at the very same time into each of our souls separately, always loving, never judging. This time I could see in those eyes that he was offering, by way of this story about his father who he dearly loved, an apology, an apology for all the times he knew he must have embarrassed us by slipping back into his local dialect while in our land of Judea. He was so incredibly humble, and I was again so incredibly ashamed. For I *had* been embarrassed on many occasions by his Galilean ways, and now realized again, on hearing this simple story from his childhood, how wrong it is to judge another without walking long and hard in his steps.

The small, sheepish smile came over his face as expected, and he continued once again. "I can still see that day in my mind, as if it were happening all over again. I was standing in the long line, awaiting my turn to approach the altar, the young lamb slung over my shoulders, as I had seen the others do, and once again my emotions began to overwhelm me. The sounds of the animals bleating in fear hurt me so terribly. I had never killed anything before, and the thought of killing this little trusting creature wrapped around my neck sickened me. Yet, the overwhelming pageantry I felt from actually being in the Temple, next to the Holy of Holies, seeing and hearing the throngs of people, made me feel small and insignificant, and proud and brave all at the same time.

"When my lamb had been prepared and put upon the altar, I felt something pull at me, not on the outside, but inside. I felt as if my Abba had touched me, as I had felt him on my distant hillside, and *I knew* that this sacrifice too would be somehow changed in time.

"With the ceremony over, my father slapped me on my back and we rejoined my mother, who was watching from the Women's Court just outside. Everyone was in a joyous mood as we retreated to the tent that father had rented for us to stay in. After a meal, and time to rest, mother dragged father off to the market place. After much begging, I convinced father I wouldn't get lost, and he let me go alone to the Temple, with many admonitions not to annoy anyone, nor get in the way. I was elated! Now was my chance to carry out my secret mission, to find the elusive priest in the temple.

"Nervously, I patted the letter that I had tucked securely in the pocket on the inside of my beautiful new robe. Oh, how special, how puffed-up, proud and manly I felt to be entrusted to carry this secret message to an unknown priest in the very confines of the glorious Temple itself. My imagination knew no bounds when it came to guessing its mysterious contents. Perhaps a conspiratorial message from a rebel leader to an accomplice in the Temple. 'What a wonderful trick,' I thought, 'the Romans will never expect a lad to carry a message of this magnitude.' I had agonized as to its contents all during the week of our trip.

"As soon as my parents were on their way, I headed straight for the Temple and continued past the outer walls directly towards the Holy of Holies, just as the old Rabbi had instructed. It wasn't hard to slip past the guards at the gates, as there were so many people, hundreds upon hundreds, asking questions and directions, that one small boy caused not even a lifted eye. My heart was pounding when finally I stood in the hall before the screen. I sat down and tried to calm myself, expecting at any moment to be arrested and thrown into prison.

"It happened quite unexpectedly. I guess I had learned to block out more of the outside world than I knew, for the first I was aware of anyone else's presence, was a gentle hand upon my shoulder. I looked up into the eyes of a kindly man, with no anger on his face. He looked back, I think equally surprised, and told me I would have to leave. Without a word, I reached into my inside pocket and drew out the letter I had guarded so carefully, and handed it to him. With a quizzical look on his face he slowly broke the seal, unwrapped it, and read its contents. When he was through, he looked at me very carefully, as if he still hadn't made up his mind whether or not he should take me seriously.

"Then, with an air of finality, he grabbed my hand, turned on his heels, and with robe flowing gloriously behind, took me in tow, retreating down wondrous stone corridors to a destination I could hardly guess. All I knew for sure was that I was following as fast as I could. We first went down a long hall, where at several locations I caught sight and sound of the altar and the people lined up to offer their sacrifices. Then, up a flight of stairs we went.

"Now it was getting darker, and I was becoming a bit apprehensive and afraid. Finally, after what seemed an eternity of passageways, halls, columns, and rooms (some with priests and scribes and some without), we entered a medium-sized room with maybe four or five men huddled in a group. My `guide' approached one of these men, whom I would guess was about my father's age. He leaned close to man's ear and whispered.

"The man had jet black hair, a peaceful face, and wore the robes of a Pharisee. The first man left us at that time, and this new charge motioned me to follow once again. We entered a small room next to the one in which we were standing. Here, he arranged himself on a rug, pulled up a low table in front of him, and unfolded the letter I had brought.

"After several minutes of reading, a smile creased his face. Leaning back against a pillow he looked up at me standing there before him, my hands hot and sweaty. `So!' he said, with his immense teeth and gums showing as his smile grew larger as he spoke, `Your Rabbi has sent you to me?' I nodded my head yes. `Well, he says that you are some kind of scholar.' There was a mocking tone in his voice. `He says that you know most of the Torah by heart. He says that not only have you memorized it, but that you understand it! Is that true, boy?'

"Again, all that I could muster was an affirmative nod. `He says that he wants me to make you my ward. He wants me to talk to your father, and arrange for you to stay here in Jerusalem to study under me. Is that what you want, boy, is that what you want, too?' The very idea of it was too immense for me to grasp all at once. Of course, I had dreamed of coming here and learning, but I never imagined that one day it would actually happen.

"My tongue finally found its way. `Yes,' I said. `Yes! Oh, yes, I most assuredly do.' That was all it took. In his mind it was settled. He would see to it that all the arrangements were made. He held the old Rabbi in deep respect, and owed him a debt of great weight that he had feared he would never be able to pay. So finally, in this request, he had found his opportunity to return some measure of gratitude to his benefactor of the past. He was quite delighted to find in me a way of satisfying his obligation of love to this old Galilean friend.

"That afternoon was one of the happiest in my young life, for my new guardian priest, Nicodemus by name, took me completely under his care, spending the rest of the afternoon showing me every wing, room and corridor of the Temple complex. I saw the doors, some of them eight times the height of a man, as one after another we passed, many of them covered with gold, silver and bronze. I saw the finest rare woods (reminiscent of Egypt), intricate carvings, rich cloth and vestments stored in the closets; and as if that were not enough, my mind reeled at the vast storehouses under the dirt and stone courtyards above, filled to overflowing with coins, and gold and silver implements of every kind. Riches beyond my imagination, all obtained from the offerings of our people, far and near, rich and poor, to our God, the God of Israel.

"I was lost that day most of the time, and completely loving it. 'Imagine me,' I thought. 'Me, a carpenter's son from Nazareth touring every nook and cranny of the Temple. Even if it ends here, it will have been grand.' Before I left that day, Nicodemus admonished me to be sure to have my father attend morning prayers in the Court of the Israelites; he would find us there, and speak to my father then.

"As you can well imagine, I could hardly sleep that night. I tossed and turned so much that in the middle of the night my father could stand it no longer, saying, 'What's the matter with you tonight, boy? Either you stop thrashing about like a sick kid, or I will throw you out on your ear!' I knew he didn't mean it, but I made sure to lie quite still after that.

"Finally morning came, and father was ready. I thought we would miss prayers altogether, it took him so long. He seemed to be enjoying my discomfort immensely. I tell you, it was quite a sight to see when Nicodemus picked my father out of all the crowd, and told him he would be pleased to see him after services. Can you imagine?" Jesus said with a merry laugh. "Can you just imagine the look on his face when everyone around him turned to stare at him, wondering why this obvious Galilean had been singled out and honored by a Temple priest.

"Father was sweating from every pore, although I remember the morning to be quite cool. He looked down at me as if to ask if I could possibly know what this was all about, then thought better of it (what could his young son know about anything so important as this?), and turned his attention back to the service, churning within himself for the rest of the hour until services were done. I am sure he didn't know whether he was to be honored or flayed behind the immensity and magic of those doors."

Jesus glanced at us and said, not unkindly, but just stating the facts of the matter. "You, being of the Temple crowd, having education, wealth, and influence, know nothing of the mystery, fear, and awe with which the country folk hold the men behind the gates of the Temple seal." He was right, for I had seen farmers, shop keepers, and many others, that had traveled to Jerusalem from the far corners of our country, shake with an excitement long lost in youth by those of us raised within sight of the City. I have seen men go mad and throw themselves upon the altar. I have even seen them loose their bowels in joy or fear when a priest or scribe singled them out for some reason, and approached them. These things my jaundiced eyes had seen, so I knew of what our Lord spoke about his father, and my heart went out to him.

"Father left me behind and cautiously approached the door that had been pointed out for him to enter. I know he was petrified, as his simple life had given him no knowledge of Temple protocol at all, and yet, he wanted desperately to please. Several men who had been nearby waited close at hand to see if they could pick up some small bit of gossip or intrigue to carry back to their friends and families. As for myself, I was just as nervous, but for a different reason. I wanted more than anything to be allowed to stay.

"I didn't have to wait that long. Father must have come to a rapid decision, for I soon saw him returning down the long marble colonnade that had been built by Herod in his ill-begotten attempt to buy the loyalty of his subjects. Father's face was white and somber, and he seemed shaken by his recent experience. He put his arm around me, and said with great gravity, `Son, let's find someplace cool to sit.' I followed him out of the Temple building and into the outer court, where we found a bench under a portico and sat.

"`My boy...' That's all he said for what seemed an eternity. His eyes were blank, deep in some mist-shrouded thought, and I was dying with anxiety. `My boy,' he finally continued, `something great and wonderful has happened. Something has come about that I do not understand. That priest...' he paused again. `That priest you saw approach me' – words were coming hard for him here, and I saw him fight back tears – `he wants you to stay here in Jerusalem and study, study under his direction. He thinks you have the makings of a fine Rabbi.' He paused again, then said, `Before I say any more, I think that as you are now approaching manhood, it is time I tell you all that I know about you, about your coming, about your birth.'

"Father then proceeded to tell me everything he knew, about the voice he heard, about the wise men and young kings, about all these things that he had held within himself all these years. He ended with the story of how the priest Nicodemus had talked to him this morning, how he had singled me out and decided that I was worthy of his teaching. I could tell that father was decidedly honored, and perplexed by being singled out by Nicodemus, but I was nearly beside myself waiting to see what my father's decision would be. Could I stay, or not?

"Finally, after a long pause he said, `I have decided. It is all too much of a coincidence, all that has happened in your life. You must be a man now; the Lord has special plans for you, of that I am sure.'

"`What father, what is your decision?' I wanted to yell at him. `I have decided you will stay!'

"I squealed with delight as I jumped to my feet, drawing the attention of several men nearby. My father, already more nervous than I had ever known him to be, put his hand to his lips (looking fervently to each side of us in hopes no one was looking), and pulled me down to the bench by the hem of my robe. `There is just one thing more,' he said, `you must not tell your mother – you must not let on that there is anything amiss. We still have two days here, I will determine a way to tell her in my own time. Is that agreed?' Of course, I agreed. This was the happiest day of my life. Imagine me, me, studying at the great Temple in Jerusalem. What would the boys back in Nazareth think now, when they heard the news?

"The Sabbath came and went, and still father had thought of no way to break the news to my mother that her son would not be returning home with her. As we walked and talked together over the next couple of days, exploring the shops and seeing the city, mother and father spent long hours (long hours for me, at least) together, all to no avail. He was no closer to telling her on the last day than he had been on the first.

"All during this time I kept looking at him, staring at him, trying to make him say something – but nothing seemed to work. Mother was happy and singing these last days, with no thought of father or me, and no knowledge of the imminent problem we had between us, and father found it impossible to break into her mood. Father had bought her some beautiful cloth to be made into new clothing for the family, and a large new pot for her to use in cooking for her growing brood. We even stopped to have some sweets prepared by a crazy roadside vender on the way back from the market streets. Sweets, however, were hardly what was uppermost in my mind at the time. Although he started to tell mother that I wouldn't be returning with them several times, each time he became afraid or stumbled over the words, changed the subject, and finally let it slide – my frustrated, infuriated skulking to no avail.

"When the evening after Sabbath ended, and mother was packing our belongings for the trip to begin the next morn, I could wait no more. I pulled father outside the tent and asked in a very exasperated voice what I was supposed to do? It was then that he concocted the most bizarre scheme to allow me to stay, and yet again forestall telling mother what was going on. `Tomorrow morning slip quietly out with your things. Do not awaken your mother, or we will both pay. I will tell her you left early, with my permission, to travel back with Joshua's family. Once we are on our way, it will be impossible for her to refuse what is already done.' This was the first time I realized how powerful my mother was, when it came to something she considered important. Although my father was the head of the family, it was the tail that most often wagged the dog." A smile spread across Jesus' face, as Miriamme and John's wife looked at each other in knowing delight.

Jesus continued, "I say I realized how powerful mother was, when it came to her family, but it wasn't until this trip that I gained a new respect for her, that I would not soon forget. In the future I was to consider her feelings and influence to a much greater degree than before. In fact, it was only a few days later that I was to get yet another warning to heed her dominant position, and this time I vowed I would never forget again.

"I had just been settled into a room within a rock's throw of the Temple and started into a routine of discourse with the teaching elders, listening, and reading, when suddenly my mother burst into a session with the teachers of the Law, my father trailing sheepishly behind. It was such a breach of etiquette that all mouths, including mine, were agape. Mother strode right up to me, her little feet echoing through the great hushed hall, looked me square in the eyes and said, `Why have you done this to us? Your father and I have been frantic, searching for you everywhere.'

"I was shocked to my roots. I stammered, `But, didn't you know that I would be here in the Temple? Didn't my father tell you that I would be in His house?' Mother missed the double entendre in her agitation, as I thought she would, but father hadn't, and suddenly I found anger rising within me. I stared straight at father, my eyes flashing with rage, as I realized, *he still hadn't told her!*

"Nicodemus was not there when my parents arrived, but was being hurriedly summoned, and met the three of us on our way out of the hall. He was able to quiet my mother, but no arguments he could make, nor statements as to my unique abilities in rendering the holy books, or my special under-standing, could avert her insistence on my return with them to Nazareth. She judged me far too young to be away from home and her supervision.

"So, it was with sad heart and resentful spirit that we once again headed north to our home. A trail that had once been bright with promise, now seemed lonely indeed."

Dawn was drawing close, and the last glowing embers of the fire were dying when Jesus seemed to weary of his memories, and so he ended this most incredible night with a statement that covered the next four years of his life, and contained but two sentences.

"It was almost a year later until my constant insistence finally persuaded my mother that it was hopeless to try and keep me away from my inner calling, and my parents once again sent me south, entrusting my care to the patient and loving Nicodemus. It was then I began to study from the most learned men of the time, Hebrew, Greek, and Hindu alike."

That last statement intrigued me, for I knew nothing of these strange people, and their even stranger faiths, but Jesus was bidding us all a fair night, and this was not the time to bring up what should be another night's subject, for we too were bone weary and needed sleep.

Little did I know that this was the last opportunity I would have to hear of my Master's childhood, in my home, from his own lips. He had divulged more to us in this one evening than he had shared with anyone else in the almost three years of his teaching, and I was honored beyond words, but my nature could not let it lay. The following week I was to piece whatever little more I was to learn of this period of our Lord's life directly from Nicodemus, now an old man like myself.

Chapter 6

After dark one night a Jewish religious leader named Nicodemus, a member of the sect of Pharisees, came for an interview with Jesus.

John 3:1

Is there a single one of us Jewish rulers or Pharisees who believes he is the Messiah? ... Then Nicodemus spoke up.

John 7:48 & 50

It was a beautiful dawn! I had risen early as Jesus had bade us do, for it truly was the most peaceful part of the day. I slipped out of bed, leaving my sweet young wife sleeping peacefully, her beautiful raven black hair spread over the pillow like a gossamer veil, and while everyone in the house slept, I went alone to the rooftop shortly before the sun stole its way over the far horizon. There, in silence, I closed my eyes and turned within to our Father, as Jesus had taught me. As the sun slowly spread its warmth upon the earth, it engulfed me in its radiance, filling my body throughout with a warming light that permeated the depths of my being, and matched the loving splendor I experienced within. The sun is indeed too bright to behold, but it dims to a pall beside the iridescent resplendence of the one God who Jesus taught us to find in the depths of our souls.

Refreshed and renewed, I looked about at the new day. Down the hill below my roof-top perch, the city was coming alive. In the distance I could hear an occasional dog barking as his stomach told him that there would soon be scraps from the table for him to eat; and when I listened very carefully, I could hear the first of the shop keepers setting up their wares at the foot of the western Temple wall. I took a deep breath of the crisp clean morning air, filling my lungs to the brim with the cool breezes that were coming up from the Valley of Hinnom, bringing with them a scent of the sea far below and to the west.

Walking down from the roof, I silently slipped past the family's sleeping quarters, then down the outside stair into the beautiful protected inner court, kept always green with the Royal Palm from Egypt, and our own native fig. The court was also filled with a myriad of wonderfully blooming wisteria, and other climbing plants clinging to the white walls with splashes of living, brilliant colors. The plants were placed in this wonderful sheltered court to give splendor to the eye as they gathered the warming rays of the sun, reflected from the two story stone walls that surrounded it. Here, the plants were protected from the frost that would not be long in coming – for autumn was close at hand.

I loved autumn, for it meant that the Feast of Tabernacles was approaching, and the Feast of Dedication was soon to follow. The weather was magnificent and invigorating at this special time of the year. Thus I thought, as I crossed the courtyard with its beautiful mirrored pool, and slipped into the room where the girls were busily preparing the meals for the day. I sat to chat with them for a moment as I ate some fruit and lightly spread bread, cold now, left over from the day before. I didn't want to wait for the fresh bread, now baking in the inside oven at this chilly time of the year, for I had set my sights on meeting Nicodemus this morning, and it was quite a walk to the Baths where I knew he would be. Jesus had left for Bethany the morning after telling us of his youth, and for two days now I had been completely occupied with affairs of business, knowing there would be precious little time during the holidays. But now, with all of that in the hands of John, I could find nothing more important than to find my old acquaintance Nicodemus and ply him with questions of my Lord.

The walk was invigorating, and even though it was mostly down hill, it was some distance, and did me good. I thought I should probably do this every morning – then chuckled aloud to myself, as I dismissed the ridiculous thought as rapidly as it had come – just another one of my good intentions never brought to fruition.

The Roman Bath, or Thermae as the Romans call it, was built by Herod in his mad attempt both to curry the favor of Rome, and spread the influence of Greeks and their combined culture throughout his kingdom. Later, when his son Archelaus was banished, the Romans enlarged and completed the Bath to suit their needs. Actually, the custom of public bathing, still thought to be a heathen activity by most of my countrymen, has many adherents among the leading families of the city.

On several occasions I have found it quite a profitable and convenient place to consummate a transaction with business acquaintances, Romans, and even to my surprise, a few of my own race.

Approaching the Bath, one must be impressed by nothing about it, but its size, for the outside is less than spectacular. But once inside, a visitor can not help but be awed by its opulence, rivaled only by the Temple itself. It is raised on a platform within enclosing walls, which houses the furnaces underneath. As you enter, you pass through a colonnade into a beautifully landscaped garden, then into the building proper. The first room is a wonderfully arched hall about which the remaining rooms are all symmetrically placed. Using the Roman convention, the hall itself has at its apex a dome more than thirty cubits high, held in place by massive walls, and Egyptian granite columns of two colors, themselves twelve cubits in height, and these in turn are topped with white marble entablatures. The mosaic floors contain geometrical patterns of incredible beauty, and the lower walls are also lined with marbles from all over the world. There are three baths, each of a different size, and each of a different temperature. The largest is a pool of naturally cool water called a Frigidarium; the second bath is of slightly warmer water (which I preferred) called a Tepidarium; and the last is a very hot bath called a Calidarium, which is housed in a most impressive domed room with clearstory windows of thin translucent alabaster interspersed along the top. Not only is the water heated in this room, but hot air also comes from the walls.

Reaching the Baths, I unclothed in the changing room

and placed round me a large towel provided by the attendant, and headed for the Sudatorium, or dry sweating room where I thought Nicodemus might be. True to form, I found him there and was greeted with warm delight. He, too, was in good spirits, delighted to converse with someone of his own persuasion, and was even more agreeable to talk about the young boy Jesus, sent to him to learn so many years before.

I told him some of what Jesus said, of how he came to be Nicodemus' ward. As I expected, this was all it took to get the old man started. I have to chuckle, for I too am his age, and can ill afford to call him "old."

"I will start by telling you that Jesus was a most unusual boy," Nicodemus began. The first thing I did when I read the note from my old friend, the Rabbi from the north, was to ask a few questions of him. These I made progressively more difficult, until I asked him a question concerning the Torah that baffles even the wisest of our scholars today. I doubt if what I asked made the slightest impact on the boy, so well versed was he in the Law. But, Asher, it wasn't just that he had memorized the Law of our fathers. It was different. It was almost as if he had written them himself. For his answers, even though they were short and youthful, were at the same time pointed and accurate. He displayed such a compassionate understanding of them that it was all I could do not to expose him to everyone right there on the spot. Why I didn't, I do not know. There was something inside me that kept me from it. Mind you, Asher, I wasn't old and feeble-minded like you in those days. I was sharp and bright."

I had not been around Nicodemus for some time, and I had forgotten his quick wit and jolly manner. Once again I was beginning to enjoy his way of telling a story, as much as the subject matter itself that I had come to delve.

We both laughed until our sides hurt, then feeling weak and a bit giddy from the steam and heat, we pretended we were thirty years younger and jumped headlong into the cold waters of the Frigidarium. It had an amazing effect. I actually felt as though the years *had* melted from me. Arm in arm we climbed out of the pool and chatted as we wound our way into the Unctuaria where we entrusted ourselves to the masseurs – slaves who were honored and treated with great respect for their special gifts of kneading and prodding, and tender ministrations that worked miracles on old, tired bodies such as ours. It was here, as we lay in flaccid peace, our sore bodies being treated as those of kings, that Nicodemus continued his story.

"I knew I had a find! For before me I had a young man with a brilliant supple mind, who with proper training, and deft handling, could be molded into the most extraordinary priest Jerusalem had ever seen. He would need a great deal of training, I knew, for his Galilean background served him ill for what I had in mind for him."

The masseur rolled Nicodemus over with a grunt, then started working on his toneless girth. Settled again, Nicodemus closed his eyes and continued. "I was mistaken, though, for I had no idea at that time just how headstrong and bright he really was.

"The first step, however, was to keep him in Jerusalem under my tutelage. In that regard, his father proved no obstacle, for he was in mortal fear of me, and the unfathomable power I represented to him. But, alas, the mother of the lad proved a more worthy adversary. Not impressed in the least with the uniform of pomp, nor the use of rhetorical logic, nor even the threat of the Lord (forgive me), she whisked him away and out of my grasp for almost a year.

"It took this long to get him back, but come back he did; thanks to my good Mentor in Nazareth, some backbone left in his father, and the lad's own persistence. He stayed here in Jerusalem for three years. Three years, wherein he received the highest wisdom and teachings there were to be had from holy men of learning in three of the richest cultures known to man.

"May the Lord forgive my arrogance and pride, for during the entire time he was with me, and that I supervised his growth, I let not any of the hierarchy know of his gifts. Because of my birth, I had no way of becoming close to the power of Annas or Caiaphas. Lord, how I resented them and their structure in my youth. But my brilliant young student, Jesus, was indeed a different story. You see, I checked his genealogy, and although of simple birth, I could follow it back all the way to David. Imagine, Asher, all the way to David!" The masseur asked to stop at this point, for Nicodemus was gesticulating and shaking his arm so violently it was impossible to hold him to the table without physical restraint.

"Calm yourself, Nicodemus, old friend." I cautioned, "You could stroke right here on the table, and wouldn't that be a pretty mess." The thought of it, for some bizarre reason, brought a tickle of a smile to the edge of my lips, and then I found I could fight the urge no longer. The twitch became a smile, the smile a barely concealed chuckle, then outright laughter overwhelmed me again at the thought of seeing the old man in death, his hand upright, and his finger extended to the sky in righteous indignation. I thought, "I shall stuff him and install him in the Temple for all to see!"

Oh, what a picture. Lord, I was laughing, holding my sides in merriment. Nicodemus, with finger and arm still waving at the ceiling frescoes above, his face frozen in righteousness, alone in his world of the past, suddenly, slowly, became aware of my uncontrolled chortling of mirth and glee. The first thing to change was his eyes, refocusing from their lofty, distant visage. Slowly coming to gaze upon another sight equally as incongruous; a half naked old man doubled up with laughter on a narrow slab of a table, teetering totally out of control, with two masseurs staring at each other in confusion and disbelief.

Still holding his godlike pose in the body denied its rightful pomp, the ends of his mouth, too, began to cleft into a sheepish smile. "Sorry," he said, and slumped limp back onto the table. When I gained my composure, I assured him that I also had launched into a pet speech or two in my time, and now I knew why my family invariably laughed themselves silly, while I flew into a rage. I apologized for laughing, reaching over and grasping his arm in friendship. I think from that day on we shared a special closeness, both in each other – and in our friendship with a very special man.

It was only after I made a solemn oath never to place him in the Temple court, should such an ignominious end befall him sometime in the future, that Nicodemus consented to continue his story.

"Anyway, Asher," he continued, giving me a wary side-long glance, "I sought to teach the boy to my ends, not his.

I planned to teach him far beyond the wisdom of any then in the service of the Temple, beyond even Hillel, whose wisdom was legendary, and incidentally, who was also of the line of David. Then, at the propitious moment of *my* choosing, I would bring him forth to rightfully claim the inheritance stolen from the people. However, my plans were not his. As he grew in years under my tutelage, he grew into manhood, and with that growth he also grew headstrong and impatient. He saw through my scheming and ended my plan, which in looking back, Asher, was from the start, a foolish and self deluding one.

"Incidentally, I understand that your son, John, has become an open follower of Jesus, and from your questions, might I deduce that you, too, are a follower?"

Although I knew Nicodemus fairly well, I did not know him as a confidant, and his question immediately put me on guard – as rightfully it should. For in the politics of the day, a careless slip to the wrong ears could mean financial ruin, and loss of influence for perhaps years for me, but it could be far worse, far, far worse.

He had just told me, in so many words, that he had once had hidden designs on the High Priest's position. What did I know of this man's ties to the *inner circle* of power? I myself had no ambitions in that regard, as I had gained entrance to the ruling body not on religious grounds, but by wealth. However, I was cautious, because there had been rumors, which I tended to ignore (perhaps inadvisably), about Caiaphas' concern that Jesus was becoming too compelling among the masses, and that he might cause trouble with the authorities, meaning the Romans. I knew Jesus well enough,

I thought, to know that he had no designs on the Temple power, nor Rome's, for that matter.

Nicodemus was a shrewd observant politician. He read my hesitation perfectly, and as we moved into the Unctuaria where our hair was shampooed, our skin scraped with a strigil, and our bodies anointed with oils and unguents, he waved his hand to dismiss his own question to me, and continued, himself, instead.

"Never mind, Asher, you should not answer that question without knowing me, and where I stand on this matter. Did you know I just saw him recently, a few days ago, privately? Did you know that your son, John, was the one who brought me to him?" He could tell by the surprised look on my face that I did not. "I saw him for the first time in twenty years," he continued, with a strange distant look in his eyes, "I had to see him again. I had to be sure that this Jesus who was teaching in Galilee, was the same Jesus I had taught so many years ago here in Jerusalem. It was he, Asher, it was he!

"Asher, my dream has come true. He has wisdom far beyond our understanding. I have been unable to sleep these past days, for his teachings have burned their way into my mind. He spoke to me of so many things, especially of a new birth for our people, one that I am only now, with great reflection, beginning to understand. I tell you, he knew me so well, and although I endured the sting of subtle reproach for my past deeds, in truth, it was milder than I had prepared for, and love was at its seat.

"His teachings were as mysterious as the source of the wind, for although I knew not of what he spoke that night, it is just now coming upon me like a gentle breeze in the dark hours before dawn. I know that he is special, and I feel that I am being reborn, not to woman, but reborn in my soul. My spirit sings a new song, and I know I must seek him out and learn from him more; no longer will I be the teacher and he the seeker, but the other way around. If I were but younger and stronger, if I had but more of the courage of my youth, I would stand for him, Asher, I would drop everything and follow him. And in that vein, dear fellow and friend, I ask you to warn him. Warn him that even now he is being watched at every quarter by Caiaphas' men. They report almost daily of his activities, and they in turn to Herod, of his sayings. Please warn him to be most cautious, lest he slip and say what he is not yet prepared to say."

Now finished, and feeling like new men, we stepped out into the bright new morning and the carefully groomed gardens of Caesar. We walked silently around the manicured lawns, each lost in his own thoughts, until I motioned Nicodemus to a seat in full view of the radiant and warming sun. Looking deeply into his eyes I said, "Before we part this day, dear friend, I wish to thank you for sharing your morning with me, and for being so candid in your speech. However, I came to find out about those years you did have him in your care. Could you tell me anything about those three years?" He smiled, a gentle smile now, and he seemed to settle a bit, as he stared deeply into the depths of the shallow mirror pool that lay at our feet. And thus he drifted back into memory.

"In our own faith, Asher, I instructed him as far as I was able. Every Law of our fathers he was taught, and of the Perishaiya, every oral tradition and each sacred rite. Even unto Hillel I led him for a month, to absorb every subtlety he could discover with his probing mind.

"Then when I judged him to be complete in Jewish Law, I led him to the Greeks. I had made many contacts, many favors were owed in kind, and so into their schools I enrolled him to learn everything he could, both myth and fact alike, to learn of Socrates, Hippocrates, Hermes, Homer and more. The ideas of the Greeks were foreign to our young lad, and like his people before him, he fought against them with a vigor I had not before seen displayed so early in youth. But the amazing thing was, Asher, he learned their lessons well, and unlike us who merely turn our backs, threaten and cajole, he turned their own weapons of tongue and mind against them, and with pure and unadulterated logic he put them in their place. Pride is not limited to we Jews, however, and after one particularly vociferous session wherein Jesus showed the pompous scholar to be a fool, he was asked, in no uncertain terms, to leave the school. I tell you truly, I have heard, and heard reported the things that he says and the things that he does, and I think that he unwittingly absorbed perhaps more than he would care to admit.

"When I was just turned twenty, I had occasion to come upon a man of strange looks, and even stranger demeanor. I had been sent to the port of Joppa to deliver a message outbound to Alexandria, and on my way back I strayed from the path set for me to see what promised to be a most spectacular view of the sea.

"I rounded a small hillock and ventured down a path, settling on a flat patch of dirt in front of what appeared to be a little cave. I had just pulled from my bag some bread, and unwrapped the fish I had purchased in the market that morning, when I nearly died of fright. From behind me came a roar of laughter, which when magnified by the acoustics of the cave, sounded to this poor soul as though a giant were about to devour me. In fact, it turned out to be a most fearsome, but gentle man, dressed in nothing but a loincloth, and a simple leather thong that was slung across his chest and under his arm. He was a fright to see, what there was of him. A man shorter than you, Asher, slight of build, he had the most amazing beard, for it stretched down to his waist, then looped up over his shoulder, and wrapped around his neck again. He wore no cover on his head, save the dirty gray unruly mop of unshorn hair, and no cover on his feet, but his eyes were more vibrant and friendly than any I had ever seen.

"At first I was so petrified that I could not have issued a sound if I had tried. My eyes grew wide and round, and my hair stood on end like a cur. I couldn't have run to save my life if I had wanted to, for my legs had turned to stone, and my bowels to water. I thought I had found a devil come to haunt me from his grave! Later, I would be thankful for my failure to escape, for in less time than it took me to regain my composure, his gentle voice and warm demeanor had convinced me to stay, and with trembling hand I ate my fish, and shared some strange hot dish that he brought out for me to dip my bread. This old man lived until just a year ago, Asher, and I visited him each week without fail during the last months when his health began to fail.

"This extraordinary little man had come from India, a far-off eastern land, once conquered by the Greek Alexander. He was full of a strange wisdom that I learned, if not to agree with, at least to respect. Incredibly, he spoke the perfect

Hebrew of our fathers, which he said he learned at his father's royal court, in a place called Punjab state. He came to our land many years ago, and never found reason to leave. He washed himself but once in each ten days, on his trip to the ocean below, and spent the rest of his time here in this small cave contemplating the manifestation of his gods from the Atman, the One unknowable being.

"It was to him that I brought Jesus last, and although I thought highly of him, Jesus would say little, but I think from him he learned much. Jesus did not have to learn to speak to God, for he already had the wonderful uncanny ability to talk to his Father directly (which, as you know, Asher, he calls Him *Abba*, daddy, a term only a child would use, even to this day). This intuitive facility to know our Father directly, I could not fathom, just as I could not understand that he and his Father were One. However, that fact was unshakable in him even at this early age, but what this wise little man was able to show Jesus was a special way to fall within, a practice of breathing and concentration that he made Jesus do over and over each day. I know of this man's ways. They are subtle, very subtle, and while this young lad of fifteen argued, stomped and stormed at being made to practice these absurdities, he was changing ever so slightly each and every day.

"I remember one afternoon slipping quietly into the little two room house I had acquired for the two of them to live in within the city walls. Jesus did not notice my presence, so overwrought was he, pacing back and forth waving his now strong young arms to emphasize his point to his teacher, who was sitting placidly on the floor against the wall with a look of extreme peace, contentment, and pride on his face. Yes, there was just the slightest look of amusement too, at the corners of his eyes – a twinkle I could recognize. For an aroused Jesus was quite a sight to see.

"'Why? Why do you insist that we must come back over and over again? Why?' he asked, looking intently at the small quiet man in the corner. I stayed quietly in the entrance shadow, enjoying the play unfold just as the old man had desired. He had been working with Jesus now for over six months, and had confided that his training was nearing an end. He told me that in India students trained for tens of years at a master's feet, and still could not come close to the depths this young soul had reached in so short a time. The 'philosophy of belief was unimportant,' he would tell me, 'it is the wisdom of the soul that counts.'

"The old man finally replied quietly to Jesus' shouts and accusations, without a ripple of agitation. 'Because, my fine young man, you have many lessons to learn, and it would be quite impossible for you to learn them all in one lifetime. It is quite apparent for example, that you haven't learned patience.'

"Jesus bent over to within a foot of the old man's face, looked at him sharply for a long moment, and then with a shrug of futility shouted, 'Patience! I've been here six months and what mysteries have you shown me? You tell me that I come back over and over. But where is the justice of it all? Look at the people, they are poor! What good is it? What possible use does this knowledge have for my people? What can I do with it? I'll tell you what I can do with it – *nothing!*'

"Jesus was now pacing back and forth, a wild-eyed youth with pent up energy that we both knew must soon find its escape. His arms were clasped behind his back, in the posture of his elders (how subtle the influence of our breeding I thought).

"'There are poor people everywhere, soldiers everywhere!' Jesus continued. 'The priests in their beautiful robes don't care! No one cares! I ache for justice. There *must* be justice, but where, oh where, can it be found?' He cried to no one in particular – yet everyone – for there is not a man alive today who has not cried this cry of our people. I knew the teachings of the old man, and I remembered too the urgency of my youth. In Jesus' youthful mind everything was immediate. I could see that he needed time to ripen. The teachings of this teacher took time, and Jesus could not wait.

"Then as I silently watched, Jesus suddenly stopped his pacing, and his head slowly bowed and cocked to the side, as if he were listening to some inner voice that only he could hear. He was strangely silent for the longest period; there was not the slightest sound in the room, as his teacher and I both watched this wonderful young soul mature, ever so slightly, in the twinkling of an eye. Jesus began to speak, and as he did, the old man slowly turned his head to me, and in his eyes I read his thoughts, 'The time of his teaching is over.' I knew then, that I had to let him go, my plans for him were ended.

"Then, with a peculiar look etched upon his face, and in a voice quite strange, soft, and otherworldly, Jesus said, 'Karma takes time... and I approve it anyway.'

"I tell you, Asher, I didn't understand what he meant then, but I do now. When I sat with him the other night Asher, I knew. He is the One for whom we have been waiting. *Asher, he is the Messiah!*

Chapter 7

See, all your angry enemies lie confused and shattered. Anyone opposing you will die. You will look for them in vain - they will all be gone. I am holding you by your right hand - I the Lord your God - and I say to you, Don't be afraid; I am here to help you. Despised though you are, fear not, O Israel; for I will help you. I am the Lord, your Redeemer; I am the Holy One of Israel.

Isaiah 41:11-14

After the celebration of the Feast Jesus took cause to leave the city, for there had been a terrible confrontation with the priests over a miracle he performed on the Sabbath, a thing I, too, thought he should never have done – oh Lord, so much I had to learn! When the trouble arose, I immediately warned Jesus of what Nicodemus had said, but it seemed to have had no effect on him at all.

Once Jesus left for Galilee, I began to listen much more carefully to the Temple gossip, which through practice I had learned to ignore in the past as I thought it petty. Now, however, I found new reason to hear, and thus newly attuned,

I found great cause to grow uneasy for the safety of my Lord. I became so concerned that I took it upon myself to ride with my servant to the north, to Galilee, to warn Jesus of what was transpiring in the dark corridors, and behind locked doors.

I am ashamed to say that I still took great care to let no one know that I was a follower of the this man called Jesus, the Galilean. I justified it in my mind by saying that he needed a hidden follower in the Sanhedrim to keep him informed of the treachery being hatched with ever greater vigor each and every day, but we both knew that was not really true. I was simply afraid; afraid of losing everything that I had worked so hard for: my position, my wealth, and of course, *my image.* I thought that I had much to lose, but for those who were not followers, there was even more to lose. There was far too much at stake for those in power to allow some "pretender to the throne," as they would say, to arouse the passions of the people against them, against Herod – or Lord forbid – even the Eagle itself.

The remembrances of the massacres and excesses that took place when the great Herod died were still all too fresh in the leaders minds. They had lived through it, and wished to avoid it happening again at all costs. So they bided their time, waiting and watching, knowing that it was only a matter of time until he would make that fatal slip of the tongue, and they would have him. I might add, in humble honesty, the leisure and wealth of we in Jerusalem depended on the peace of our little nation, such that it was, and on how well we were able to get along with our *master* from afar, for we were truly just pawns, and spoils of war.

In any case, it matters little what I say in my own defense.

You will judge me as you will. I know I was weak, but I have been more harsh on myself than on any other, so I am able to continue and share with you if you will allow. Because he taught me by example to open myself to others, to expose myself to others, no matter the risk, no matter how much of a fool I appear to be, I will tell you of my life with him in hopes that it will help you to understand him. I do it willingly. He used to plead with us to *hear*, if we had ears to hear, and to *see* if we had eyes to see. I ask you to do no less.

Jesus was a soul who suffered more, and loved more than we can ever comprehend. Come to Galilee with me, the Galilee he loved, and see him as I saw him, talk to his disciples as I talked with them, open yourself to him through an old man's heart and eyes. I know you will hear many other stories, some from my own son to be sure, but these are the special times I had with him, that I thought you might like to share.

I found Jesus without trouble. It was never hard to find him anymore, for wherever he went there were crowds, whether in the towns, on the lake, or in the hills – even in Judea I could find him, if I but knew the general area. So when I arrived at the lake in the afternoon, at the mouth of the Jordan river, we simply rode westward, then north, following the shore to the northern end of the lake. As we rode past Tiberias, a place Jesus would not go, we began watching the low lying hills until at last we found a crowd that had gathered about a man sitting on one of the slopes.

The Sea of Galilee (or the Sea of Tiberias as it is lately called) is one of the most beautiful areas in all the land. In late fall, as it was then, it was most pleasing indeed – neither too hot, nor too cold – for Galilee is the most gentling of places to be. The sun shone brightly that day as we skirted the edge of the new city of Tiberias, built by Herod's son Antipas, past Magdala and Gennesaret. Then we dropped back once again along the shore line, and found the lake absolutely calm, like a piece of polished glass, reflecting the pastel pink-gray clouds from above the eastern hills. The closer we got to Capernaum, the lighter my spirits became, and as we rounded the north end of the lake and headed east, I could barely keep from singing with joy, for this was his city, and I knew he would be close at hand.

A short walk west of Capernaum we spotted the group I had expected. Numbering nearly fifty, they gathered at the top of a small rise, a short distance up from the shore. I spurred my lathered steed up the hill, carefully guiding him around the large black basalt stones that littered the hillside and hid in the tall grasses, stones which could lame the unsuspecting man or beast walking unwarily off the beaten path. The stone, which is common all over the area, had been spewed about the landscape in ancient times by a long forgotten volcano, from a time of fire and fury long before man ever set foot here, and it added an unusual quality to the otherwise beautifully peaceful countryside.

Jesus watched us approach. He could see us coming at a far distance from his vantage point on the hill overlooking the shore and the placid waters below. As we came close enough for him to recognize us, I could see a smile spread over his face, for he was genuinely delighted with our arrival.

Afraid of disturbing those who had gathered, we dismounted a distance away and closed the gap on foot. He waved at me to come close, then bid me come through the crowd to sit by his side. With a gentle smile on his sunburned face he clasped my arm and pulled me down to sit upon a robe that had been spread upon the ground for him to rest. His eyes hesitated just a moment in mine, and I could see the smiling laugh lines that were being etched upon his darkening face, so much outside was he now these busy days. In that moment's pause, a love passed between us that would have made a trip four times as far well worth the while.

Still smiling, he turned to the people seated about him, enjoying this scene of welcome for an old friend of his, and introduced me by saying simply, "This is my beloved disciple from Judea. He has come this far to see me." The crowd was warm and relaxed, and murmurs of welcome could be heard from them as he continued. "He has come to warn me of the trouble I am in, haven't you, Asher ben Ammi?" I was startled to hear him discern the cause of my trip before I had time to even say a word in reply to his greeting.

I was surprised, to say the least, but before I could question him, he held up his hand for silence, and cocked his head listening. The crowd heard it too. It was the sound of a rapidly approaching rider atop thundering hooves, appar-ently hidden from our immediate view by a row of bushes and trees up the hill to our rear. Because Jesus and I were the only ones facing the water, I had to turn to see who came this way alone, off the normal path. I heard Jesus say in a very low tone, that carried a sense of authority, control, and a total lack of fear, "No matter who rides this way, I wish you to remain calm, watch me, not him, and listen to the words I say." No sooner had these words escaped his lips, than, I saw a surprised rider pull his steed to a halt as it came around the row of trees and onto the mass of people sitting in his path. The horse, not expecting the crowd, shied as if it had come across a she-lion in its tracks.

With nostrils flaring, the beautiful beast reared and pawed at the air with powerful hoofs. Its bit tore into its foaming mouth, and its reins jingled taut as the owner pulled back violently to keep from being thrown to the rock strewn ground.

The rider immediately soothed his high-spirited horse with expert hands; then, holding tightly back on the reins, he slowly pranced the nervous animal the rest of the way down the hill to where we sat. There he stopped, looking down imperiously from atop his horse at the seated man of no apparent means who held the assemblage tranquilly in his hand. All the while, Jesus, impassive to the commotion, calmly kept the rapt attention of the crowd with easing words meant to soothe the troubled and worried among them. Because I was the only one, save Jesus, with my back to the rider as he came upon us, I was the only one turned completely about when he asked us to ignore him. I also turned my attention away from the rider, but not before I identified him in my mind for later use.

The rider was a Roman of very high rank, judging from the cut and colors of his tunic, and the quality of armor he wore. This ominous intrusion was of the most dreaded kind, for one never knew what a Roman might do in this situation, and common sense would dictate that no one should provoke him in any way. Our very presence was cause enough to bring about his fury. The faces of the people, however, rather than being wide-eyed with awe or fear, showed no immediate reaction of any kind, so commanding was Jesus' presence upon them.

The Roman's name, I was later to find, was Placidus, a Tribune, elected to uphold the rights of the plebeians against the patricians. I met him some months later in the Baths, wherein he approached me, saying that he recognized me, too, from the one chance meeting on that lonely hill in the backwaters of Rome's far flung Empire. Placidus, if not a follower of my Master, did become an admirer of his, and wished me to tell him all I knew of "the man with the strange eyes," as he called him. Placidus so impressed me with his sincerity, that I met him on several occasions just to share what I knew of Jesus. It was thus, in meeting with him quite by accident, that I was to hear his point of view of the chance meeting that afternoon in Galilee. The story, as it tumbled from the lips of this Roman, showed me once again what an incredible effect our Master had on all those who came into contact with him – both friend and foe.

Placidus was on his way to Jerusalem, but instead of going directly there from Rome, he landed instead in Tyre three days earlier, for he carried instructions to the Tetrarch Philip, son of Herod the Great, from the emperor and the senate. He had ridden hard all the first day to reach Caesarea Philippi by nightfall. He then spent the rest of the day, and all the next consulting with Philip on matters of state. He had enjoyed the mild day in Caesarea Philippi and wished he could have stayed longer before heading south, but duty called, and he wished to be done with this trip as soon as possible, to return to Rome and the post that awaited him there.

While in the newly built and beautiful city, however, he

was determined to make the best of it. In the afternoon he rested in the spacious quarters provided to him for his use. And in the cool of the evening, before the dinner in his honor was to be served, he enjoyed walking the terraces with one of Philip's daughters. The terrace below his room overlooked the sweeping plains of Gaulanitis, and hung suspended directly above the tree-lined banks of a beautiful stream, meandering its way rapidly to the Sea of Galilee in the south. The city of Caesarea Philippi had been constructed by Philip upon the Greek city of Panias. He named the new city after himself, and spent quite a bit of his time in this lovely town. Built on a high grassy plain at the foot of a large cliff, it was the northern-most fortification of Philip's kingdom. From the base of the cliff sprung clean, pure water, as if from a magical source, and the water flowed with a delightful rush into pools below. In the face of the cliff, just above the pools was a cave dedicated to the god Pan, and several rock-cut niches still housed statues of his nymphs.

But that was yesterday. This morning, up and on his way before the sun, Placidus started down the easy slopes toward Capernaum, feeling the wind in his face, and under him, the powerful steed that carried him easily on his back. The Roman was happy and curious about this land of which he had heard so much.

As he loped the morning away, he took bread and meat from his leather bag, and sipped at the wine in the skin. Idly, his mind wandered, and his thoughts turned to the reason he had been sent. Then, as minds do, he thought of the steed that carried him on his way, for he was a military man, and had spent much of his life on the back of a horse. "What a fine horse they have given me," he told me he exclaimed to himself, "I shall have to ship it back to Rome. What shall I name him? Zeus! By the gods, I shall ride into my next battle on the back of the greatest god that ever lived! Let me see what he can do. `Fly my beauty!'" he said he yelled into the wind, and the horse sensing his desire, flew across the countryside. "`My, how he moves!'" he remembered thinking, as he watched the animal's great muscles rippling, as he galloped across the countryside. "`Now, easy boy, let's slow to a comfortable gait,'" he crooned to his new steed, "`What a war horse you shall make. I will wager you can travel like this all day.'"

On and on he said his mind adventured as he descended down the hills into the valley to the south. "I wonder what these people will be like? I read that they're a stubborn and excitable lot. They don't accept us even yet, after all these years, and with all the autonomy we have given them. Strange, I hear that we conquered them, yet in their own minds they are free. Strange qualities, these Jews. How can they say we've never conquered them? They are under our fists, aren't they? Already, I don't understand them – but I will – by the gods, I will!"

He was quite a story teller, and although I cringed at the words he used, his perceptions of my people, and our land, I showed it not; nor did I voice any objection, for he was Roman, and I a Jew. Had it not been for the teachings of my Master, I would not have been able to listen to the arrogance of this man. Even though he meant nothing by it, it cut deeply into my skin. To him, Rome was the world – so I rendered unto Caesar his due, and taking a deep breath, opened my ears to hear him continue his tale anew.

There was a slight change of direction, as he left the well-marked route and struck out across the open hillside to skirt just north of the town of Capernaum, along the northern ridge. He didn't want to be held up by any minor functionary in the border town that marked the line between the two tetrarchs Philip and Antipas. These minor officials were always trying to court the favor of Rome by being nauseatingly nice to anyone of rank who happened their way, and he wanted none of it.

His horse carried him along the high ridge overlooking the lake, that now spread out before him like a blue, mist-covered jewel. Breaking past a fence-line of dark black stones, he turned his steed down hill toward the water. As he cleared the last small hillock and carefully guided the horse through the rock-strewn field, he whipped his horse into a gallop, seeing his day's goal, Tiberias, in the mist-shrouded distance. Then, seemingly out of nowhere, as he broke past a heavy line of trees, there appeared a gathering of about forty or fifty people.

The unexpectedness of this find frightened his horse, which reared and pawed at the air. Placidus instantly soothed and stroked to his newly found friend, as the great beast nervously snorted, pranced, and side-stepped in wide-eyed terror, fighting against his new owner's practiced, calming hand. Placidus made a mental note that before he took Zeus into battle, the animal would have to be better trained, and learn to ignore this kind of surprise, that is, if his rider and he were to come out of even his first skirmish alive. He slowed his horse to a walk as he came perilously close to the seated crowd, affecting all the grandeur that his Roman presence commanded, and expecting an immediate subservient response.

Placidus couldn't believe it! No one moved, as their attention was riveted upon a man of about thirty years of age seated on the ground before them. This man was speaking in such a low voice that Placidus could not hear. "They're not paying any attention to me!" he thought. "How strange; we bring fear wherever we go, but I have no effect on them whatsoever. That's some power the young man has over them," he admired. "I am Rome, and yet they are all ignoring me. So is their leader." As he jerked his horse's reins to stop its pacing, he studied this young man more carefully, and thought with startling humor, "He uses a lot of hand gestures; he would make a good senator."

He watched the young man in the center of the crowd for quite a while. Nothing was said. He just watched. Placidus told me that he felt compelled to just sit there and stare, he didn't know why. It was as if the man had cast a spell. Jesus never slowed his speech as his head started slowly to turn in the stranger's direction. Then it happened! This Jesus, a simple man of no means, a quiet man, on a quiet hill, in the fall of the fifteenth year of the rein of Tiberias, met the Roman's eyes – and held them.

"By the gods, look at those eyes!" Placidus' mind roared. "He's possessed! I have to get out of here. There's no fear in those eyes. His eyes are burning, burning into mine! 'Go Zeus,'" he commanded, as he dug his heals into the sides of his terrified horse. "I must leave this accursed place. I must go!" his mind screamed at him. But he couldn't move, for Jesus' eyes were slashing their way into his skull – into his soul.

I remember that day as if it were yesterday. The air was electric with the tension.

As suddenly as it began, however, it ended. Jesus slowly lowered his eyes to the people seated about him, each of whom, including me, held his breath, not daring to breathe, not alone to chance a guess as what was about to happen. Now suddenly free of my Master's will, the Roman wheeled his horse about and spurred him into a headlong run for the freedom of the sea. "I will find you again, my man," he yelled back across his shoulder, "I know not who you are, but someday I will find you again."

As the dust settled, the sound of the galloping horse was lost into the valley beyond, and the peace of the hill returned. You could hear an audible sigh from the crowd. Jesus once again turned his attention to those who awaited him, enraptured and terrified by what they had just witnessed. Never before had anyone seen a Roman flee before a *Jew*, and in their minds the people began to ask themselves who this man must be to perform a miracle such as this. But Jesus, sensing that they thought to make him a leader of man against man, sought in a subtle way to change their minds by example. For the people still looked for a warrior king, and I knew enough of our Lord by now to realize that his kingdom was not one of this earth. Not this man.

Jesus spoke to them in a soft voice filled with concern, his brow wrinkled as he tried to express what he needed them to understand. "The Romans are like beasts of prey," he said. "So I ask you, if you are cornered by a beast of prey, do you show fear?" He stopped, waiting until he knew they were all following him, "No, he will attack. He will sense your fear and attack. I say to you, look them in their eyes, face your tests with calmness and no fear, and they will not attack. The Romans, as you have seen today, and those like them, are wild beasts let loose in the world today. You must learn to live with them, you must not fear them; they are not of *our* world, for *our* world is with our Father, and He watches over you with love, beyond your understanding.

"If you lived in the forest, and it was here you wished to stay, but you found the forest filled with wild creatures of the land, then you would have to learn to live with them in harmony and peace. You would learn to give them space, you would know not to antagonize them. You would learn their ways, and you would learn to avoid them. Yet in this forest there can also live the hunter, who lives to curse and kill the animals of prey. He lives to struggle with them, and he misses the sweetness of the day. You can live in the same realm as the hunter, and in the same forest with the beasts of prey, and yet be touched by neither of them. Do as I have taught you if you are confronted. Did you see what just happened with the Roman? Did you understand? I ask you, did he stay? Did he hound you? No, he rode his way!

"I am the way. Do as I do. I will teach you a better way. A way to live, a way to love, a way to be free. Loose the thongs that bind you. For too long the scribes and the Pharisees have bound you to laws of fear my brothers; loose them, and throw them away!"

Jesus was sitting cross legged, bent forward holding his arms upright and out as if he had just been cut free of his imaginary binding. His expression was tense, his eyes pleading.

"Don't you see? You can be free. Loose your spirit, for God is only love, and He loves *you*. God loves you as he loves me. I am not different from you, *I am you*. Do as I have shown you each day. Loose the thongs that bind you and you shall be *free!*"

Some of the people were smiling gently now. A look of peaceful ecstasy had found its way across their faces, the strain and fear so real a few moments before had vanished, melted into thin air. Some too were quietly crying, tears silently rolling down their brown, weathered cheeks. In some magic way, everyone there was being touched by this incredible man of peace.

"Lift your eyes to your Father; he is everywhere. He loves you as you love your own children. Look there," he said with the kindness which bespoke the tender loving he had for these simple people who followed him. He pointed to a tender young woman who was holding a precious young child fast asleep against her breast. His voice lowered and softened to a compassionate whisper. "See that woman, with her arms around her child? Think you not that our Father loves you much more then even she can love her babe? I say to you, He can, and does. He cries with you, he loves with you. He has given you life, he breathed it into you. Think you not that he rejoices in your living of it fully and warmly?

"Throw down your burdens. They are worth nothing. Go within, to the quiet places, as I have taught you. That is where you will find your Father. Lift up your eyes to the high places, and your hearts to the mountain tops. I say to you, take this step into the starry night sky, take my hand, let me be your guide, and we will fly. We will fly, as the angels do, as I have shown you. Ye shall have no fear. Your father in heaven is a loving God, not someone to fear."

Then Jesus looked at a man who sat a little way down the hill, and off to one side. "Look at that man with his son, the son who sleeps quietly in his lap without a fear, without a care. Become as a child, trust as you did then. Curl up in your father's arms and he will surround you with His light and love.

"I say to you, love one another as I have loved you. You feel my heart, you know my love. Feel *His* love, which is greater than mine. Go to Him in the private places of your heart. He will be waiting."

There was silence then, as each, in our own way, thought on his words, thought of our own lives, thought of our own fears, hopes and aspirations. And I loved him. I simply loved him.

"It's time now," Jesus said with a tone of finality that meant we were coming to the end of his time with us this day. "It is time that I go, my Father calls me. It is time that you, too, go back to your work, back to your villages, to your husbands, your wives, your lovers – but know in your heart, that God is your only true love.

"For those of you who have lovers now, think on what I am about to tell you, and for those of you who have known no lovers for a long time, remember back. What pleases you more than anything when you are in love?" He paused to look for one to another. "I will tell you." he gestured for emphasis. "It is doing something wonderful for your lover, something that will bring him or her happiness.

"God is your lover. He can find nothing that brings Him more joy than to bring *you* happiness. He does not shut the door, he seeks a love affair with you. Open your door at sunset, in the calm of the evening, or in the quiet morning hours before dawn. Open your door and find him waiting there. He will bring you the purest of love, beauty and happiness that you can imagine.

"Go now. Go in peace. I will be with you always."

The crowd slowly began to rise, the older more slowly than the young, and after sitting for a long time, I understood their plight, for my joints had become stiff and sore – the riding I had been doing hadn't helped either. Jesus brushed the dust and grass from his stained robe that had been spoiled from the horse stopping too near. He walked a few steps over to where his disciples were standing in a little knot talking among themselves, said a few words to them, patted Peter on the back with a smile, and returned to me. "Asher, you rode a long way to be with me, let's go." With that, he abruptly turned and headed west down the hill away from Capernaum. I turned to find my horse, only to see that Peter had grabbed his reins, and was leading him and my servant away in the opposite direction. I turned back to Jesus, who was now striding rapidly down the hill ahead of me. "Wait Lord!" I cried, and hurried my short old legs down the hill after him.

When I caught up to him I was out of breath, and had to stop, bending over with my hands on my knees, panting and gasping for air. Jesus leaned over to look at me, his mature muscles in their prime, hardened by years of hard work lifting and plying wood, and now almost a year of walking in the open countryside of Galilee. It surely made me wish for my youth again. "I am sorry, Asher," he said, "my mind was occupied with a thousand things. I will walk more slowly."

With that, he sat back on his haunches, waiting for me to recover.

No longer in a hurry, he stared out upon the placid waters, now showing the deepening warm yellows of the late afternoon sun. In a wistful voice, still staring out over the land he loved, he reminisced. "I used to be able to come here alone, when first moving from Nazareth. No one came nearer than the foot of the hill. From here I used to watch man and beast making their way to and from the mixed blood of Capernaum; and alone, I could find time for my Father. It was here, in the beginning, that I gathered strength. But peace is no longer mine. It seems I can't find it anywhere. Unless I leave far before dawn, and climb high into the hills to seek my Abba, my beloved Abba, they will find me, hound me for *miracles*. Miracles, that is all they want! Cannot they see Asher, I seek not to give them a meal, I seek to teach them to fish the plentiful waters themselves. I seek to take them to their Father who provides *all* things."

Looking up into the deepening blue of the sky, he intoned, "Oh, God, you have taught me in such a loving way. You are in me – I *feel* your presence like the softest dream. Never do I speak without feeling you as One with me. Oh, beloved God, I am caught up in you, and in my Oneness with you. I gather them to me to teach them, to help them feel your touch, to make it as real to them as you are to me.

"But, it comes so slowly, dear Father. Do I have time? Month after month, and with most of them, those I will have to depend on, I seem no closer to opening them than I was the first day I found them again. Dear Father, talk through me I pray, help them to see you and know you as I know you. Help them to see you through my eyes."

I had never heard Jesus sharing the intimacy of his heart and soul this way. I felt almost as if I was eavesdropping, hearing him pray to our Father this way. I didn't know if, in this strange mood, he remembered that he wasn't alone, that I was standing by his side as he squatted, staring out over the now placid waters of the sea. I had not experienced this closeness with him before, and knew no one who had. This glimpse of my teacher was so rare, so precious, that I didn't dare move. I scarcely wanted to breathe. I felt so honored to be here with him at this special time, and I felt so sorry for him. He was always giving, never taking in return, and yet in Judea, there were some who wanted him out of the way.

Of course now, as I sit to write, I know that the greatest cruelty of all was yet to come.

Chapter 8

*Then one day Jesus came from Nazareth in Ga-
lilee, and was baptized by John there in the Jordan
River. The moment Jesus came up out of the
water, he saw the heavens open and the Holy
Spirit in the form of a dove descending on him, and
a voice from heaven said, "You are my beloved
Son; you are my Delight."*

Mark 1:9-11

When my Lord finished praying, he sat forward, arms
wrapped about his knees, staring at nothing I could
see. Then he blinked, and kind of shivered, as if a chill had
run through his body, smiled at me with that sheepish little
grin, then stood up and slowly stretched the whole length of
his body. It had been a long day, from before dawn until now,
late in the afternoon, and he still wasn't done. He couldn't
rest, because now he had me.

He turned to face me. "Ready?" he asked. I nodded my
head yes, and we headed down the hill toward the water once
again, but this time in a leisurely manner that leads to an easy
communication between two friends who share a special love.

"Did you talk to Nicodemus, Asher?" Jesus asked, as we slowly approached the shore and turned west away from Capernaum, toward Gennesaret.

"Yes, Lord, I did. He was very helpful to me. He told me everything that he remembered, up to the point of your leaving Jerusalem. He was the one who set me to listening and watching in the Temple for any plots the priests were hatching against you. I have also employed two others I trust to do the same in my absence, Lord. I will get word to you as soon as possible, if I feel it is important."

He didn't say anything, just sadly shook his head, then bent down to pick up a flat stone and skip it across the water toward Tiberias in the distance. "I used to love to do that as a child," Jesus said. "There were such few good stones like that in Egypt, so it was a rare find indeed, for there was mostly sand, and more sand. A rock like that was not one to be wasted on oneself, but savored for showing off to a friend."

Once again we just walked quietly along the shore. I felt that there was something he wanted to say, or share with me, but I couldn't pry, so I was quiet, and waited. After walking the better part of an hour, we approached the outskirts of Gennesaret. He motioned to a large black boulder near the water's edge, and there invited me to rest. We put our backs to the large, time-worn stone, and finally my beloved Master began to speak. For me, hearing his voice was like hearing the angels sing. I was far too old to worry about position or place with him, as most of his disciples did, nor could I walk with him on the long, hot, dusty roads between towns as they did. My only joy came during the quiet times with him. But, dear God, these were the finest hours of my life, for at these times he, too, was relaxed and introspective, and in a sharing mood. I was simply a friend he could trust. I was not one he had to prepare to send out among the wolves. I was simply one to listen to his thoughts.

As if he read within me my feelings, Jesus said. "The quiet times are most important, Asher. Make sure you are your own best friend, so that you fear not being by yourself and going within. I had to learn that again, Asher, after returning from Jerusalem, I had to learn to be alone all over again.

"Asher, do you know what it was like to come back from the holy city, after three years of study with the finest minds in the land? Three years of intellectual straining and growth – then Nazareth – a carpenter shop – and nothing!

"I almost went crazy. This was truly my time for growth and testing. Others think the testing of my will and strength comes now, but I tell you, this is no test. The testing is past. Now I see the end, and there is nothing this world can throw against me that will stay me from that light. Please, Asher, let me tell you of that time between heaven and hell, the twenty years of waiting."

I felt a sense of urgency in the way he spoke, as if he needed to tell someone, and relieve himself of the burden before he could get on to his other work. The telling itself didn't take that long. It was the feeling that came from him that utterly overwhelmed me. In telling, I pray you put yourself in my place, along that same rock strewn shore, at the softest time of the day, and hear his words the way I did that day.

"When I returned home I was sixteen, and considered a man," Jesus told me. "I took my place in the Synagogue, and

I took my place in my father's growing home; there were now four brothers, the last boy being named Judas, and a sister, with one more yet to come, and all had to be clothed and fed. That was the year I met a girl in Cana, named Julia, and although I saw her only once, it was love in my heart that I felt for her from that day on. It was six months more before we went to visit relatives again in the village, and all the long days as I wrestled with the wood and learned my trade, the thought of her was what kept me alive, kept me at my work in the shop.

When I look back now, I am sure it was God's hand which gave me this time. For I know also that I would have gone mad with boredom and run away, if it had not been for the thoughts of winning the hand of that maiden, who in my heart loomed larger than anything I had learned in Jerusalem. In my wonderfully imaginative youthful mind, I dreamt of becoming the finest craftsman in all of Israel, earning fees from the wealthy and powerful, so that I could make for her a home. It was she who kept me at the bench all the long days after my return.

"I think it was God's hand too that held me from going back to the nearby village of Cana for as long as He did. For had I gone back I would have found that she had been betrothed shortly after my first visit, and it was not meant to be that I would know her touch, or feel her arms around me when I needed to be held. The fire within me burned strong and bright, then died as quickly as it had come. As time went on, I was to understand that if I had not wanted this woman more desperately than I had wanted anything before, if I had not known how the thinking mind can loose its sway, if I had not yearned for her in every way a man can yearn, I would never have been able to understand those same feelings in another.

"But I do understand, Asher, as it is with you. Your beautiful Miriamme is but half your age, for which you have taken much abuse, yet when I look at the two of you I see only the true love that binds you." I looked at Jesus, and in his eyes I found the incredible understanding and deep love they were capable of. He judged me not that my sweet wife was but a girl of twenty, and I an old man of sixty, for I did love this woman with all my heart, as she did me. The wonder of this simple man named Jesus, who could share a part of himself, and make each and every soul who heard him feel that the sharing was meant specially for him.

He sighed deeply, then leaned back against the stone. Fearing that he would stop, I begged him to continue, if it wasn't asking too much. He turned his head toward me again, smiled a smile of yielding, and continued on his way.

"After Julia, nothing meant very much to me for a long while. I did what was expected of me, but I fear that my father was at his wit's end with me. Nothing that he, or any of the family could say brought me joy. I am ashamed to say that I reveled in my unhappiness, and I fear that I learned to enjoy the attention I derived from it. I had become an insufferable, self-centered, brooding young man. I also developed a religious snobbishness that was unconscionable. I knew I was better than any in that stupid little village, and in the synagogue I showed my knowledge of the Law with smugness, to everyone's distaste. I was not sharing what God had planted there for all to see, quite the opposite. I was using my

knowledge to make them realize their own stupidity.   I was
worse than the worst of the Temple priests.

"Now, Asher, do you see why I lash out at them when I
have the opportunity? I see in their smug priggishness – me."

Of course, I recognized what he was saying right away.
We Pharisees had a way of making everyone think that we
were better than they. We had started our sect to make the
Law of the Sadducees more livable for the common man, but
ended up making more laws than he could ever live with. And
for the "uneducated of Galilee" we even made special
dispensations; otherwise, none of them could have entered
the Temple "clean".   Although he told the story on himself,
as I have said, my conscience burned with the lessons learned.
I am also sure that my Master knew of all this, even though you
would never know it from his look, or the way he spoke. Jesus
had difficult lessons to learn in his youth, but learn them he
did, for this man was now a soul of infinite love. Yet the other
side of him was certainly not unknown for he could deliver a
tongue lashing like no one else I knew, when he felt that it was
necessary and due. But let me continue, for it was about here
in his narrative that we watched the giant red orb, we can the
sun, slowly come to rest over the hills to the west, approxi-
mately where Nazareth would lie, then sink it did into the
very hills themselves, as if being absorbed in some magic way.

"My father became very sick when I was eighteen years,"
Jesus continued, "and lingered ill and unable to help until I
was twenty-two, when I became the head of the house – a
position that suited me ill. It was this event that caused me
once again to reevaluate my life. I loved my father terribly,
and to see him wither away in my sight, day by day, had the

most sobering effect on me. This, too, I give thanks for, for it was in my love for my father that I learned to lose myself in someone else's pain. It was through the love that he had poured into me, that I was finally able to see that truly, it is in forgetting ourselves that we do find ourselves, indeed.

"Lessons come so hard for us all, dear Asher, we add them one by one, and the hardest lessons of all are probably the most lasting. In the long years that followed, I learned that each lesson was like the leaf of a tree. With each lesson we add a leaf unto the tree that is us, and when all the leaves of a lifetime are added up, we add it to the limb which goes upon the trunk. With each life then, we continue to add a branch, until some day we become complete, the beautiful full tree that God intended us to be. And the most beautiful tree of all," he said, with a large smile on his face, and his arms upraised in a gesture of humble supplication, "is God!

"Come, Asher," he said, reaching out to pull me to my feet, "you are my guest for a change, and a feast is being prepared for *you* tonight."

I smiled with heartfelt gratitude toward this man of miracles, and held out my hands to meet his. He lifted me to my feet with one easy motion, for I was but a feather to this strong carpenter from Galilee. We started walking back eastward toward his city, but we did not hurry. As we walked, we stayed close to the water's edge, where its tiny lapping sounds upon the stones made music in our ears. As we walked I asked him questions, for there were many holes in the fabric of his life I was weaving. "Lord, I know much now of your growing up. But tell me, these last ten years or so, what have you been about... and, what took you so long?" I added with feigned reproach. "If you had started ten years ago, I would have been young enough to enjoy you more!"

My Master stopped dead in his tracks, then with a howl of delight said, "You'd better get running, old man, lest I throw you in the water this night!" With this admonition, he made motions of throwing me into the lake, and I for my part started to run as if for my life. "You had better run, you old fool," he shouted at me in a mocking manner, shaking his fist. "If I had come ten years ago," he yelled after me, "you would have been too busy counting your money to have even seen me to your door! And I, old man, I *would* have thrown you in the lake!" He took four giant leaping steps and was on me. The look of rage had melted into a belly-aching laugh. He dipped his hand into the lake and sent a cascade of water into my face.

Wiping my face with my robe, we held each other as brothers do, and together, arm in arm, we walked back into town.

There were no more serious discussions that night, for Peter and his family had provided a scrumptious meal, delightful company, and the most wonderful sleeping mat I had ever slept on (or so it seemed to me that night). Perhaps I was just tired, and having reached my destination, I could finally slacken, and relent I did. I didn't wake from my little room until far past the hour of work. Upon entering the family room the next morning, I found everyone had gone except Peter's mother, and John, son of Zebedee, whom Jesus had asked to stay behind and wait until I woke.

Counting this day, which was the day of Sabbath eve, I stayed nine more days. These days of warm sunny weather and cool evenings will remain with me forever, for it was during this period of time, away from family and responsibilities, that I relaxed and listened and watched and waited. Each afternoon save two, Jesus walked back to town with me alone from wherever he was teaching that day. I was also able to spend much time with John of Zebedee, and learned much about him. He turned out to be my watch-mate for I was not as young and energetic as the young men surrounding Jesus, nor Jesus himself, and my Lord made accommodations for me by way of John. I would rise when I felt refreshed and after my morning fruit and bread, John would guide me to Jesus that day. I found John to be young enough, and I old enough, for him to be open and totally honest with me about his understanding of the teachings of Jesus, and his feelings toward him, especially because of John's special place as a disciple – one of the twelve.

As these beautiful days wore on with Jesus, I gained more and more insight into this special man whom God had sent here to us, to teach us of His love. My leisurely afternoon walks gave Jesus time to explain much of what was rolling around in my mind, and that I had been wondering on. I also found him almost compelled to tell me of his life, in a way I never heard him speak when with the crowds, nor even when he was alone with his twelve. It was as if my age and years of experience afforded me a special vantage point, a certain perspective with which to look upon his life.

One day, as we walked back to Capernaum from the countryside of Bethsaida, he hung back to be out of earshot of the rest, then began to speak to me in such earnestness that I had to take particular note. As he spoke, I felt that he had a special need for me to understand him. It was as if everyone who was close to him (his followers and disciples), were so awed by him that he could not truly have a friend – just a friend to share both his joy and pain alike, without pretense or judgment. At this particular time in his life, I was humbly honored to fill that role, for although I was impressed with the miracles, I came not for that reason, and paid them little heed – for I came to find his soul.

I could tell that he was already deep in thought as we walked along, for suddenly, without looking up from the dusty path we traversed, he opened the conversation between us, almost in mid-thought, saying: "I had to fill that empty hole in my soul!" He looked at me as if pleading for me, for anyone, to hear and understand him. "Can you *understand*, Asher? It gnawed at me like a wild animal, a wild animal never able to satisfy its hunger. It almost drove me insane. No one I knew had that gnawing pain, that hunger inside – for God, or woman, I knew not which. I only knew that there was a yearning in my soul, a fire that needed to be fed, and the more I fed its flames by living, the more the fire grew, until it raged within me without ceasing. And I was pent-up and could speak of this to no man, no woman; with no person could I share what was hidden there within me. There was no one I could talk to! Neither my mother, who loved me, but could think only of my sick father and our large family that had to be fed, nor did my brothers or sisters care to understand.

"The weight of providing for the family was overwhelming to me at that time, and I wished to flee the wood shop whenever I had a chance, yet my guilt for not doing just a little bit more for my family, to earn just one coin more, wore on me more and more. Fortunately, by the time father died, my brother James was able to do everything that I could do (and quite a bit better I might add), and Joses wasn't far behind, although, like me, he wouldn't ply the trade once full grown. Then in the next ten years, Simon and Judas grew into the trade, and my load was lightened considerably, until finally I was away more than I was there.

We stopped. This time it was I who pointed to a place to sit and talk, for I wanted to give my Lord my undivided attention, which I could not do while we walked along the rocky path. He seemed more than willing, waving on the others, when they looked back to see what made us tarry. I spread my robe down upon a grassy knoll, and in his supple, easy manner he dropped down upon the ground and lay flat out upon his back looking up unto the heavens, the heavens that he tried so hard to share with us, but as yet only he was able to see.

"I know that God put me in my particular family," Jesus told me, "without a wife, and without position, so that I would yearn mightily for Him, so that I would desire Him more than my life itself. And I did. I knew I was the One who was to come, Asher. I don't know how I knew, I just knew, and that is a terrible burden to carry. I knew of all the Scriptures that foretold of the coming, I knew them all. Yet there were so many missing pieces yet to fall, and I felt my chest constrict with the pain of constant waiting. I would pray, 'When? Oh, God please tell me when. Show me a sign dear Father, show me a sign!' I pleaded over and over, night after night, month after month, year after year.

"And when my lessons had been learned, and I proved

myself strong in His ways, he showed me a sign – and the sign was my cousin John. He was howling in the desert, and from that desert wild, I could hear him whispering my name. I heard him, no it was more, I could *feel* him. I could feel him pulling me, and I had to drop my tools and go to him.

"When I stepped from the crowded shore into the water, and started to wade toward John, I was already in ecstasy, my whole life had focused on this point in time, my time of initiation, my time of opening. At this appointed place, at this tiny, green strip of land along the river called Jordan, the whole of the universe stopped for an instant, as God reached down through the heavens to touch one simple human soul, me, a poor Jew of no import; and in that instant, His son and He became One.

"As I approached the crowd lining the banks of the river, it was as if they were not there, so centered was I. Every cell of my being had prepared for the opening that came. I saw only John... and the Light. I walked slowly toward him. The crowd began to part in front of me, I know not why, and slowly into the unhurried, hip-deep current, I waded. John saw the crowd parting, and saw that they were watching someone approach. Mysteriously, one by one, the noisy voices silenced as I stepped down into the water. It was then that he recognized me. I had to be opened, and for that purpose it was that John had come. He reached out as I neared him, and touched my forehead, and my mind exploded with light and love, wonder, and joy! And as I told John there, I saw the dove of light descend. It was a light like you have never seen. My beloved Abba had finally come. He finally came to me!"

At the edge of Jesus' voice there was the same hint of

incredulity and wonder I had detected when I first heard him tell the story of his earlier life, before the warming fire in our home a few months prior. It was as if he still had difficulty believing it had actually happened to him. As for me, I had no trouble believing it at all, for he was the most wonderful person I had ever met.

He shook his head again, at the marvel of it all, and once again continued the most astonishing story I had ever heard.

"From the banks of the river He then sent me into the wilderness of the desert wastes, and there I lay entranced in paradise, day upon day, so many I lost count. It was there He told me of my future, and He told me of my past. He showed me my people, whom I had so carefully trained, and He told also what I must do. And as I lay there, I was grateful, and I cried, `My God, my God, you have finally fulfilled me. I am finally whole!'

"He gave me my task, which I pursue; a mere outline only, and He gave it to me to fill in the gaps as they appear before me, to use my senses, my knowledge, my feelings, my memories. It was then that I finally knew what I must do, what I had to do to fulfill the prophecies.

"Then, as mysteriously as it started, it was suddenly over. I raised myself as from the dead. It was then, for the first time, that I noticed the total barrenness of where I had been. I was black from the long days in the relentless sun. I was parched and needed drink, but my mind was singular in its purpose, and so I set myself upon the Path He had given me. And each day since then I have followed the plan as it was set before me – and I will follow it unto the end."

There, on a distant shore, I sat next to the most holy man

our one God had ever made, and I wept. I wept for the feelings of my Lord, for the feelings that were now mine. I wept because on that special afternoon in late fall in the land of Galilee, I, too, found my God. I found him in the words and feelings of my Master Jesus. I sat there, and wept. Jesus watched me intently as I sobbed uncontrollably, then unexpectedly he reached out and hit me a blow to my head. I fell back against the ground, dumb-struck, unable to move. And there, I now too, found rapture in Him of whom he spoke. I cried within, "Oh, God, why me, an old man, my life gone to waste?" And, it was then that I also knew what I must do.

It is in the sharing of this time, and these words with you that I am finally able to honor my love for Him – and also for you.

Chapter 9

"Tell everyone to sit down," Jesus ordered. And all of them - the approximate count of the men only was 5,000 - sat down on the grassy slopes. Then Jesus took the loaves and gave thanks to God and passed them out to the people. Afterwards he did the same with the fish. And everyone ate until full!
                                                            John 6:10-11

Jesus replied, "The truth of the matter is that you want to be with me because I fed you, not because you believe in me..." They replied, "You must show us more miracles if you want us to believe you are the Messiah. Give us free bread every day..."
                                                            John 6:26 & 3

I had mentioned earlier, that one of the reasons I felt that Jesus and I had become so close, was that I never sought him out for the miracles he brought. The reason I sought him out lay within him, not without – but that was not true of everyone, as I was soon to find, to my distress. And, in this lesson that soon came, Jesus once again found a way to bring the message home for those who had ears to hear, and an open heart.

For two days after I had fallen into the blissful state of ecstasy, and therein seen the Lord God in all His brilliant light, and felt His compassion total and complete, I could function little, and think none at all. I allowed John to take me to and fro, but my consciousness was not of this world. I drifted in a shimmering haze of resplendent luminous love which filled me through and through, and I knew evil not during those days. When I looked upon the Master I saw only the most dazzling shimmering flame; and some of the people, when he spoke to them, would begin to glitter and beam and glow, as if they too by heaven's light did know. So powerful was this man who, but slowly, grew toward his destiny.

The thought came to me that I would never awake from this beatific dream, but upon saying this to Jesus, he only smiled knowingly, and laughed at me in a kindly way, saying, "Just wait, Asher, just wait." So it was, on the third day I arose to find the world once again as it had been before. But it mattered not, for in those days that I had walked His path, I had learned much, and I had changed. I had truly changed inside.

But now, just as I thought I had all the answers to the problems of the world (vision sent), I was to find that the world of *man* means so much more than I knew or understood. For this was the day of the loaves and fishes. And the day after that, came even more.

We left early, I along with the rest, for Jesus wanted to cross the Sea in time to teach along the pilgrim's path. There, he taught the morning through, as the crowds gathered and grew, until by noontime the crowd had grown to be the largest I had ever seen come to hear him. I stayed on the outside of the gathering to let others come close to see him, some for the first time. And too, I wanted to talk to some of the people arriving, and tell them to hurry to his side and also learn from this most amazing rabbi. This was a new experience for me, not hiding my discipleship, but rather displaying it in the open, and I was finding it exceedingly joyous indeed.

As noon came close I wondered if he would break to allow those who had not brought food to hurry on to Tiberias, or back to Magdala, to find their meal. Then as I started to work my way through the throng, to get close enough to my Lord to offer up my purse to feed the lot, I saw at once that Jesus had already started to distribute a few loaves and a few fishes his disciples had rounded up amongst themselves. Then to everyone's amazement, the basket holding the meager supply kept circulating, back and forth, row after row, back to where I was standing. As it came, the wonder of everyone there grew. With my trader's eye, I tried to discern where the food was coming from, and although I found that some souls shared what they had already brought, this in no way could account for the total lot. I, along with the multitude, looked in wonder at what miracle my Master had performed, and with joy in my heart, I foolishly called him "King" along with the now unruly mob.

Such a ruckus was being raised that Jesus realized any more teaching was out of the question that day. In fact, the people pressed in upon him so hard that I began to fear for what the crowd might do. They were screaming now, hysterically; some wanted favors granted, some wanted the healings they had heard he could perform, and others carried the idea of "Messiah-Savior-King" to the fore, with more vigor than he could allow. Then, as I had often seen him do when things were not to his liking, he bid his disciples to hold the crowd at bay, while he retreated off alone, taking with him only Peter to walk with him awhile, to protect him from any who would persist by stealth, to follow.

We thought that he would be returning in the early afternoon, but as the day wore on, and it became clear that he would not come back in time for them, the crowd became restless, and some even angry. So, while some stayed behind with one of the boats to wait for Jesus, I joined the others and headed back to Capernaum, for I was weary to the bone. The wind was also picking up, and the locals were saying a storm was coming from the south, which I wanted to avoid if I could. Being caught out in a small fishing boat in a gale was not something I wanted this night (nor any other).

When we returned, it was almost dark, and the impending storm could be seen fast approaching. It appeared as a solid foreboding, gray wall in the twilight, coming across the lake toward the north. As the others pulled the boat safely up upon the shore away from the now choppy water's edge, I walked to town upon the stone path rising from the shore. The light was beautifully eerie as the last rays of the sun streaked through the black gathering clouds in brilliant shafts of gold and gray-pink light. As the cloak of night silently settled, I nervously watched through the small window as the first pellets of rain spattered against the dusty ground, and the storm slipped moaning in upon the land. We all worried for the remaining

boat that stayed behind alone, waiting for our Lord. As for
me, I could not rest, for as the storm struck with wind-swept
fury, and howled about the house, all I could think was that
I had left my Lord for my own comfort. I was self-found guilty
of thinking of no one but myself.

Finally, I could stand it no longer. I pulled a warm robe
about me and headed out and down to the shore. I didn't
actually think that I could do anything to help, but it was one
of those times that I just had to do something, anything to ease
the ache of worrying within me. The rain was not falling as
hard as it had first seemed, for as I picked myself down the path
to the water, I noted with gratitude that I wasn't getting as
soaked as I had expected to be, for the rain had now settled
into but a heavy mist. The wind, however, was gusting with
great force upon the water, and a dense fog had descended,
bringing intermittent swirling blackness, and an eerie silence
with it, making it even more dangerous to be at sea. I could
see that vision of more than a short distance would be
impossible until the storm let up. I knew that a storm of this
nature was not unusual, and often blew away as rapidly as it
came, leaving no trace of its vengeance and fury in its calming
wake. The only thing that made this storm different was that
everyone that lived near this inland sea knew enough to stay
off the lake when the winds approached. Jesus and his
disciples were out in this storm, and in the convoluted path
human minds take, I wished that instead of Jesus, it had been
me, lost in this night's black sea.

As my mind whirled in a murky world of worry and self-
pity, I lost track of where I had been walking. Then realizing
that I had been out for quite some time, I stopped and tried to

get my bearings. The only sound I could discern, beyond the wailing wind rushing around my ears, was the crashing waves breaking at my feet, along the rocky shore. The murky, swirling mists were flying about me in a nightmare's dream, when suddenly the clouds parted for an instant, and it looked as if, about twenty paces distant, a lone man stood in front of me. I was so taken aback by fright, so fearful of the aberration, that I could scarcely breathe. There, out of the black and blue-gray vaporous foggy haze, stood my Lord, looking intently out to sea. Then, as a gasp escaped my throat, Jesus strode straight out into the water's inky blackness. It was as if he had seen something I could not see, or heard something my old ears could no longer hear, for he did not hesitate one second, once he knew his course. Then, when I thought my lungs would surely burst, my breath escaped with a sigh of gratitude and relief, for there, out of the mist came Jesus, with a boat in tow. Not just any boat, but our boat, the boat with the disciples aboard.

What joy I felt! I ran to the water to greet them as they leaped ashore, and helped them pull the boat the rest of the way onto the land. Everyone was laughing and crying at the same time. We hugged each other in gratitude and relief, for the cold, wet disciples (and I also) feared that they were surely dead. Throughout this whole tumultuous affair, with all of us leaping and talking at the same time, Jesus stood back and simply smiled in the most calming and peaceful way, as if there had actually been nothing to fear at any time. Each man came in turn and thanked their saving Lord personally, before Jesus sent them running off down the beach into the night toward the town, to garb themselves in dry clothes, and assure the rest of the family of their safety.

When the last of them had left, save my Master and I, he put his hand on my shoulder, then with a grin on his tired face, he slowly shook his head and with a note of weariness said, "It's been quite a day hasn't it, Asher ben Ammi?" It was then that I noticed his clothes were soaked up to his waist, and I urged him on to the town, so that he too could change. He stopped me, and turned me to face him. The storm had passed, taking with it the clouds that had hidden the full risen moon, and I could see his calm concerned face, and those incredibly deep, clear blue-gray eyes shining in the light.

"Asher, tomorrow is going to be a very difficult day; there will be a falling away of many. I must speak the truth tomorrow, Asher, and it will cause much trouble among some of my followers. You will see, by tomorrow morning, this night will have become a miracle; and soon, if I don't stop it, that is all there will be to my being. That is all they are interested in now, and it must be stopped if we are to succeed. You have *seen*, Asher, you have seen what I am about. You have felt His touch. I need not explain it to you. Yet today, even *you* wanted me king.

"I must stop it, for if even you cannot see beyond the passing of His hand (not mine, Asher, not mine), then what chance have those who have never seen my Father, nor felt His touch? It is for them that I have come. Do you understand? Through me they will learn of the Father. I am the way, if they will but follow. I am but His servant who holds the lamp to light the path, so that they will not lose their way – the path that each and every one of us must ultimately travel alone someday, if we are truly to become One with

Him."

He paused, his face changed, then he said, with a mischievous grin, "The truth is, Asher, I am freezing, and it is *you* who has kept me out here on this cold beach talking, when I could have been warming myself by a nice fire in my own home by now." His arms waved back and forth in pretended exasperation.

"You are wrong, young Lord." I countered, "It is the impetuousness of youth that has kept you jabbering in the cold night air, not I. For I, my dear Jesus, have grown wiser and more patient in my age, which is the only reason I have tolerated your madness for this long. Indeed, I judged you to be possessed, and mad over an hour ago."

With this we laughed together, the easy laughter of friends who can banter back and forth, comfortable in each other's respect and love. When the laughing stopped, however, Jesus sent a chill through me by saying, "Asher, you leave for Judaea in two more days, and there is still much I must teach you before you go. Things will become very difficult for me soon in your land, and I do not know if I will have another chance to spend this much time with you again. Come to my home this night. We will talk till dawn." As he spoke I felt the hair on my neck stand on end, and as he finished, with his eyes speaking, as always, more vividly than his words, saying, "Asher, please stand by me tomorrow when the others leave. Please stand by me, if you can."

My God, what was he saying? I felt the sting of tears as they welled up in my eyes, and I felt a painful lump growing in the tightness of my throat. "Oh, Lord, you know I will. You know I will!" was all I could say, before he turned and headed down the beach to his home, with me pattering along behind, trying to keep up on my short old legs.

When we arrived at the home where Jesus stayed in Capernaum, we found that the fire had already been built, and dry clothing had been laid out for him to change into; for in this, the women who followed our Lord, made sure that he was taken care of as if he had a wife. And, I knew him well enough to realize, that no matter how busy, or how trying the day was to be on the morrow, he would find the woman responsible for this caring, and touch her with his thanks, for the littlest things escaped him not, and the tenderness of the women touched him most.

We settled onto a bench in front of the fire, and while the magic warmth of the dancing flames worked into our bones, the deep shadows etched their fabric upon my mind for later days and easier times.

After he had sorted out his thoughts, Jesus said, "Asher, I need for you to understand the nature of the miracles that are wrought in my name. For the things that happen are special indeed, but they are not of my doing. I and my Father are One, and that does make me special; but, Asher, you have touched Him, and you are *special*; and some of those who follow me now will touch Him, and they will be special; and some yet who follow later in our footsteps will touch Him, and they will be *special* too. Do you understand, old friend? Anyone who truly seeks Him with a humble and trusting heart can find Him. He is *within*, Asher, not without. He lies within each one of us. This is what I have come to teach our people. He can not be purchased with lambs or doves, He is not found in the laws of the Pharisees, nor is he found in the *miracles* that the people so demandingly seek. He lies within."

He paused, so I dared ask a question that had been bothering me since earlier that day. I was not immune to the excitement of the crowd, and I, too, had been carried away by the magic of the feeding of all the people with the most meager of supplies. And although I now heard his warning against pursuing miracles for their own sake, I didn't understand their harm. Even more, I didn't understand how he did them, how they came about. I had not seen him heal people with my own eyes, but I had heard the astonishing reports of those who had, and in one case I had personally questioned a poor man in the Temple grounds who claimed to have been lame all his life until Jesus had cured him of his deformity at the pool, just to the north of the Temple grounds.

"Lord, if you will permit me to ask... what is a miracle, and how do you bring it about? And if I dare one further question, I would ask, if you heal one poor soul, why, Lord, do you not heal the rest? For there are so many who need your help." I didn't know if I was being too forward, or brazen with my questions, but in my own mind I needed an answer. I felt also that I was unworthy of his special presence and attention, when after being with him in God's radiance just three days prior, I could be so stupid as to try his patience again.

Yet, instead of showing annoyance at my foolish questions, he seemed to be warmly affected by my earnestness, and more than happy to be afforded the opportunity to explain to me the mysterious happenings that surrounded him so much these days. It was as if this amazing human being found it rare indeed, to be able to just sit and share with another soul who wanted nothing more than to genuinely learn, who sought no gifts, healings, or favors, save his company alone – for he was besieged these days with people everywhere he went who wanted nothing more from him than the gifts I mention.

For a man who but a few hours ago wished nothing more than a meal and bed, I was now vitally alive with the anticipation of learning the most hidden secrets of my Lord.

"I will tell you, Asher, so that everyone you touch will also know the key to that which lies within me. I will tell you so that those who follow us will know that they, too, can touch our Father in the same way that I have, and that you did. I will tell you so that they will know that they too can be One with Him, and know His special grace. For it is by His grace that any healing occurs, *not by mine.* I merely open myself to Him until I am overflowing, and then He can work through me to touch those in need.

"How many come to me each day, Asher, to be healed? How many?" It was a rhetorical question of course, and needed no answer, so I waited for his answer. "Tens, hundreds, thousands, I do not know. I do know, that if I had my way, I would heal them all. For I cannot look at any of their twisted bodies, their useless eyes, their mad stares, without wishing with all my heart to take their afflictions away. But it is not my way that brings Him pleasure. It is His way. And, it is in doing His will that I have come. For it is in healing some, and not others, that His loving work of teaching the lessons we must learn is done. There is a universal law that governs everything, and no matter how we would wish to change it, it will stand forever and govern us all. To attune ourselves with it, is what we must learn. As I have told my gallant men who fish these shores: we are the fish that swim in His ocean, and

He is the one true fisherman. He bids us welcome to his boat. The hook is set, and whether we fight it to the death, or swim to join Him, is up to us.

"Our people are ignorant, Asher, not just those here in Galilee, but all our people. Our people's minds are full of evil spirits, demons, and curses that find no place in fact. Over half the people I have touched belong to this class. They are afraid, old friend, they are so very afraid. Life is a fearful mystery to them in all respects; so much so, that if one comes who is strong, and loving, and cares for them, it helps – it takes away their pain. The secret is no secret at all, for this technique I learned from the Greeks and their physicians. Notice what I do. I must myself be calm, then I must get their total attention, which is not easy because of their fear, but it must be done. Sometimes it can be done in a crowd, but at other times I must get them alone, isolated, perhaps in a small room, there to gain control. It isn't magic. It is knowledge of crowds, people, and how they are made. I take them apart to separate them from the fear of the crowd – which is very real. I hold them firm in my hands, which are strong, and I speak to them in a calm commanding voice, that they *must* believe; and lastly, I speak to them with my eyes, for with the eyes you cannot lie. If the problem is with the devil, or the evil eye, you will cure them, for it was placed there unwanted in their mind by an ignorant people and an ignorant time."

"That covers some of the miracles of which I speak, Lord, but what of the rest? What of this day with fish and bread?" I quizzed.

"Ah, that my beloved disciple, is a mystery of the greatest order, and remains that way to me yet. For from the very beginning I have sought an answer, but none have come, save this. I have told you that if it were up to me, I would heal each and every one who comes to me, but that will never be recorded as happening. You must go within, and this is the one thing I teach my twelve continually, you must go within and become One with our Father's will. In that way it is His will you seek in purity, not the subtlety of our own, instead.

"This other half, the victims of diseases and twisted limbs, of blindness and parasites, they suffer the results of a thousand things that medicine doesn't even know the name – not the least among them, lust and greed and shame. Their afflictions are caused by disease and dirt, and ignorance of the ways of health.

"It is for those too that I come. I walk among them, and lay hands on many; some the Lord God heals, and I can feel it, because it has a purpose. God knows who needs to be healed, and I can feel His light pouring through me, and this thing we all can do. This is why you must go *within*, Asher. You must become One with *His* will. It is in this way He can walk with you, and use you where there is need. And most importantly, you must understand, you must not judge, for the one He chooses might be the least in your eyes, but in His, the greatest. Sometimes you can feel sympathy for the one He chooses, and sometimes you cannot. It must be His will, and not yours – and thus the greatest healer is often judged by his peers to be the least among men.

"Walk among our people, Asher. Reach out and touch the least of them, if you are to learn the secret of His will. See what goodness is in them, open yourself to the Father, and miracles will abound!"

This was a heavy load he had handed me – so much to understand – and yet he was by no means through.

"After I fed them today, I tried to tell them what I tell you now, but that is not what they came to hear. They came for the spectacle, for the sport, and it is this insincerity that I will not tolerate. I will go not to the place where I taught yesterday, for they seek only a show, and this I will not give them. I will tell you what more will happen on the morrow, if you wish, if you have need to know." Now Jesus was becoming more expressive, once more falling into his habit of talking also with his hands. As I watched him, his eyes had become distant, as if he were actually watching what was happening on the morrow, not like I, in the here and now.

"When I left you to be alone, I knew there would be no peace in the area of Tiberias where we had been, so I left to reason the happenings of the day, and what very deep changes must be made. I walked north to Magdala, where I found a boat that would take me back to Capernaum. I have been teaching here for over a year now, Asher, more than one whole year, and although there are now many times hundreds, and often times even thousands, who gather (as you saw today), they are not interested in the words that I give them, nor the ways that will bring them everlasting peace. With each day that passes they have become increasingly less interested in the ways of our Father, and more and more demanding of the ways of the earth.

"The old covenant with our people is dead! They must understand this: I come not to take the land by force, I come not as a man of miracles, I come as a light shining in the darkness, leading them on a path that will take them to their

Father's land. And in His place they will find everlasting light, total peace, and they will drown in His all-encompassing love. This simple beauty is bitter medicine for we Jews, but it is what my Father has shown me, and it is true, and it is what I must teach to them, until they can understand.

"There will be a great shaking out tomorrow, but those who stay, will be those who have felt His touch within themselves, and can do no less than follow the Path to the end, no matter where it goes. For it is for those few among many that I have come, and it is for those few that my lamp shines brightest to lighten their way. Truly, no one can come to me unless my Father, who sent me, draws him close enough for me to whisper in his ear. Now is the time that I must go among the fields to hoe the weeds free of the stalks, so that the grain that is left shall sink its roots deep into the earth to drink freely of the living spring, and turn its face to the sun to be guided by the spirit, and therein it shall grow strong."

Oh, I loved this man so much. If I could but tell you what it was like in those days, to sit next to this man who had such incredible power within him, that sitting next to him was like being in an electric storm. I was like a trusting child when with him. I guess that is the feeling I am trying to express. I was like the most innocent, trusting child. And I was also like a sponge in his presence, absorbing his radiance into me like the warmest, most wonderful dream.

Yet, that still does not convey the meaning, for it was more than that. It was like being with your most intimate lover, whom you have grown to completely trust over the long and hard times you have had together. It is as if you were with him or her, on a very special night, when everything was right, and you felt safe enough to finally open up your most closely guarded parts, and lay yourself totally bare – you trusted that much. That's what it was like that night, alone with my Lord. He had such an amazing capacity to love those who came to him with simple and open hearts, yet he knew that if his mission on earth were to succeed, he could not be all things to all people at all times, and the events of the next day proved to be that exception to his softness, and went to prove the rule.

The next morning the storm had completely passed, leaving no trace, save on the minds of men. It dawned crisp and clear and so exceedingly bright that you had to guard your eyes from the hurt. The early morning yellow light reflected from a myriad of tiny drops hanging tenaciously from the tips of the barren twigs, and sparkled from a thousand hiding places amongst the rocks, only to drop into the rainbows of puddles and slippery mud that we picked our way through so as not to mire our sandals in their deep. The freshness of the air was draped with the rich pungent fragrance of the wet earth below our feet, as we walked the short distance to Peter's place to take our morning meal.

Capernaum was a busy place where taxes were gathered from travelers, both near and afar, and strangers and friends alike were hard to tell apart. I enjoyed it because the mix of peoples seemed to have struck an easy accommodation with each other's customs that was rare in our land. This town was at the far edge of Antipas' rule and close at hand to the land of Philip, the easiest of Herod's brood, which made it less difficult for our Lord to live and teach in the way that he did.

For myself, strange as it may seem, I felt more refreshed

and alive than I had in years. I noted it, because I couldn't understand it, what with the lack of sleep and all the physical and mental strain, it seemed absolutely wonderful to me. The other disciples too seemed in unusually good spirits, as they gathered about him to hear of the day.

Meanwhile, across the lake, the throng which had gathered to hear our Lord on the day before, had once again come together, expecting Jesus to be there. When neither he, nor any of the disciples arrived, they hired boats from the small port just north of Tiberias to sail them across to Capernaum, where they were told that he would be found. When these people arrived, Jesus was sitting in the synagogue with perhaps twenty or thirty of us, among them the twelve, and more whom he had specially chosen. Now, when those who had come from across the lake entered the synagogue, they asked straight away, with no courtesy at all, why Jesus had not come back for them, to teach as he had the day before.

I held my breath, for I think only I knew what was about to happen.

"Why do you ask for me?" he demanded. I could tell by his hard tone that the ordeal was about to begin. The sharp edge to his voice was totally unexpected by the disciples gathered about him, and caused them to look up in surprise. Others, chatting a short distance away, turned abruptly, questioningly, while yet others exchanged shrugs and hidden, wondering glances.

These truly simple folk who had come from across the lake with their demands, knew not that this gentle teacher, could turn uncompromisingly rock- hard when he felt his purpose was God driven. Little, too, did they know that from this "simple carpenter's" mind could come arguments that would turn the *wisdom* of the finest minds in all the land into sand slipping between their gold bedecked fingers; so these self-styled miracle-seekers, and king-makers were nothing in his hands. The skirmish had commenced.

"The truth of the matter is that you want to be with me because I fed you, not because you seek what I teach, nor because you believe in me." There was stunned silence in the synagogue as he began to purport to them much of what he had warned me of the night before. He told them about himself in a humble, yet forceful way, for he could speak nothing but the truth, and the truth was that he was *the one* who had come as the prophets had foretold.

Instead of believing, though, they were aghast, and began to whisper amongst themselves, "Who does he think he is?" And the boldest among them spoke out against Jesus directly, saying in a belligerent voice, "If you want us to believe you are who you say you are, then show us more miracles!" His challenge was given in a cynical, mocking tone, and was accompanied by snickering and laughter from the others in his crowd.

The ill-advised man was not, however, finished. He continued his challenge to Jesus by saying, "Give us free bread every day, as did our father Moses! Only after you do this, will we believe."

Now, at last I thought, Jesus will put an end to this affair, for I had never heard anyone speak to him this way, and I knew Jesus could lash out with vengeance when he was of a mind. But, instead, feeling still that there were among them a few who might be able to hear, he changed his voice to an almost pleading note and tried one more time to open himself to them, to teach them, trying to explain that it was only through his teaching that they would find freedom from the Law, and find Him whom they call their Father.

He continued with lessons such as they had never heard, knowing all along, I think, that the crowd which challenged him would reject the mysteries in it, yet knowing also, that the real recipient of the lessons this day were those who already called him Master.

Toward the end of his talk, to my surprise, even his own disciples began to question him to one another, so difficult were his teachings for them to understand. For he held nothing back this day, but gave them wisdom that is beyond understanding, in hopes that they could *feel* this truth within them.

At times his teachings were incredibly subtle, but that was not the case this day. Even on a superficial level, he cut like a knife into their hearts. And, at the same time, I understood their problem in comprehending because Jesus' teaching brought with it a whole new way of thinking for those of us raised in the Law of Abraham and Moses. Jesus taught us to find our faith within, and not from without, and it was precisely that to which we were not accustomed. Our laws had been handed down for over a thousand years and interpreted for every man on every occasion by the great rabbis who studied and knew them best. But now, now Jesus brought with him freedom from the tyranny of the intermediary, the scribes, the doctors of the Law, the very priests themselves. Through him we could find our Father within our own hearts. No priest need tell us right from wrong! We needed only to love our Lord God with all our hearts, and all our minds, and all our souls, and love our neighbors as ourselves, and in this one law we would find His loving gentle peace within our souls.

More than once during this day I found myself going back to my awakening, and the feeling of complete Oneness with God that was its result. I knew what my Lord Jesus meant when he said that he and his Father were One, and I knew also that if any of these people would but trust him, he would take them on a journey they could never forget. They would be changed forever.

Once when the crowd grew very upset, he looked my way, and out of the corner of his eye I thought I found in its sparkling glint, the barest hint of a smile. I smiled back at him in a way I had learned from him, and in so doing, I hoped I would reassure him when the crowd was turning against him. In truth, however, I think he knew all along who of us would understand, and who would not. For I was to find out that he was about to choose seventy from among those here, and others of his followers, and he needed to find them out with absolute assurance before calling them to his needs.

Before this day was over he would find several who loved more than most. He would also find those who would not, or could not, for at this point many of his disciples turned away and deserted him completely.

Then the most startling thing of all happened. As the now confused and angry mob milled about, and the level of arguing and loud talk rose, he turned to the twelve whom he held most dear, and asked with an angry edge to his voice, "Are you going, too?" It was a most disquieting moment for us all, for no matter how I had pictured this day, I could not have imagined that he would have challenged the loyalty of one of us, and most especially one of the twelve. For a moment, confusion reigned among the chosen twelve, who were now looking from one to another, hoping someone, anyone, would speak, save them.

It was left to Peter, the strongest leader among them, to answer our Lord. "Master, to whom shall we go? You alone have the words that give to us all the eternal life we seek. We believe in you."

With that, Jesus swung about and called forth from the crowd, in addition to the twelve, a number to equal about twenty-three in all, and leaving John, the son of Zebedee with me, departed with them to teach them what they must know.

Jesus swept through the crowd toward the door, as if riding a whirlwind. As I watched him go, his face appeared to be set in stone. His robes were flying out behind him as he hastily strode out the opening of the building with his shocked and worried disciples hurrying to remain in tow. For just an instant, as he stepped over the threshold of the Synagogue, one foot on the ground outside, he stopped in his tracks, and cocked his head. It was as if a momentary thought had crossed his mind, or he had heard a pointed comment from the crowd, and thought for an instant that he might pause and answer the unheard. In that moment the sun caught his head, and it shone like something I had never seen before, as if illuminated by some mysterious and wonderful source. It was at that time I thought him to be the most beautiful and radiant being in all the universe.

Whatever had happened, it had passed, and he was gone,

leaving John and me behind with the arguing and hostile mob. I motioned toward the door to John, and we silently slipped out into the fresh cool air of autumn.

Chapter 10

A little farther up the beach, he saw Zebedee's sons, James and John, in a boat mending their nets. He called them too, and immediately they left their father Zebedee in the boat with the hired men and went with him.

Mark 1:19-20

John, the son of Zebedee, along with his brother James, was a fishermen like Peter, but by their nature they were of a completely different lot. As rough, open and robust as Peter was, the sons of Zebedee were the opposite. So different were they, slight of body, quiet, reserved, and introspective by nature, that Jesus often made fun with them, pursuing them, and trying to draw them out. He called them the "Sons of Thunder."

When asking his twelve for an opinion, or urging them to interpret a story or parable, Peter's voice could be heard first among them reverberating through the valleys and over the hills as he gave free vent to his unshackled spirit that knew few (if any) bounds. This unbridled display of energy and devoted emotion delighted Jesus over and over. More than once I saw a twinkle in Jesus' eye, as this mighty man, who he rightly called, "The Rock," took it upon himself to give orders, or expound in an exaggerated, unyielding way upon a "hidden wisdom," the meaning of which he felt only he could rightly judge or view. He never lacked for conviction. He would speak with fire in his eyes, his body as unmovable as a mountain. Standing like a giant boulder, with hands on his hips, he was like an angry lion that few ever cared to challenge.

After giving Peter free play to his will for a while, Jesus would turn to John or James and say, "We have heard from quiet, gentle Peter. What say now the Voices of Thunder?" Of course, John and James would turn beet red, and stumble for words, to the howls of laughter from the rest of those gathered. Jesus was never mean, but he loved to banter when there was easy time with his few. I am sure he also wished to encourage these timorous apostles to stand forward and be heard – now – before the going became hard. And, as Jesus' days began to dwindle, Peter too, felt the sting of his Master's words from time to time, for Jesus knew that if his teachings were to survive, it would be upon this stone called Peter he would have to build his house. Yet, the supple qualities of the enduring reed were also going to be needed if Peter were not to be crushed to dust under the might of Jerusalem and Rome. And so he pursued the others as well with great vigor, yet with tenderness and understanding.

I will speak of Peter's training at the hands of the gentle one in a moment, but first let me tell you of the man who on this trip had become my constant companion – John, the son of Zebedee.

I found that, although I would not have chosen this young man to be my companion, I was grateful that Jesus paired us together, for John was exceedingly interesting, and lent me a look inside one of those that was closest to Jesus, without really prying. For in the innocence of his youth he was totally open to me. I write of him here, because he was so different from me, that I thought his perspective might be exceedingly valuable and timely. Thus, I will try to encompass hours of quiet talking and feeling into a story of this young man's searching, and fears, and pain.

I will try to speak of them to you with all the deep, strong feelings with which they were related to me, for I believe that in his unburdening, we too, will remember, that at one time or another, we have felt the same yearnings, great insecurities, and deep needs. He was a delicately sensitive young man who loved his Master very much, for I think in many ways that Jesus was like a father to him.

Interestingly enough, I also learned that during much of the years he spent with Jesus he was absolutely *petrified*. He was afraid of everything, it seemed. He lacked the total faith that some of the disciples had, and being of timid nature, his shortcomings were only accentuated. Like many of us, he also struggled with Jesus' teachings, which seemed so foreign and arcane to him. To his way of thinking, however, it appeared that he alone, could not understand what his Lord wished him to see. Yet he stayed, month after month, year after year, walking hundreds of miles in the Master's steps. Jesus' voice, his captivating eyes, the chance to be special, *one of the chosen*, and the infinite love that poured from Jesus into this young man, were more than enough to stay him from ever leaving.

On the first morning I was in Capernaum, I sat at the breakfast table after a wonderful night's rest and gathered my strength from the long ride just past. John was sitting across from me at a rough, hand-hewn table, his elbows squarely on the boards, and his chin propped upon his hands. Although it looked as though he was trying to let a beard grow, as of yet his young baby-like face was ill-suited to cooperate. I would have guessed him to be of about sixteen or eighteen, but when I asked, he said somewhat defiantly, "I'm almost twenty! That's pretty old isn't it? I've been a man now for a long time!"

I sensed from his reply that he was a trifle insecure, and drifted away from any more intimate questions that I thought might embarrass him. "Tell me, John, how did you meet Jesus? What prompted you to follow him?"

I was genuinely interested in how this young man, who was one of the very first people Jesus called, had come to drop his work and his life on a moment's notice on the same day, and in the same manner as Peter and Andrew had done when Jesus first appeared out of nowhere to call them. His answer was interesting and insightful, if a bit circuitous (as I was later to find his speech to be), yet I recorded it later in the evening to tell others who might also question, like me. I leave this poor Galilean's language as it was, even though I cringe to reproduce it in this manner for you to read.

"You know what Jesus' brother James says?" John answered in reply to my question. "He said that Jesus changed when he went to see John, the one who baptized thousands in the river Jordan. He said, before that, he didn't think he was anything. But something happened when he went to John, but he didn't stay with John, he was *baptized* by John. Something special happened he said. Then he went away – nobody saw him for a long time – I don't know how long, and then he came down, and he was down by the sea watching the fish and the fishermen. And, you know what? He walked right up to the fishermen like he knew them..." A cloud seemed to pass over John's face as he paused to remember the scene. Whispering half to himself, he mused, "Maybe he did know them. I never thought of that." Then, deciding that the apparent mystery would have to wait for later musing, his face cleared, along with his mind, and he continued.

"He walked right up to the edge of the water and called them, and he said, `Come with me!' He *yelled* it! Can you believe that? I mean they were right out in the water, and they were picking up their nets, but he told them to come in. And I thought, `Is that strange!' You know I was just sitting there by my father and I saw that. Then they did what he said, they came in and they talked to him a few minutes and started to walk away with him – but one of them didn't. I jumped up from the nets we were working on and ran down to the water's edge where he was just standing, watching the rest walk off down the shore. I grabbed the one who didn't go and I said, `Who was that?' He said, `I don't know, but my brother's leaving with him. He must think he's *somebody*.' And, uh, I said, `Do they know him?' And he said, `I don't think so. I don't know who he is. He's strange, isn't he? Did you see those eyes?' And I said, I hadn't, I wasn't close enough, but I followed him anyway. They didn't go far, they went down to the village and up the street, and the fisherman (Peter) took him into his house, and I hung around until he got out, and I looked at him. Oh, my! He looked at me and you know what he did? He grabbed me by my head on both sides by my ears like this..." John reached across the table and grabbed my head at this point, quite hard, "...and he looked right into my eyes, and he was older than I was. He looked right into my eyes and he said, 'Son of Zebedee, I have come for you!' And, it was incredible! I mean, what do you do, right? So I've been with him ever since. I left with him, that was all I could do."

By the time John had finished his story of meeting Jesus, I found that I was enthralled by the events in this man's life. Here was a young man, hardly out of youth, fascinated by the same characteristic as I – Jesus' eyes!

I rose from the table, walked around and gave John a big hug, and thanked him for being so open with me, then we gathered the food that had been prepared, and the wine, and headed down to the shore where a boat was waiting to carry us to the other side of the inlet to the lake where John assured me we would find Jesus.

We climbed into the creaky wooden boat that was swaying gently from side to side. As I clumsily tried to find a place to sit, John haggled over the price of the fare to the destination he had in mind. To me, the sum asked wasn't worth arguing about, but for John, the price was an insult, and he felt it his duty to come within shouting distance of the price he had in mind. Finally, when all the arrangements seemed to have been worked out, two men pushed us out beyond the lapping waves and jet black rocks to waist-deep water beyond. There, the breeze picked up the sails and we were on our way at last.

John came back muttering under his breath, "That

stinking fisherman! He charged us too much for his boat. We are too easy with them. Jesus won't let me drive too hard of a bargain, he says they need the money – but so do we." With that said, he sat down beside me in a pique. It was all I could do not to laugh at this funny young boy trying to be a man. Then he pointed almost straight ahead of us across the top of the lake to a barely discernible spot far across the hazy water. "He told us to meet him on the far side, uh, there's pretty hills there, that's where we are going to meet him later."

I wondered at the timing, when we gently leaned off to one side, then another, as the boat plyed its silent way against the eastern breeze. The only sounds were of the water rushing against the side of the boat, and creaking wood rubbing against wood in the joints. The sturdy wind blowing in my face made me feel refreshed, and I was anxious to reach my Lord. I took the opportunity to fill the silence by asking John how his parents felt about him leaving home to follow this unknown rabbi from Nazareth.

"They hadn't seen me for so long after I left that day. I've only been home once since I started following him. He sent me home to see them and stay awhile. My parents were so glad. They were so worried, but they had heard where I was, and they made sure I was all right. I'm not a bad son," he added, looking at me with a worried expression on his face, as if I was a visiting relative come to test his sincerity. "What could I do? I've followed him... But I don't always understand him. You know, I haven't been to school or anything."

I found that almost all Galileans sorely felt their lack of education, and although I had often made fun of them in the past, listening to this young man try to explain his ignorance, made me ashamed. I was ashamed for not feeling another's pain, humiliation, and desire for the same things that had been handed to me without my lifting a finger.

"I know the Torah pretty well, but that's all," John went on. "We don't have a rabbi in our village. Sometimes one comes, and that's nice. We men get together for the Sabbath, but I don't really like it when the rabbi is not there because we're not very good, and nobody can really read it very good. It's kind of dull." Then, the thought of Jesus and his teaching came to his mind, and John's face lit up with the thought of this rare Galilean who made the scriptures come alive for him. You could sense the pride these men had for one of their own kind who could rival the knowledge of the best minds in all of Israel. "Jesus knows! You know, he can take any part... I mean people come to him, you know, they'll say, what about this or that, or something in the Torah, and ...*he knows!* He makes it so clear." He shook his head at the wonder of his teacher. Little did he know, little did he really suspect, how very special this teacher of his was.

We were both quiet now as the small boat started to turn toward the shore. As we watched, for some unknown reason, a little knot of people gathered up the hill from the village not far away. John turned to me with an anxious smile on his lips. "It takes so long when you want to see somebody you love, doesn't it?" Then he turned back again to watch the land slip by. How simple this man, yet how exquisitely elegant! Nothing complicated – he just loved Jesus.

Still facing away, he said, "You know what's strange?" It was a soft, quizzical, far-off voice. "I don't even know why I love him. I think... I think I'm going to be someone special."

There was a pause, then, "Maybe not, I don't know, but some of the people, they say that he's going to take the Romans by storm. I don't think so. He never talks about... about war, but he is interested, you know that? He keeps some people around him that scare me to death. They've got knives. They tell him where the Romans are, and Herod's soldiers too, and so we stay away from there. Really, we don't go near them. Maybe that's why he keeps them around, because, you know, they know *everywhere* they are. They know before we get there." John glanced nervously at our shipmates, then leaned close to me with his hand spanning the gap between his mouth and my ear, and said, "They have spies everywhere."

We were fast approaching land now, and John finished his story by saying, "Some of the Romans aren't that bad, but a lot of them are brutes, and they smell." What brought this up I will never know, but in listening to John that week, I learned he had a particularly keen sense of smell, and a very small range of tolerance of what he considered acceptable. He continued, "What do they eat to make them smell like that? Most of them don't like us, and we don't like them. I only saw them once in our village – just once. I really don't know if they're good or bad, but everybody down here hates them. They are here all of the time, I guess." With this he made a leap at the rocky shore, and turned in time to catch the rope one of the fishermen tossed to him on the way. Then with the naturalness that comes from spending years on the water, he helped the others pull the boat safely up upon the gravel. There they held it firm while I shakily, cautiously climbed out upon firm ground.

Hesitating only a second, John then began to push the

boat back out into the deeper water where the fishermen could start their journey home. I must have been daydreaming for I didn't notice him striding back up the beach toward me until he started to speak: "This is the very spot where I was standing when I first saw him."

His voice jerked me away from my deep wondering thoughts of the morning, and suddenly I realized that he was standing right in front of me. "I'm sorry, John," I apologized, "I didn't hear what you said."

"I said, this is the very spot where I met Jesus," he repeated.

"This is it?" I exclaimed surprised, suddenly waking from my absent reflection.

I looked about me, smelled deeply the wonderful pungent odor of the fresh, dew-drenched earth mixed with a faint, elusive stench of rotten fish. I stared out at the water as the small fishing boat slid away, and thanked God for the glorious morning, and my part in it. I stretched my old body from side to side as far as it would go to get the kinks out of my bones. Suddenly, I became painfully aware (not being accustomed to travel on the water) that I must have been holding myself tense and tight the whole morning through. As I arched my back to get the muscles working and relaxed, I felt my advanced age wash over me as inexorable as an incoming tide.

"What a wonderful way to be spending the day," I thought, as I looked around at the stunning countryside, and the Sea of Galilee that reached out to the horizon far beyond me. The water reflected the light rippling blue of the late morning sky, and through the last of the distant haze rising from the choppy sea, I thought I could just make out the sparkling white ramparts of the city of Tiberias shining in the crystal clear air.

"Come, sit where my father used to sit," John said, as he motioned me to a natural, water-etched seat among the gray and ebony-black rocks. "This is where we used to mend our nets together." He pointed around us where I could see the remnants of more than one fisherman who used this place to while away the day.

"Where are they now?" I asked.

He pointed south, and said, "The fish run there at this time of year." Looking up at the sun with an experienced eye, he added, "They should be tied up somewhere near the mouth of the river now, waiting out the day. They'll be back at dark, after fishing the waters at dusk."

The thought of fish reminded him of food. He reached into the pouch he carried slung over his shoulder and handed me a dried fish and a small loaf of bread. He shook his head as he handed me the midday meal, grinning apologetically. "We sure eat a lot of fish, don't we. Wish we had more money so we could eat something else. I like it when we visit his rich friends like *you*, because then we get good food." To this we both laughed. It was then I realized that this was the first time I had seen this young man laugh. After what had happened earlier in the synagogue, it felt good; the laughter, the food, the cheap wine and bread, all seemed to break the tension of the morning past that still hung over us like a cloud.

I was wondering what Jesus was doing right now with his disciples, and when we were going to join him, when John burst in with thoughts of his own. John was still young, and the thought of food was not so easily dislodged from the forefront of his mind. He began to giggle as he leaned forward and whispered (so the rocks wouldn't hear, I suppose), "I ate pork once! It's good. I didn't die either, and Jesus still loves me!" This seemed like the most wonderful joke to him, and he laughed and giggled and laughed again, until I thought he was going to choke on his food. I couldn't help myself either, for his good humor was infectious, and I joined in the lighthearted fun, slapping my thighs and wheezing with delight. When we gained some semblance of order, he continued, wiping the tears from the corners of his eyes.

"He does strange things sometimes – Jesus, I mean. You know, I think he tries to make them mad at him or something, because he does things he just shouldn't do. On the Sabbath for instance..." He took a huge bite of bread and fish at the same time, and I marveled at how he could speak, eat, and breathe all at once. "He'll keep on doing what we do every other day, and it makes them furious!" "Who?" I asked. "You know, the priests, the Judeans, the people from Herod.

"The people love it though, because they're so sick of it – all the rules and all." By now I was marveling at John, for I just couldn't believe that this slight young fellow could eat so much. I wondered incredulously how he did it. Finally assuring myself he wasn't going to choke to death, I relaxed, and whiled the afternoon away listening to him talk. "The people love it, because he just stands right there and no matter what they ask or say, he has an answer. And, the men who come to test him, or catch him saying something he shouldn't, they go away furious. The people love it because they have all been humiliated by them, because they are poor and have no learning, and have no money. We have nothing, you know.

Jesus doesn't take money. I mean, we're taken care of sometimes, but – and I know we must have money someplace because we have to buy bread and stuff – but there's very little."

He paused, then in his own manner of speech, he suddenly changed the subject in mid-thought. "They all want the Messiah! You know what? He is the Messiah... I think. I think he is. He's strange. He doesn't come out and say anything, he just tells us stories. I understand some of them, but not all of them. He's so confusing to me. Timothy just, well, he just feels from his heart, he doesn't need to think. I wish I could do that a little more – just trust him, but I keep thinking, I keep wondering – we're just a motley little band. What are we ever going to do? We've got to get a lot of people. We've got to get a lot of the people and grow and grow everywhere, because they are so strong."

I assumed that the vague "they" he referred to was the existing power structure, which, if he could think clearly about it, probably included me. The poor young man now began to actually tremble as he told me of an incident that had happened not too long ago, perhaps during the last hot season, I would judge, from the freshness of its telling.

"He's so mysterious!" John sounded frustrated at not being able to understand this man who often spoke in parables. "Why doesn't he tell us where we are going? I remember once, we were heading for Caesarea, I knew that much because we were approaching the sea. But why? I didn't want to go to the coast. The Procurator was there because it was so hot every-where else; and then we heard that Antipas was to be visiting there too." John now began to wring his hands in fear. How this young man stayed with Jesus I will never know, for Jesus never shrunk from a confrontation if he felt that it served a purpose.

"We were getting closer and closer to the city. It was so hot and dusty. I was covered with sweat, and wished only to rest and cool myself under a tree. But Jesus kept up a horrid pace all that day, and the one before. Then we saw them. It was just as we came over a rise, the city lay before us, and behind it the sea. Still there was no relief from the heat, no breeze to cool us this day, but worse – what I feared most – soldiers! I couldn't tell whose they were from this distance, but what did it matter, we were dead! Two of the disciples were carrying daggers (not me of course), but Judas and Simon – they are... *Sicarii!*"

The word *Sicarii* hissed from his mouth, as if saying it were in and of itself an evil; a word not to be mentioned in anyone's presence for fear of reprisal.

I knew the meaning of the name, of course, and the very mention of the term Sicarii sent waves of dread through me, as well as John, lest I too be counted among their many victims. For the Sicarii were a party of killers drawn from the Zealots of our land. They were bent on the destruction of everything we had built. This secret group of Jews, from all parts of our country, kept daggers beneath their robes, and when mingling in a crowd, silently, cowardly, slipped their poisonous deeds between the ribs of an unsuspecting Roman, Greek, or highly placed Jew like me. They wanted the Eagle of Rome out of our land, and one's race meant nothing to these despicable men, if it served their needs. I myself had great cause to fear and loath these evil smelling jackals.

I knew that Judas and Simon were Zealots, but I didn't know Jesus counted Sicarii among his disciples, and I must admit that the thought disturbed me.

John actually had tears in his eyes as he continued with the story, so incredibly frightened was he that Judas and Simon would be uncovered. It was almost as if he were pleading with me to understand how frightening it is to travel in the company of some of those closest to our Lord.

He started again. "As we got closer I... I could tell that the soldiers had seen us. We were going to be stopped. Oh, God, why would twelve men be traveling together at this time of year if they were not up to no good? If they search us, they will find the knives. We are dead. We are dead!" he moaned.

There was a long pause as John once again gained control. He then apologized, quite embarrassed for breaking down like he did. I assured him that I was just as afraid as he was of the dreaded Sicarii, and this seemed to make him feel quite a bit better; in fact, it seemed to cement our relationship even more closely in his mind than before. I asked him if he could finish his story, and he nodded his head yes.

"Actually," he said, "there's very little else to tell. I believe it was a miracle as surely as many of the healings I have seen. Jesus spotted the soldiers long before I, and as we approached, he began to speed his walk, so as to reach them before the rest of us got too close. Immediately upon reaching the dreaded men, he began an animated conversation, of which to this day I know not what he said, but to be sure, it was one of the best stories he ever told. I suspected that the story was meant for the soldier's ears only, and judging from the manner and extent of their laughing and gesturing at us

I would guess the story to have been of a vulgar nature – and we undoubtedly were the brunt of the joke. I fairly wet myself with fear as we silently passed them by. We were so close that I could smell their foul breath, and even more, their foul bodies. They wore armor, and in this hot weather, smelled like the pigs they ate. I held my breath, and glanced at Jesus, who was walking in the lead as if he had not a care to his name.

"I don't understand him, Asher, I try, but I just don't understand. Why we even made the journey I do not know to this day, for when we reached the city he went straight to a most specific house, knocked three times, and we were immediately let in. Once inside the court, Jesus further disappeared inside the house, and was gone from our sight for the rest of the day. The servants brought us water and wine, figs, grapes, and food of every kind; but why we came, that we did not know, nor would he ever share."

It seemed that John was in no hurry to join Jesus as yet, I was sure by instruction, so to ease his agitation from the emotion in his story, and the locking once again of my stiff joints, I urged John to join me in a walk along the shore. This we did for a while. Then, as I had seen him do before, John looked heavenward to the sun, and said, "Come, it is time to go."

I was curious. "Where do we go, John?" I asked, trying to keep up his pace.

"Jesus asked me to bring you to him late in the afternoon. He bade us join him at supper time. Come, your needs have already been seen to, you will stay the night in the open with us." With that proclamation, we headed north, following the river that flows from the cliffs of Pan. It was not a difficult journey, for John, deferring to my age, slowed the pace as the afternoon wore on; thus, the trip became no more than an easy stroll, even though we seemed to be continually climb-ing. As we walked, I quizzed my host for more stories of his years with our Lord. He seemed as anxious to tell someone about Jesus as I was to listen, for I think few among the most intimate paid John much due.

"What do you wish to hear?" asked this slight bearded man with a face of tanned leather from years of wear in the sun.

I replied, "Tell me, as you travel about the country, he surely doesn't have followers in every town and village. How do you eat? Where do you all stay?"

"That's easy," he replied with a twinkle in his eye, "it's his charm, with the women!" A big grin of dubious origin slid mischievously over his face. I didn't know at the time, but I was soon to find out that John held women in a somewhat different light than did Jesus, and this was reflected in the manner in which he told his stories, and the content thereof. In fact, that same night I was to hear Jesus deliver a lesson in this regard, much to John's discomfort.

Wary of the look upon his face, I asked, "What do you mean?" Whereupon John contentedly continued, aware now that he was *teaching* this wealthy Judean, and he was begin-ning to enjoy his new and prestigious role.

"Let me ask you a question," he said, his voice deepening, and his hand raised in gesture, as I am sure he had seen Jesus do on many occasions. "If you arrived in town, perhaps in the afternoon, and you wanted to let the people know that you were there, where would you go, who would you tell without standing on a roof-top and yelling `I am here'?" I had to admit, I didn't know. "You go to the well!" he exclaimed with an exaggerated flourish, and lordly flash of eye, communicating to me that he felt himself the purveyor of a delectably obvious truth. "Jesus' first stop when we arrive in town is the well. And, who is at the well?" I shrugged. "You don't know?" he said with a mocking exaggeration, and a shocked look on his face. "I will tell you then. Servant girls! The servant girls for the wealthy come in the late afternoon to fill their jugs at the well (and swap stories about their mistresses of course)." This caused John to chuckle for a while as we continued to climb the winding trail. I know not of what he thought, nor why it was so funny. Plus, I must admit that I was becoming tired, and a bit annoyed. A few moments later he continued.

"Jesus comes up to one of them and asks if they would kindly let us drink from the jug of cool water they have just drawn. He has such an easy warm manner about him, that I have never seen him refused. Then as we are washing away the thirst from the dust of the day, Jesus begins to speak to them. You know, Jesus can look into someone, and right on the spot tell everything you guard as most secret and dear. By the time we have finished quenching our thirst, and have begun to look for the cool shade of a tree, the women are already scurrying off to tell their mistresses of the wonderful stranger they met, with the deepest blue-gray eyes. And, oh yes, he just happens to mention that his followers have need of a place to eat and rest for the evening."

I knew the story from there, for I myself have seen many times how Jesus can come into a home of a complete stranger, and within a few precious moments capture, not only the women of the house, but everyone. An ordinary dinner becomes a feast if he is your guest. Within an instant he knows the hearts of those present, their needs, their hurts, their most secret desires and wants. Then, like no one I have ever met, he can weave a story like a flower with a thousand petals, the outermost of which fall at the table as he speaks, but the youngest and most tightly wound to the tender bud fall later, in a quiet time of reflection. Sometimes, days and weeks later, these petals of wisdom suddenly fall before their eyes, and reveal their moral with an intuitive flash back to the special night with my beloved Lord, and an awakening response takes place within their hearts as if he himself were there right there with them.

It was late in the day when we reached a shady spot to rest, and lean against a tree. John said that we would stay here and rest until sundown, then head up the hill a bit farther, where Jesus and the others would be waiting. I nuzzled up to a fallen tree, and wearily eased my tired bones down, closed my eyes awhile, and listened to the peaceful stream at my feet. I wasn't the only one feeling the effects of the long slow climb, however, for John, lying flat upon the grass and looking up at the mellowing sky commented, "I love this time at the last of the day, because the sun's low, and it's never so hot. My feet are sore!" That was the last I remember, for when next I opened my eyes, the sun had fallen another notch from the sky and wrapped itself around the gnarled tree on the distant hill. The sky was alive with streaks of gold and red that was deepening to wine, I noted, as I rose and stretched.

John was perhaps fifty paces ahead, up on the crest of the nearby hill, looking intently at something at which these old eyes could only guess. When he saw that I was awake and about, he waved at me to join him up the path that wound its way to the top of the hill. When I finally joined him, it was obvious that I had not as yet gained my second wind. As I bent over and tried to catch my breath, I suddenly felt every one of my sixty or so years complaining as if it were their last gasp before they all let go of my feeble frame.

It was a good thing we did not have too far to climb, for I was totally exhausted when we came upon the group Jesus had taken that morning from the synagogue. He was sitting, as usual, a little above them on a log atop a small rise, so that they could all see him and hear him, equally well. Two of the disciples were off to one side, quietly working on the evening meal over a spit and fire, and something they were shoving in the coals. Jesus was talking quietly to them as we approached, so we merely picked a spot and sat down to listen with the rest. We were at the rear of the group, and I found it difficult to hear. My quizzical look at John set him off, and from then on he felt duty bound to keep up a running commentary on what Jesus was saying, whether I could hear him, or not.

"He's talking about someone they met today. You wanted to hear about girls, huh? Well, here it is, he's talking about a girl again." I glanced sideways at John, wondering what on earth he was talking about. What little I heard of what Jesus was saying, had little bearing on the interpretation John was giving me in my ear. "You know, I don't understand that," he decried, "they don't count. Girls I mean. He seems to think they're just the same as we are. Listen to him." I was trying... I was trying! "'She's... so *sweet*.' I've heard that so many times. 'Did you see her eyes?' I've heard that so many times!" John's voice was mocking Jesus, and I found that my temper was beginning to rise a bit, despite myself. I remember that a rather crude explanation presented itself to my mind as to the cause of John's discomfort with women; however, it best remains only my hidden thought.

Jesus started speaking once again, and John (much to my despair) started up his commentary again. "I think that they love him so much because he likes them. I wonder if I'm jealous? Maybe I *am* jealous. Wouldn't that be awful. What's got into me? I must be tired." I continued to try and ignore him.

"Did you hear that, Asher? He said that he saw her in the crowd, and he saw that her heart was pure and sweet. He must have called her up out of the group, I think that's what he must have done. He's asking if the others saw her, saw her eyes." John was now leaning over next to me, whispering in my ear, to my great discomfort. "He's telling about her. He's saying that she'll probably be in heaven before most of us will, because we don't understand, and the girl understood. See... he keeps saying that! He said the girl understood him, and *we* don't!" John was becoming quite agitated, and several others were looking around at him and giving him looks that clearly meant for him to quiet himself – all to no avail I might unfortunately add.

"What does he want from us? We're with him every day! In fact, I've been with him almost every day for almost two years now. I don't understand. You know, I'd do anything he asked. What does that girl do that makes her so special? After all I..." He was now quite loud, as his agitation grew.

At that point Jesus looked John's way, and stared at him

for a moment, without saying a word. John began to moan, "Oh, it's so difficult to understand." Nervously he began to look around, as Jesus turned his attention elsewhere again. "Oh, its getting dark, and I'm afraid again. I know it, I just know we are going to get caught someday. Arrested! I'm so glad we've got a large fire going." With that, he clutched his arms around his drawn up legs, and began to rock back and forth and moan unconsoledly. He reminded me of when I was a child, when the events of my little world became too much for me, and I would grab my dog, hold him ever so close and rock to and fro. Somehow, it seemed to help (me, not the dog).

Jesus was through speaking for now, and the group was breaking up, most of them heading happily toward the warmth of the fire and food. I began to look about to see if anyone could help me with John, when all of a sudden Peter was at my side, and Jesus at John's. Jesus gently lifted John to his feet and put his huge arms around him, and held him – just held him ever so tightly. Tears were streaming down John's face as Jesus handed him some food and gently led him to a seat by the warm, friendly fire. Before Jesus left, he held John's face in his hands and John *knew* that he was loved. And, in that instant, I knew why John followed him. It was the same reason any of us followed him, it was his unconditional love.

No matter what our heads told us was right or wrong, no matter what we had been taught, no matter how many called us fool, when Jesus silently stood before you, and looked into your eyes, you felt wrapped in the most intense love you have ever known. Nothing else mattered after that, nothing, save to do his will. Yet, we all knew, he was but a man, and it was not his will that he sought accomplished, but his Father's instead. He sought that each and everyone of us grow, in the ways that he showed us, closer to our God. He urged us with every tool at his command to use all the strength that we could muster in our search for Him who gave us life and reason to live. He taught that we were just as he, and that those things he did, we could do, too, with grace and humility. And, on special nights like this, I believed in my specialness, and his, with all my heart and soul.

Peter, sensing my inner thoughts, and sharing my adoration for our Lord, smiled warmly at me, and together we walked over to the fire where we were handed plates loaded to overflowing with food. Peter motioned me over to a large rock by the coals, and silently we began to eat together. The sun had long set, and only the faintest trace of cobalt blue held back the coming cold black of night. The first star could be seen near the horizon, and the quiet of the hillside was broken only by the muted voices of the men who had gathered here to be with their Messiah. I was feeling the welcome warmth of the fire when Peter, piece of bread in hand, pointed at John and quietly said, "I remember another time when I saw Jesus do that." I looked at him questioningly. "Hug a man like that I mean. He was a cripple named Timothy." I watched him in the flickering firelight.   His chisel-like features, and his cracked and weathered face took on the look of the ancient earth itself. I could see the valleys and ravines, the upturned furrows of a new beginning, all etched there for anyone who cared to see.

I also understood now why, after Jesus, Peter was the leader of this diverse band of men; for even speaking as quietly as he could, as we sat by the fire together, his voice was like the low rumble of an earthquake before the ground begins to tremble and shake. His face, lacking the softness and inner peace reflected in Jesus', had instead a hard look which, accompanied by his massive voice, and out-going personality, made him a natural leader of men.

"We were walking along the road one day," Peter started softly, a far-off look in his eyes, "when suddenly we came upon a man, who was crippled. The poor man's lifeless leg dragged behind him uselessly, making a furrow in the dirt as he made his helpless way along the hot dusty path toward some distant town. As our band of maybe eight or ten, came upon him, he moved to the side of the road so as not to block our way. I still remember his face; it shone like an angel. There was no fear, nor hate, or resentment there. He had found a gentle peace in his affliction, that was a marvel to see.

"When Jesus came close, he looked into the poor creature's face, and saw no malice there, absolutely none, and his heart went out to him. Jesus, fascinated by this person, turned to us to say, `This man's suffering has ended! No more has he a need to carry this leg about; his lessons have been well learned.' With that, Jesus' overwhelming love poured into the man. He put his arms around the astonished cripple and held him tight, so tight that the man screamed out in pain, but Jesus would not let go. Then, when Jesus had worked his way, he let him free, and the traveler was crippled no more!"

I don't know why this story touched me so, but I suddenly felt the sting of tears welling up in my eyes, for I knew what the healing must have meant to that poor soul. Now, the man would be useful, he could be employed. No more would he be a burden to himself, nor to his friends, or his family. He would be whole.

Peter, seeing the wetness of tears glistening in the fire-light, looked at me and smiled knowingly, saying, "The man you seek is there." He pointed across the fire to a figure sitting opposite me, who had been listening silently all the while to Peter's story. The man looked at me, and the most gentle smile came across his face.

Peter quietly said, "Yes, Asher ben Ammi, it is he. I want you to meet Timothy."

Ancient Memories

Chapter 11

No one lights a lamp and hides it! Instead, he puts it on a lampstand to give light to all who enter the room. Your eyes light up your inward being. A pure eye lets sunshine into your soul.

...If you are filled with light within, with no dark corners, then your face will be radiant too, as though a floodlight is beamed upon you.

Luke 11:33-34 & 36

The next morning dawned crisp, clear, and bright. This was to be the day that I was to take my leave from Galilee and from the man who made my life sing; I approached it with mixed emotions and feelings. So many memories crammed into such a few short days – experiences that will remain with me forever.

He touched me on the shoulder shortly before sunrise, and motioned for me to follow him past the eastern rise. Several of the others were beginning to stir as we quietly crept out of camp and headed for the hill. Once out of sight of the rest, Jesus put his arms around me and held me for a while.

There was a strange sense of sadness that I felt as he held me on that lonely mountain top, yet at the same time I could also feel the hidden power of his indomitable spirit flowing into me and making me whole.

He stepped back and looked at me with a small grin, saying, "There, you look ten years younger than when you came. This outdoor life must agree with you." I held up my hands in protest, for although I may have looked ten years younger (which I doubt), my bones felt ten years older after having slept on the hard ground all night. He clasped his arm around my shoulder, and together we climbed to the top of the rise. Once there, we sat next to each other, wrapped our robes tightly around us to keep out the morning chill, and fell within that sacred part of our souls where only God doth dwell. There, on a deserted hill I sat with him, and felt the warm sun sweep my face, then drench my body with its vitality and warmth, and my soul *sang*.

I opened my eyes to capture one of the most wonderful and poignant pictures I had ever experienced, one that lives in my memory as clear today, as it was that morning on the Galilean hill. I opened my eyes in time to see the deep yellow rays of the sun illuminate Jesus' bearded face, and there for me alone to see, was a man of consummate peace, lost in the highest realms of ecstasy. In that rare glimpse of my Master, I saw the heights to which we all aspire. I saw him in a state of rhapsody.

He must have felt me watching him in adoration, for slowly his eye lids lifted, and a strange smile of *knowing* crept over his face. Suddenly, a shock went through my whole body. My face turned ashen white, and I shook violently for a second, not knowing what the cause. It was as if the icy grip of death had passed through me as swiftly as a breeze. "Yes, Asher, you feel it too. Our time rapidly approaches, my dear disciple, for too soon both of us will be at death's door. Remember, there is a sweetness in passing, and now that you have tasted heaven, you know there is nothing to fear." These words sent more tremors through me, and I pleaded for him to stay away from Judaea, where his healings and teachings had drawn such hatred from the priests. "Don't worry, Asher," he said, "I will not come south until the Feast of Tabernacles next, and then I will come in secret. I will get word to you somehow."

Those were the last words we had alone together until he returned to Jerusalem, preceded by a messenger, the following autumn. Silently then, we rose and walked the distance back into the camp of his *chosen*. There I was surprised to find my servant waiting with our horses and our baggage to begin our long journey home. When I saw the horses prancing in the morning air, pawing at the ground in anticipation, I shot a glance at Jesus, and saw him smiling as he turned away to tend to his little flock.

❋❋❋❋❋❋❋❋❋

Over half a year had passed since that day, when late one evening, a knock was heard, and a man entered and asked for me. I alone from among my household would have recognized him, for it was a man who once was a crippled beggar, until my Master passed his way. It was Timothy. "Come in, my dear friend, you have walked a mighty way. Please, my home is yours. I want you to meet my family. What a wonderful surprise for all of us here." I had told everyone about our meeting that night with Peter around the campfire, and they all wanted to question the poor man at the same time, and on the very night that he had arrived. I insisted that everyone leave him alone until he had been fed and was able to catch up on his sleep, then I left it up to Timothy to defend himself.

He stayed two weeks with us waiting for Jesus to arrive, as he had been told; then, after only one night to rest, Jesus and he both struck out together to be with others of Jesus' followers whom I had secretly alerted of his coming. I then swore my son, John, to secrecy, and sent him on his way to alert those who were to know that on the morrow he would arrive.

The following morning then, after a good night's sleep, I escorted Jesus and Timothy as far as Lazarus' house – and that too was an experience to behold.

Friends since their youth, Jesus and Lazarus were inseparable whenever it was possible for them to be near, and so it was with a great deal of anticipation that each awaited the arrival of the other, whenever their paths came close enough together.

Lazarus' home is in Bethany, just a short distance from Jerusalem, and it didn't take us long to walk. As we circled around the hill of the Mount of Olives, we saw a man running toward us waving his arms excitedly. It was Lazarus! As he approached, Jesus said, "What brings you here?" and laughed uproariously, as they embraced. "I was waiting for you, Lord." Lazarus said, bending over, trying to catch his breath from running. "And what of your sisters?" Jesus continued. "They wait for you too, Lord. We heard from Asher and Timothy here, that you were coming. I'm so happy – so happy Lord! We were so *joyous* when we heard of your coming. I ran all the way out here Lord, to be with you just a few moments sooner. We're so delighted that you're coming to grace our home again."

He turned to Timothy and me now, waving his arms to include us too, saying, "You're all welcome. The women are making bread and baking for you. And, the wine merchant, I've told him to bring wine. It's a happy day, Lord, that you've come to visit once again. I even bought this new robe to honor you. Isn't it beautiful!" Jesus, Timothy and I were all laughing heartily now, as Lazarus spun around and around in the dust showing off his new clothes in child-like glee. He was totally unaware of the spectacle he was making in the road, much to the equal delight of the passers-by, for honest, lighthearted joy is truly infectious, and makes everyone happy to be a part of it.

We couldn't have calmed Lazarus even if we had wanted to, as he continued to happily babble on as we headed down the well-traveled road toward his home. "It's been so long, Lord, months, and we haven't heard from you. Come, make your steps light, we welcome you all." Lazarus turned and walked backwards a few steps, to better see his boyhood friend. Jesus started to turn red at the ears with all the unusual attention. Timothy and I looked at each other smiling, and exchanged a wink of delight. "Where have you been, what have you been doing?" Lazarus asked. "We hear that there are many more with you now, Lord; where do they come from?" Jesus was about to say something in answer, when Lazarus held up his hands and said, "No, wait. Save it for Martha and Mary, they want to hear too, they don't want to miss *anything*." Then, leaning close to Jesus, he said in a conspiratorial tone, "However, you can tell *me* just a few things can't you; things they wouldn't understand, just man to man, eh? After all, they don't have to know *everything*!" I think this was a private joke, with a meaning just for the two of them, for they both began to laugh merrily.

"Lazarus, my friend, it has been good, and it is good to see you. My dear brother, your eyes do sparkle so. It's good to see you so happy. Now, tell me of your sisters." With that query, Lazarus leaned close to Jesus' ear again. What he said, I do not know. However, whatever he said brought peals of laughter from them both. Then Jesus groaned and said, "She shouldn't wait for me. I love her, but if she waits for me, she'll wait forever!"

"I've told her that a thousand times, Jesus, but she doesn't believe me, does she?" Lazarus shook his head and shrugged his shoulders in resignation.

"Oh, well," Jesus continued, "it's all right, I'll talk to her again tonight. I'll make her understand somehow, but you're right, it's nearly impossible, isn't it." With that, Jesus changed the subject away from the personal, became more serious, and went back to the way we are used to knowing him – teaching.

"Yes, my friend you have heard right, we have gathered more about us. Oh, Lazarus, my brother, if only I could..." Jesus was suddenly serious and silent. For a moment, he paused and looked at his friend as if he were about to tell him something of monumental importance. Then, shaking his head, he said, "No, there is no way I can share this with you, no matter what I wish." No one knew what Jesus was speaking of, least of all Lazarus, yet we were all immediately concerned, for our Lord's seriousness lately frightened us all more than any of us cared to openly admit.

I stepped up to Jesus, and put my hand lightly on his arm. He turned to me to look me in the eyes, and I found a sorrow there I didn't know existed. He patted my arm. "It is a wonderful thing, our Father's work, I mean," Jesus expressed, as much it seemed for himself, as for us. "Just think," he went on, "all those years growing up, all these years preparing, and now the moment is at hand." Jesus seemed to be carrying a frightful burden; you could see it in his eyes. "All these souls, dear one," he was still holding my eyes transfixed in his, "...all these souls. Some nights they weigh so heavily on me. So many souls, so many that I cannot touch them all! My time is so near, I just can't touch them all!" The hair on my neck stood up just as it had on that last morning in Galilee.

Then, I believe, sensing that this was neither the time or place, Jesus caught himself, took a deep breath, shook, as if ridding himself of a deep chill, and changed the mood as rapidly as it had come. He was again light and bantering.

"Wonderful, Lazarus, everything is wonderful." He slapped Lazarus on the back, and together they started off again on the road to Bethany. He glanced over his shoulder, and his look told me, "Later, later I will explain." Meanwhile, he picked up the happiness of the day as it started, saying joyfully, "They flock to us, more and more brother, in greater numbers every day. You'll have to come and spend a week or two. You can take the time. You will just have to come and see for yourself, and let me introduce you to many of them.

"But, for now, it will just be good to be in your home, dear brother, and to relax. Can you make arrangements for my followers as they come? Food, lodging, and so on?" Lazarus said that it would be his delight. "But please, find them lodging in a place other than in your home, for I need the rest. I can tell you that brother, I *do* need the rest."

With that, Jesus stopped, for we had rounded the last hill, and there, higher up the path leading from the road, were Mary and Martha, waiting and waving. Seeing them, Jesus pointed and exclaimed happily, "There are your dear sisters! Look at them waving. Ah, it's going to be good to see them and to forget everything for awhile." Jesus rushed forward to throw his arms around them. The greeting was tumultuous and wonderful to be a part of.

Later, as I stood to the side of all the activity, leaning against the back wall of the living room, in this small, simple two room home, watching the happy homecoming, I thought about what had happened on the road; and for the first time it occurred to me that no one, not one of us worries about him – Jesus – we worry only about ourselves. Here we have a man who gives of himself totally, each and every day, and yet when have we ever heard one word of complaint? When does he rest? The thought had never even occurred to me before. When he has walked all day, and he takes his "rest" in a friendly home, when his disciples take their ease of food and drink, what is Jesus doing? He is teaching. Teaching. Teaching. He can never allow himself to stop, for continually in his ear he hears: "Help me, Jesus," "Tell me, Lord...," "Why me, Jesus?" "Teach us, Lord," from early morning until late at night. It never stops.

Thinking back, even when he was at our home, could he rest from the constant questions, even there? The answer was, unforgivably, no. For even there, my son, or his wife, or my wife, Miriamme, or I were always occupying his time with questions. No wonder he could not stay with us when, as now, he needed to get away from the crowds, the questions, and the pleadings. I felt again the pang of shame.

As I stood there in the home of Lazarus, in the back corner of the room, watching, I remembered back to just before we arrived, while we were still on the road, how Jesus' heart gladdened upon seeing the women, for he had grabbed Lazarus and said, "What would I do without you? Oh, sweet brother of mine, you have always treated me just the same. Since our boyhood in Egypt, always my friend!" Then laughing again, he admonished, "Tell me, is your sister going to get emotional again tonight?" Lazarus responded, "You have to deal with her tonight Lord, not me." "I suppose I do, I suppose I do at that, you're right. All right, but no stories late at night, understood? You tell her that. I'll be here for a few days, and there will be plenty of time to talk. I need rest tonight." Then Jesus, looking up at Mary jumping up and down and waving again, winked at Lazarus and predicted, "I fair say, she's going to wet her pants if she doesn't stop jumping like that, eh!"

Mary loved Jesus with all her heart, and I wager she would have given her life to have been allowed to take this man as her husband, but that was not Jesus' lot in this life. He came not to grace but one; instead, he came to give everything he had for us all.

Mary's love touched me though, and reminded me of my dear Miriamme. Once in the living room and seated on cushions spread about, Mary came to Jesus, bowed before him, sunk to her knees, bent over, grasped Jesus' feet in her hands, and began to sob. Once again I struggled to hold back my emotions as I watched this woman, who loved this man so dearly, try to wash his feet with her tears.

The room fell silent, as each of us watched this heart wrenching scene.

"No, Mary, no... please don't," he spoke softly to her, and tried to lift her gently to her feet, but she was determined in her love. "Don't, Mary, not with your tears, Mary, please," Jesus pleaded. "I know they are tears of joy, but you mustn't." Mary continued to worship her Lord in the only way she knew – *totally*. Jesus' eyes were filling with tears now too, as he tried again to dissuade her. "No, Mary, dear one, I understand, but please, enough." Then, bending forward, he touched her still bowed head, and said, "Dear one, I love you with all my heart. No one has ever loved me so much as you, and I will repay you this love very shortly." He shut his eyes very tightly and murmured, "Oh, God, if she only knew how soon it will be, if she only knew." There was that far-away look in his eyes again, as I moved deeper into the shadows, and wondered at his words.

He released her bowed head from his gentle hands, and Mary started to back away from him, to leave, to help with the preparations for the evening meal. Jesus lay back against the pillows with a sigh, and said, "Let me lie here for a moment, just one moment, please. Don't leave me, Mary, sit by my side. Your sister works well enough for two; please, just let me rest a moment. My poor body grows heavy, and feels the walks more acutely each day. The days seem to get longer, and the path shorter all the time. It's all rushing so fast, so fast now Father, so fast." His voice began to trail, as my precious teacher slowly sank into an exhausted sleep. You could barely hear him intone, "The words... the memories... Abba, Abba, I love you... Guide me, Lord, make me strong. They all drain me so Father... Abbaaa."

With a heartfelt sigh, his breathing deepened, and he dropped into sleep. Mary was curled at his feet, as I silently slipped away, and I headed for the loneliness of the silent hills.

Chapter 12

Jesus was moved with pity for them and touched their eyes. And instantly they could see, and follow him.

Matt. 20:30 & 34

Then Jesus placed his hands over the man's eyes again and as the man stared intently, his sight was completely restored... Jesus sent him home to his family.

Mark 8:25

As he was walking along, he saw a man blind from birth... Then he spat on the ground and made mud from the spittle and smoothed the mud over the blind man's eyes, and told him, "Go and wash in the Pool of Siloam"

John 9:1 & 6-7

Now begins a period of months of anguish for me, that ended in the death of my Lord, which I could do nothing to forestall. I know now that it was ordained by our

Father, and carried out by His son with a degree of timing, and a sense of eloquence incomprehensible to any of us at that time. Jesus set about to prepare for the culmination of his teaching, and we, along with him, were mere players in this play of life, death, and then life again. For, from the period of the Feast of Tabernacles (in the autumn), through the Feast of Dedication (in early winter), unto Passover (in the spring of the following year), Jesus taught in the Temple, and throughout the surrounding area of Judaea, without returning to his native Galilee.

As he taught, he healed; and the more he healed, the more he became the focus of the people of Israel; and the more he became the hero, the prophet, the Messiah, the more the priests and rulers wanted him out of the way. Within a week of his arrival, I was visited at my home by a very agitated Nicodemus. My old friend was beside himself with grief, worry and rage. I no more than got him settled down, and asked Miriamme to pour wine, when he spurted out the happenings at the Temple that day.

"As you know, the rumors have been rampant that Jesus was somewhere here in Jerusalem, and I among them wondered, too. Well, I was in the Temple today, as is my custom, when to my surprise there began a commotion in the outer court which grew to such an intensity that we all left the buildings to find the cause. Lo, before me there was Jesus!

"People were running from everywhere as word spread that the *miracle worker* from Galilee had arrived. Most of my colleagues, too, pushed their way close to hear what this fellow they had heard so much about (who was rumored greater than the Baptist) had to say. I tell you, Asher, he made no hiding of it, in fact he fairly shouted it out. You could not dispense with his words without knowing that he was declaring himself to be heaven-sent, and special – yes, maybe even the Messiah himself. Yet, so clever was he in his words and deeds, that any who heard would be hard pressed to stone him for blasphemy. But, so close did he come, and so aroused did the crowd become, that the Temple guards were sent to stop him and bring him to Caiaphas for questioning.

"We were all watching the fortress nervously for signs of what the Romans were about. With the Temple full to capacity during these holidays, a confrontation had to be avoided at all costs (lest we forget our lesson at the hands of Archelaus). But, arrest him, this I could not stand! So, when the officers returned empty-handed, I gave a silent sigh of relief. He had escaped them, Asher, and I was glad." With this, Nicodemus most uncharacteristically downed an entire goblet of wine, placed there by my wife in the form of a refreshment, and he did this in one swallow. "Oh, Asher, then I did a most terrible thing." he continued unabated. By now, I had lost all semblance of patience. My worry was escalating throughout Nicodemus' never-ending story. "What, Nicodemus, what did you do?" I yelled. Miriamme tugged at my sleeve, urging patience. "I'm getting to that, Asher, patience please." I sank into the chair and thought, "He will never tell me – *never*!"

"Old Annas was there," Nicodemus finally continued, "full of righteous indignation, and said mockingly, `Is there a single Sadducee or Pharisee among us who truly believes that this carpenter king from Galilee is the Messiah?' No one uttered a sound, as he looked from one to another. `The stupid crowd will believe anyone who will heal an ache or a pain. I spit on them anyway!' Then he bid the officer of the guards to go again and arrest 'this man called Jesus.' I could see old Annas' son-in-law, the High Priest Caiaphas, lick his lips with delight. I was so incensed, Asher, that I did something I can't believe as yet – I stood and challenged Annas. Can you believe I would challenge the High Priest past, and the entire house of Caiaphas!"

"What did you say to him, Nicodemus?" I said, gritting my teeth. Miriamme refilled the wine goblet.

"As the officer started to walk away to do the high priest's bidding, I stepped in front of him, and said, 'You shall go nowhere to arrest anyone this day!' The officer looked at me in surprise, then turned to see what his orders would be. While there was a stunned silence, I grabbed the moment and asked, 'Is it legal to convict a man before he is even tried?' Annas screamed, 'Are you a Galilean too, Nicodemus? Search the Scriptures and see for yourself – no prophets will come from Galilee!' Still angry, I continued undaunted, 'He was born in Judaea, like you, Annas, and from the house of David – not in Galilee!' This so upset the crowd that they all began to argue among themselves. Annas realized he had lost everything for the moment, and with a quick glance at Caiaphas for his approval, he dismissed the guard, and ordered everyone out."

"You did very well, my friend." I told Nicodemus (I really was quite impressed and surprised). "Very well indeed. Why do you appear so worried now, though?"

"Because, Asher Ben Ammi, that was only the beginning, just a skirmish. They will kill him, Asher, believe me they will kill him. And now that I am counted along with him, I have lost the element of surprise, I will be counted as one with their enemies. No longer will I be privy to what they hatch behind their people's backs. Please, Asher, find him and warn him, that the priests will not tolerate too much more."

With this warning ringing in my head, I saw poor Nicodemus to the door, bid my man-servant to see him safely home, which was not far away, while Miriamme called for John, and together we sent him heading for Lazarus' house in an attempt to find Jesus. As for me, I headed to the Temple, glad that I had remained a hidden disciple, or at least not an open one here in Judaea, for I planned to listen to what I could behind the closed doors of the Temple gates. But my plans fell by the wayside, as I inadvertently picked up my Lord's trail in quite an accidental way.

I came to the aqueduct, which I had to go under before reaching the bridge over the valley leading into the Temple grounds. There, at the intersection, close to the market, stood a mixed crowd listening intently to a man, a poor man, by the looks of him. I pulled my cloak about me and started to hurry on my way, when I was halted in my tracks by the name, "Jesus." I swung on my heels, suddenly interested in this man wrapped in rags, an Arabian I would guess from his looks, but certainly not a Jew. I could hear enough from the edge of the crowd to learn he had been blind in one eye all his life, could see but poorly out of the other, but now he was on his way home, *healed*, in both eyes, because of a man named Jesus.

I found someone in the crowd whom I knew, and paid him to fetch the poor man and bring him to my house. "Tell him that a follower of the man who healed him wishes only to see him fed, bathed and sent on his way home after a good night's sleep." Then I anxiously covered the short distance left to the Temple, and knocked on the massive doors for admittance. The temple was closed at this hour of the day, save to those of us who had paid our way well through the years. And so, without further ado, I was admitted into the sanctuary where I spent the better part of an hour trying to ascertain from the priests, and those I could still find, exactly what had transpired that day. From what I learned, it appeared that Nicodemus had not exaggerated. He had made a few enemies that day, but won some admirers as well (for few there are that will stand up against the fury of the high priest – or his father-in-law). Upon leaving, I had pretty well assured myself that there was as yet no coordinated effort to bring Jesus up on official charges. So, at least for now I felt relieved, and headed home wondering what luck John had in Bethany and whom my strange guest would prove to be.

Upon returning home, I met my son, John, just coming through the stable gates with news that he had seen Jesus, and that Jesus had given him his assurance that everything would be all right, that we should rest easy. He had told John that his time was not yet come, and that although there would be much furor over his preaching, there would be nothing done that would bring him harm during this holiday.

Much relieved, I clasped my son around the shoulders and explained what I had learned while he was gone. Together we entered the courtyard to find the stranger just coming out of the guest quarters, where my man-servant had garbed him in one of John's finest robes. I saw the startled look on my son, and saw the blood of anger start to rise to his face. With mocked gravity, I looked at him with concern, and said, "John, I am surprised at you. Have you forgotten so soon what Jesus has taught you, that it is more blessed to give than to receive?"

I caught him more by surprise than I thought, for now his brightened skin was from embarrassment. He apologized to me, and strode ahead to meet our guest with open arms. Our guest's name turned out to be Maston; he had little or no education, but I was right about his heritage; he was an Arabian of mixed, but very handsome blood. In fact, quite to my discomfort, I noticed Miriamme's eye more than once that night glancing this good looking stranger's way. But, ignoring that, what a story he told! One that I could hardly believe. I think, if I had not seen the multiplication of the loaves and fishes with my own eyes, and heard of the healing of Timothy's dead leg in his own presence, I would have dismissed this man's testimony as being too far-fetched to be true. Yet, I will let you judge for yourself – as you must anyway.

"Please understand," he started, "I have been blind in my right eye since birth. I had never seen out of it. Although, at one time, I could see with my other eye as well as you, about a year ago it started to go bad too. I saw so poorly that it was of little use in plying a trade or making a living at anything at all. I came to Jerusalem, the holy city, to find a cure, to find some hope for me. I came from the desert, where my home lies, and that is where my family awaits my return, someday.

"For almost a year I sought a cure for my eyes. I went from one doctor to another, but I searched in vain. I was out of money, and had no way to earn enough even to return to my home again. I was reduced to lying by the healing pool, waiting my turn to get close enough so that when the water boiled, I might be healed. Have you been there? Have you seen what it is like?" I had to admit that I hadn't. I tried to stay away from places like this that only served to depress me greatly.

"It is a filthy place. The small pool is maybe forty or fifty paces across, and suffers the refuge and waste of hundreds each day. It is more a wallow than a pool now, and the water is the same color as the mud around it – kind of brown, or greenish yellow. The ground around rises up to about the height of a man or two, on three of the sides (the fourth provides the outlet and is covered with bushes of several kinds), and from there it levels away. Any ground cover has long since been worn away, or trampled into dust by the teeming mobs that come each day to be cured or saved. It is said that when a miracle is about to happen, the water begins to boil. From my position atop the ridge, I could hear, and vaguely see people of every ailment and infirmity (except the leper), lining the dirt, awaiting the movement of the holy water below. I had seen it happen only once. *Experienced it*, is a more accurate description, for at that time, the stampede of people became so intense, that the healings were far outweighed by the trampled bodies that were left behind to be hauled away. Yet, even as I say this, I feel little remorse, for it was only by someone's death that any of us could move our allotted place any closer to the water. So it was, that when the miracle made the water boil, we willingly threw our bodies into the water, no matter what the risk. So miserable had our lives become that death was preferable to this living hell within which we lived."

My stomach reeled as my imagination filled in any gaps in this poor creature's story. In my wealth, I could not, no matter how I tried, imagine what it must be like to live as this man had.

We urged him to continue.

"As we sat there day after day, our lot became worse, through lack of food and care. Once in a while people would come as an act of charity, and bring us food, but that was rare. As for myself, I stayed alive by walking each evening to the village and begging. I also picked up scraps of food that had been thrown out from behind the homes. Day after day I'd be there again, barely staying alive. Meanwhile, at the pool, each of us had our spot, you know. We would have fought and killed if someone tried to take it, thus everyone knew their place. I had no idea how long it would take to find my way to the bottom of the hill, and into a spot that might allow me to throw myself into the water should it begin to rise. For up to now, I had been too far away to get to the water and even try.

"Once in a while someone wealthy would come with their retainers, and sometimes soldiers would come with their men. They would simply wade in and clear a path. They would just throw us away! It was easy, because most of the people were so emaciated, they couldn't weigh more than a small bag of salt. They just threw us away, as if we were less than animals lying in their path.

"I remember one poor man, who was the only exception to the rule of position. When they brought him there, they picked him up by his rags and threw him down the hill, caring not a twit upon whom he fell in this human refuse pile. His legs didn't work. Nothing worked at all. He just lay there for the longest while, face down in the dirt. It was hard to tell if he was alive or not. His legs were just bones, there was no meat on them at all. But slowly, ever so slowly, he lifted his head; then stretched out his arms; then with the strength only of his will, he dragged his body inch by inch, with his fingers clawing at the earth, down the hill. Closer, and closer to the water's edge he went. His legs I remember so clearly, because they were the thinnest things I had ever seen. Each and every one of us, no matter how terrible we felt, began to hold our breath as he worked his way agonizingly closer to the water's edge, dragging himself across the ground, and bodies too, that happened in his way. As he would pull himself over a poor wretch, he'd look neither left nor right, but with glazed eyes stared straight at his goal, hearing not his dead legs thud and crack as they bumped and bounced over rocks and bodies alike. Nor did he feel the blows delivered by some of those that he crossed. I am sure he had made up his mind that he would be healed, or go to the bottom of the pond. It mattered little to him how it ended, just so that it did.

"As he got to the edge of the pool, he couldn't throw himself in. He had only one way to move, and so, slowly, deliberately, excruciatingly, he began to drag his torn and mutilated body into the water, head first, the only way he could. Then, he took a breath, and dropped beneath the surface. Thank God some poor wretch like himself took pity on him then, for he would surely have drowned before his legs flopped in. A man with crippled arms and back gave a mighty growl, and kicked the rest of him in.

"At last, I thought, the agony has ended. It became deadly quiet. Everyone's eyes were riveted on the unmoving water. Then, when everyone thought the drama had run its course, we suddenly saw his head begin to emerge from the pool! Then slowly, steadily he started to rise. He started to stand! It was like a lost continent, ponderously starting its rise from the depths of some great murky sea. He didn't say a word. First his head, then his shoulders, then still staring straight ahead, his waist broke free. We thought a demon was holding him up, and many in his way began to shake and back away in terror and fear.

"He walked out of the pool on his own two feet, that although bloody and bruised, and still thin as a sliver of wood, were working and strong. He walked over the top of the rise and left. We never saw him again. There wasn't anything said for the longest time. We were so shocked. Then, it was awful!"

The poor man in front of us began to break down and cry as he finished telling of this grim scene. "It was just awful!" he cried again. "They came by the tens, by the hundreds, all rushing and clamoring to get into the water while the magic lasted. The stronger fought over the weaker, and the weaker died. That's when the man kicked me. That's when he kicked me in the eye! Water gushed out of the socket, and Oh God, it hurt so terribly. He kicked my blind eye out, and he didn't even care! I never got to the water. I simply lay there, staring into the flaming pain."

We were all sobbing as we listened, but hardly comprehending this poor man's story of abuse, and terror beyond anything we could understand. Miriamme became sick, and had to rush from the room, but Maston kept right on with his story, seemingly unaffected by our loss of composure.

"I had lived that way for a month and a day, existing on scraps those around me gave me to keep me alive – though I barely cared. In fact, today was like all the rest. I didn't even notice the man when he came. I lay on my back and looked up at the sky with what was left of my one ill-seeing eye. It was a hazy morning, and I remember that the sky was a light, eggshell blue. I just lay there and watched the one fuzzy, wispy cloud off near the horizon as it changed into a hundred different shapes before disappearing into nothingness. The sun was bright, and the air warm. Nothing else entered into my consciousness, nothing, it was empty. For the past few days I had been laying like that; staring into nothingness, caring little when the end came. Until somewhere, an urging inside told me that something was amiss.

"All of a sudden I knew what was wrong: the noise; the arguing, the chatter, the moaning and the wailing of the people had stopped. I propped myself up to see what was happening. It took a minute for my one eye to adjust, for the ground was dark in comparison to the livid sky, and my sight was hazy at best. And, there was the man – the man called Jesus.

"He was wearing just his loincloth, that's all. Someone off to the side was holding his robe for him, but now, he was up to his thighs in the water. He stood there, right in front of me, but I couldn't figure out what made all the people quiet, for although I could see the man from this short distance, I couldn't understand what brought about the unnatural hush that had fallen all about.

"Then I noticed. He stood there in an easy manner, his arms were limp at his sides - *but he was looking straight at me!*

I mean, there were hundreds of people there, but he was looking straight at me. There was not a sound to be heard, except the roaring in my head as I realized that for some reason I had been singled out of the crowd. Then he held up one hand in my direction, as if he expected me to come and take hold of it – and still he stared. Then he held two hands toward me.

"I had to get up. There was nothing else I could do. I thought I was going to be killed. I thought, `They will stone me, they know I am not a Jew. That is why he has singled me out, he has come to have me killed.' I started to walk, if you could call it that. I stumbled and slid down the rest of the hill, because my legs were so weak from hunger. I fell and got up again, and fell again, then reluctantly entered into the water. Ever so slowly I walked toward him, trembling as I went, tears streaming down my dirty, mud-caked cheeks.

"I saw his robes being held by his men, and I knew that he was a Jew. I was panic stricken; I wanted to run, but there was no place to go. I pleaded, `No, Lord, I'm not of your race. Please, you're a Jew; they'll stone me, they'll stone me for sure!' Inside I was wailing, `Doesn't he know he's killing me? You might as well drown me, I'm a dead man when they get hold of me.' I stepped into the water. The pool was hot! And, the deeper I went, the hotter it became. I struggled to keep my balance on my tottering legs. They were burning so bad that I cried in pain. Then my agony was over, for I was in front of him, and now I knew I was surely to die. I remember I was up to my waist, and he up to his thighs, so I knew he was taller than I.

"He put his hand on my head, over my face and my eyes,

and I could feel that he was slowly opening my bad eye. `Don't!' I shrieked, `Don't, I'm blind! Please don't, oh please, it hurts so. Don't open my eye!' I *screamed* for the last time, in a mixture of terror and agony. At the same time he was slowly pressing me down into the water. I knew I had finally met my end. I could not have resisted him if I had tried, but I did try, with all my strength. `*OPEN IT!*' the man shouted in my ear. `*OPEN YOUR EYE!*' I was whimpering, and gasping for air, but he wouldn't let up. `*OPEN YOUR EYE, MASTON!*'

"Slowly I sank beneath the agitated waves, as the sound of my name rang in my head. `How did he know my name, how?' The water was over my head. I couldn't breathe, yet longer than I could hold my breath he held me there without letting me up. I let my breath out with a gasp, and started to sink into oblivion, when all of a sudden I was standing again, facing him, and he was talking to me, but this time... *I could see!*

"Then ensued a strange conversation with this man in front of me who had just miraculously brought back my sight. `Who are you?' I gasped, `You can't be a Jew, or you wouldn't have done what you have done to me, a non-believer. Who are you, Lord? Who is your god? Tell me so that I may worship him. My god could never do this. I will follow your god anywhere. Just tell me who you are, and who he is, so that I may follow him.' Then for the first time, this man of miracles spoke quietly to me. `Maston, your god and mine are one.' `But, who is your god, Lord?' `Maston, your god and mine are one, neither is better. I say again, they are ONE!' Suddenly I was afraid for this man who had brought me back my sight. `No, Lord, don't say that. You'll be killed along with me for saying that!' `Maston, was your eye blind?' `Yes, Lord, you know that.' `Maston, do you now see?' `Yes, Lord, you know that, too.' `Maston, your god and mine are one. When you go away from here, you will know there is only one Lord God.'

"'Master,' I said, `I will proclaim that – but they will kill *you* for it!' Then, putting his hands on either side of my head, I suddenly saw a brilliant light, and speaking very slowly he said, `Maston, can you now *see*?'

"'Yes, Lord, they *are* One, Lord.'

"'Yes, Maston.'

"'Then they will kill you, Lord.'

"'Yes, Maston, they will kill me.'

"'Then not from my mouth will they hear this.'

"'Maston, you won't have to watch long.'

"'Watch?'

"'And when I am gone, then you can tell.'

"'How long will I watch you, Lord?'

"'Maston, have I not given you eyes to see? Go now to your home, tell your wife, your family.'

"'You won't ever see me again, Lord?'

"'Maston, have I led you this far only to lead you astray? Watch after me, Maston, and when I am gone, come to my people and tell them what you *see*.'

"I started to sob uncontrollably. `Yes, Lord. Thank you, Lord. I can see. I can see!'

"I am still confused, noble Asher ben Ammi," Maston confessed. "He left me then, just walked away without saying another word. The people paid me no mind, for they were screaming for him to heal them, too. And those who could still walk followed him, as I stood looking after him. I didn't know what to do, so I started walking across the pool and out. Then I found my way into the city on my way home, and that was when you found me."

A cold fear ran through me, a fear that I felt once in Galilee, then again last week in Bethany, a fear that I could not quite isolate, but which struck me as an emptiness in the pit of my stomach, a void so immensely deep that I felt it could never again be filled.

I forced my thoughts back to the frail, handsome, middle-aged man in front of me. What a change from the dirty street beggar I had seen just a few hours before. How many more would we welcome into our homes without question if only someone cared enough to help? Maston was speaking to me. "Did I do right in telling you as I did?" He was more pleading than asking.

"Huh? Oh, yes. I'm sorry, Maston, my mind was somewhere else," I apologized. "Yes, you did right. But I will ask you to fulfill your promise to him as he asked. Cling to this man's teaching, my friend, and I think in time you will understand his message to you. Yes... I am afraid you will understand all too soon.

"Come, Miriamme, dinner is waiting, and our guest has not had a decent meal for a very long time." I took my wife's hand and led her into the next room where the evening meal was being served. On the way out the door I could not help myself from saying to my guest (just loud enough for John to hear), "My, that robe does become you. It was an ill fit on its previous owner anyway. I swear, if you keep dressing like that, Maston, we will make you Jewish yet." Everyone laughed, save my son, who shot me a dirty look in return, and I might add, plotted his little revenge.

The next morning, after I came down from the rooftop where I customarily meet the new day, my guest was waiting for us in the court. "If I may be so bold, sir," Maston started, "what do you do so early on the roof of your house?"

"My friend, you have a bright and curious mind. When once you greet your family and friends, and have a proper time to settle your affairs, why don't you return. Bring your wife, and children too, if you have any, and return to Jerusalem to join my household and serve me in any capacity you might choose. There is much to teach you, if you have a desire to learn. Then I will tell you of my Master whom you met yesterday at the pool. I think you will find that your stay will be most rewarding in many ways, and I think you might be most happy here too."

"You are too kind. I accept your offer only too willingly. Thank you. You will see. Someday I will return." With that we joined John, his wife, and Miriamme for a light morning meal. Then giving Maston enough food for his journey home, we set him upon a horse and sent him on his way. I bade him farewell from the courtyard, entrusted him into my son's hands, then climbed the stairs to the roof to watch and wave goodbye from there.

I couldn't believe my eyes. Was I seeing right? As Maston flew from our stable yard, he was riding my own black gelding, not the horse I had selected for him the previous day. I ran all the way down the stairs, yelling at the top of my lungs, and when I hit the bottom stair I started running across the stones toward the courtyard door. "He's got the wrong horse!" I screamed, as John opened the stable door. Pushing him out of the way, I started for the stable to get another horse to chase him down. "You let him have my horse! I just can't believe it!" I fumed as I turned the corner going out the back way. Five steps did I take before the last of John's soft words sunk home.

"I think the horse goes so well with the new robe, don't you?"

Chapter 13

I am the true Vine, and my Father is the Gardener. He lops off every branch that doesn't produce. And he prunes those branches that bear fruit for even larger crops. He has already tended you by pruning you back for greater strength and usefulness by means of the commands I gave you. Take care to live in me, and let me live in you. For a branch can't produce fruit when severed from the vine. Nor can you be fruitful apart from me.

John 15:1-4

I don't have much more time to talk to you, for the evil prince of this world approaches. He has no power over me, but I will freely do what the Father requires of me so that the world will know that I love the Father. Come, let's be going.

John 14:30-31

Thus began a week of foreboding, alarm and torment for me. Each day found me at the Temple early to wait for Jesus to arrive, and each day found Jesus preaching to the people, whose numbers grew proportionately with the days that went by. Nicodemus and I could only shake our heads, for Jesus spoke out mightily against the leaders among us. Not one was spared the lash of his wit and sharp tongue, and we (all of us who followed him) were desolate that we would ever be able to save him once the time came for the high priest to seize him. For in the end, we knew that it would not be the rabble that would build him a power-base, but rather we who were at the source – or so I thought.

When word of the blind man's healing reached the crowds, with those who had seen the miracle witnessing to all those who would hear, the crowds that sought him became almost unbearable. And as the story grew, as is natural, so did his "followers."

They were not his true followers, I well knew, for as soon as the holy days were finished, they would vanish with the wind; back to their homes, their towns, their villages, and their tents – then where would he stand? I was very bitter and discouraged during this time, for the man I saw was not the gentle man of Galilee, with whom so short a time ago, I had spent the happiest moments of my life.

I was sick with what I saw happening, and powerless to stop it. The problem was not with the people, for truth and hope are hard to fault, and the people were more than happy to follow anyone who would lead. In their desperate need, they saw in him the promised power, wealth, freedom and fame that had escaped them in their own rulers' greed. So they encouraged him and cheered him in this futile aim.

If it had not been for these very masses, that everyone feared could easily be whipped into religious fervor (bringing the Roman might into sway), and the Zealots (the Sicarii among them), who now surrounded him wherever he went, he would surely have been stoned for blasphemy, much to the priests' delight. As it was, almost nightly those of the inner-council met to plan his death. They waited only for the right moment, for just one miscalculated deed, and they would do with him as they had with other messiahs, and even with John before him – they would have his head.

As the holy days ended, and the people began to disperse, Jesus disappeared. He just vanished. I, as well as others, sought in vain for word of his whereabouts. Neither he, nor his twelve could be found. I sought an answer, and so it was that I inquired after Placidus, to see what he had heard. Had Jesus yet attracted undue attention, I knew that the Tribune Placidus would have heard. Desperate times call for calculated risks, and so I ventured to the Baths to find this Roman who, although as yet would admit it to no other, I believed that he had become a secret follower of my Lord. Anyway, I had to take that chance; and if need dictated, I felt that Placidus would be discrete in his questioning of the proper authorities, and answer me honestly if the news were bad. Yet, being the Jew that I was, I could never have expected the tidings that he brought.

I found him in the Frigidarium, the coldest of the baths. I never could fathom these Romans who put so much stock in the appearance of their bodies. Upon gaining his attention (which wasn't hard, for I was the only Jew about) and motioning him to come my way, he agreeably swam over to where I was leaning at the edge. "Please, Placidus, I need a word with you in private, if I might." He nodded, and said he would meet me in the garden as soon as he could get dressed.

I was pacing nervously back and forth when, true to his word, he approached me alone across the green of the garden. "Placidus, my friend," I started hesitantly, "my heart is troubled, and I know not where else to turn. There has been trouble in the Temple, and I fear for Jesus' life. The high priest Caiaphas would see him dead, if he has half a chance." I caught myself pacing again, and wringing my hands, which, as soon as I noticed I stopped, and with great difficulty held my calm as best I could. Just being put into this situation of confiding in a Roman made bumps stand out on my skin. "To make matters worse, he has disappeared with his closest followers, and we know not where he is."

Placidus could not conceal his surprise. "Why, Asher, I am amazed, for I saw him just last night, at a dinner party thrown by Lacayus. He seemed fit and well, and provided the most wonderful entertainment I could imagine."

His shock at my question was more than equaled by my own at this stunning turn of events. Had my Master lost his mind? If the priests heard this news, it would surely seal his grave, for no Jew would defile himself by going to a drunken dinner party at the home of our unclean, heathen masters. The thought was too excruciatingly painful to contemplate. I turned ashen as the blood drained from my face, and Placidus, fearing I was about to stroke (and being ignorant of our deep-seated social and religious prejudices against dining with the Romans), sought only to seat me more comfortably upon a bench before I passed away.

Thinking he was cheering me up with this new and wonderful news of my Lord, that I had not as yet heard, he was only too happy to begin telling me everything that went on at the dinner, in the most minute of detail. I tried to conceal my feelings, but the thought of Jesus at a *Roman party*, of all things, was most difficult for me to understand.

I tell you of this event now, because it is only now that he is gone, and I have time to take within me the impact and the detail of Jesus' planning, that I see those things I could not see as they took place then. Only now, after speaking to Peter, am I able to fill in the last gaps to the mystery of these last months of his life. But this must wait for you to see for yourself. Be it enough for now, that I tell you of the events that took place that night.

Jesus had been invited to this gathering of wealthy patrons of the Roman Lacayus. He came to the home with two of his disciples (Peter and Judas – the reason of which I will try to make clear). He found before him both men and women of great means, each at ease, lounging on couches and taking their meal. Most had eaten and drunk too much already, and Jesus knew that he had been invited by Lacayus more for sport, than for any lessons he might give.

The dimly lit chamber was heavy with shadows, and noisy with alcoholic laughter, as Jesus looked about the room. Jesus' eyes stopped when he spied the young Greek diplomat named Theodore, whose eyes were glazed with drink, and whose mind was full of lascivious thoughts. His blurry eyes tried to focus on the man who had just entered the room. Jesus was glad to find the Greek. He would purposely address his comments to him, for compared to the Romans (whose minds usually missed the subtleties of his teachings), the Greeks were possessed with insight and intellect.

The Romans, thick of mind, envied and imitated the Greeks; and Jesus knew that if he drew young Theodore into the conversation, then the interests of the Roman guests would soon follow. A keen judge of people and events, Jesus could size up a complex and difficult situation such as this in an instant, and accomplish what no other could.

The Roman Lacayus thought that this Jew, who he had heard was an intellectual of the highest order, might prove to be a wonderful surprise for his guests. If he was as witty as he had heard, then it would provide interesting entertainment, indeed, for Jews were honored for nothing, except their ridiculous stiff-necked religious tendencies. If, on the other hand, he made any slips at all, he knew his young Greek guest would lick the spittle from his arrogant lips, and devour him alive with his own words. This is why Lacayus had made sure this young sharp-witted, and equally sharp-tongued guest, had been invited.

Theodore, however, had only one thing in mind for the evening; he had accepted the invitation to the Roman's home because he had been advised that the lovely, and unbedded, Diana was to be there. Never shy of his skill at winning favors from women, Theodore saw the slight, young, delicious Diana as a challenge he could not pass.

The wine of the evening was already beginning to rise to his head as the proud young Counsel to Judaea first noticed his host welcoming in three of the dirty, smelly, unkept Jews he so detested. What nonsense had this idiot Roman planned for the evening? He thought, "If he spoils my evening with this beautiful girl, now that she is within my grasp, I will have his head."

But the crafty, if not overly bright, Roman had read his guest perfectly. He greeted the rabbi and bid him to sit on the couch next to his. He glanced at his guest who was swinging his lean well manicured body into a listening position, with obvious enjoyment beginning to show in the tenseness of his manner.

Lacayus' attention was snapped forcibly back from his social scheming, as he heard Jesus address him in a soft, yet forceful voice, "Where are you from?"

Slightly annoyed with the unquestionably, ridiculous query from this Jew, he answered with little thought, and a pride that was impossible for any Roman to hide (which served them both well, and ill, in their conquered lands). "I am from Rome!" he proudly exclaimed, with an arrogant obviousness that delighted Theodore no end, as the Greek sensed, by intuition more than word, a trap being set by this unknown rabbi for the simple-minded Lacayus.

Theodore's quick mind was leaping ahead now, as he relished the game, and sought out an opening in the conversation to join the fray. Already now, he was positioning the pieces well ahead of the present moves being made by the Jew. There was a flash in Jesus' eye, and Theodore thought for just a second that the rabbi had glanced his way as he spoke, aiming his words and barbs directly at him – could that be? Was it just his imagination? Could this simple Jew truly be setting a trap? And, if so, was it for him, or the idiot Roman? He would soon find out.

Jesus remained silent, and looked at the Roman, studying his face as if he were still waiting for him to answer. Becoming uncomfortable when Jesus didn't respond to his simple declaration of origin, thinking him perhaps dull of wit, Lacayus repeated, "I am a Roman, I am from Rome!" Then, more out of duty as a host than anything else, he added, "Where are you from, rabbi?"

Jesus answered softly, "I am from my Father."

Suddenly annoyed by the ridiculous direction the conversation had taken, the Roman barked with an irritated air of finality, "We all come from our fathers, what kind of an answer is that?"

Jesus answered so quietly that every eye and ear was now tensely straining to hear him as he said, "But, you do not claim my Father as yours, why is that?"

The silence was deafening, as Jesus held his host's eyes with his own, as only Jesus could, saying not a word. The quiet in the room lasted forever for poor Lacayus. He had no idea what to say. None of this made any sense to him. The sweat began to pour from under his arms, and his proud forehead beaded with moisture as he sensed every eye on him now, demanding an answer.

"*Because, he is not the same father!*" he yelled far too loudly, which annoyed him even further, as he heard his voice echoing through the hall. He noticed with great discomfort that even the eyes of the guards, trained to ignore everything, turned as he startled them with his outburst. He was in over his head now, and wondered how he could ever have been so ill-advised as to have invited this filthy Galilean to his home. "I am a Roman, and you are a Jew!" he blurted out, trying to control the volume and anger in his voice.

Jesus, a master of people, and of the moment, paused for the barest second to gain the attention of everyone present, then said with now gentling eyes, "Our fathers are *not* the same, as you point out, yet our Father is One. How can this be Lacayus – if we are not brothers?"

The obvious skill with which the riddle and the lesson had been delivered was greeted with great delight by the guests (including my friend Placidus), and approving sounds spread throughout the room (not shared, of course, by our poor host, whose head was now splitting with the throbbing pain of humiliation).

Sensing that he had better grab the moment away from Lacayus before the buffoon, seething in embarrassed rage, had his guards do something impetuous, Theodore stood up, and with the practiced ease of an experienced orator, clasped his hands behind his back, and slowly began to pace the center of the room. Once he was sure he had everyone's attention he said mockingly, "Tell us more, rabbi. Everyone's attentive to your words, teach us please."

Jesus smiled warmly at Theodore, then said, "I have no father, no mother, yet with my Father I am One."

Without pausing, Theodore responded, with derision in his voice, and barely pretended respect, "Sir... this father you speak of, could he be Zeus?"

"No," Jesus said softly, knowing very well the pattern this conversation would take.

"No? Ah, then would it be Mars, the god of war in whom the Romans believe ?"

Jesus again spoke, but so softly so that every ear was straining to hear. "You toy with me, sir, ask your questions that have meaning."

"Ah, then you understand me, sir. I have been told that

you Jews believe in but one god. If this be true then tell me, why does your god blind some, and make others see? Why are some poor, and some wealthy? Why does he make some dumb as an ox, and others as bright as a star? Tell me the answer to that if you will, rabbi." Theodore turned to his delighted audience, and was grinning broadly now, very proud of himself.

"I will answer you in a different way, with a question of my own," Jesus said pausing. "Why are there a thousand flowers on the road? Why do some flowers have fragrance, and others rare beauty? Why are some homely, yet they attract bees, and others as beautiful as a crystal, yet attract nothing with their scent? Why are some plain of color, and yet others emanate beauty from every pore. Tell me, my dear Theodore, why are there so many flowers? Is one more precious than another?"

Theodore knew at once that the rabbi had had his way, and he could respect him for that. He answered forthrightly; "Why, no, they are all beautiful in their own way."

"Ah, then you *do* see, my wise Greek," Jesus said, a widening smile now coming over his face, his eyes sparkling in the reflected firelight of a hundred torches. "And, so it is with our Father."

Placidus congratulated himself on his judgment of character, knowing now that he had not judged this strange man wrong, when first he met him on the hill, shortly after he arrived in Israel. He was indeed an unusual man.

"Well done, Master. Well done!" Theodore graciously bowed his head in respect, as the crowd clapped and roared their approval. Walking up to where Jesus was sitting,

Theodore invited him to sit with him and share his table. Lacayus was more than glad to turn this unpredictable guest over to the Greek, and although he had no idea what pleased his guests so much about the dirty Jew, he relished in the praise that now came his way. Placidus overheard him tell the couple next to him, that he was just toying with Jesus all along. Placidus' next comment on Lacayus' parentage is best left unsaid.

"What a party this turned out to be," Theodore mused, as he shepherded Jesus over to his couch. "First I have Diana, now I have you.

"You speak well, Rabbi, you have learning."

"And you speak well, too, noble Greek, you have learning." Jesus chided, as they sat down laughing, and began to take their food together.

"Fair enough Rabbi, let us drop the testing, and enjoy each other's company." With that they settled into an easy conversation that lasted well into the night.

Thus ended the story from Placidus. He told me everything he knew, he had taken it as far as he could go, and I had to wait in agony for nearly a month before, without warning, Peter showed up one night at my door. Jesus had sent him to fetch me to Jericho, to the house of Lazarus' sister, Ruth, at whose house I had first met my Lord face to face, and in whose house I had first broken bread with him. Jesus left Peter with instructions to start the journey back to him that very night (for Jesus was still in hiding and wanted no one to see us set on our way).

We had a moon, though not full, yet light enough to make travel along the well-worn road safe enough for those who knew their way. Peter had walked to Jerusalem that day, but now rode somewhat tiredly and uncomfortably beside me on the way down the Judean mountainside. By the time we had gone a short way out of the city, it became clear to me that Peter was far more used to the bob and sail of his small wooden boat, than the jarring ride on the back of a horse, so I slowed to an easy walk and engaged him in a conversation that took him back to the night of Lacayus' party. Peter, relieved that we had slowed to ease his painful and jostled insides, seemed more than willing (as he usually was) to openly tell me of an experience with Jesus.

According to Peter, all during the dinner he and Judas remained in the entrance shadows, silently standing, neither talking to any there, nor taking of any of the defiled food that the Romans proffered. As long as they had been following Jesus, they still were unable to understand why he periodically associated with people who were unclean; whether it was a prostitute, or a Roman, or a Jewish collaborator – it made little difference to them. It was certainly not done to gain popularity among the followers he must win. And, to Judas, who had sworn an oath to rid his country of the hated enemy, even unto his death, joining Jesus this night in the camp of the enemy was particularly galling. Earlier, when they realized that Jesus was actually going to take them with him, out of hiding, here into the house of a Roman, they tried their best to dissuade him from this folly, but he would hear nothing of it.

Now, after standing all evening waiting, their nervous and sweating hands never far from the daggers hidden beneath their cloaks, they saw that Jesus had finally finished his meal and was heading toward the door, looking for them. Seeing one of the guests making ready to leave, one of Lacayus' servants started for the door to open it for Jesus and his disciples to leave. Suddenly, Jesus put a hand on the servant's arm, stopping him in mid-stride. "Hush," Jesus warned, "there's someone outside the door. We wait until they are gone." The servant looked at the other two, hoping for some explanation, but receiving only impassive stares, he waited patiently with them, until, at last, Jesus said it was safe – then out the door they went.

Jesus was in upper Jerusalem, in the wealthiest section of the city. This Roman house was surrounded by the richest and most powerful Jews in all of Judaea, and he did not want to be discovered associating with Lacayus and his kind as yet. He had dropped out of sight of the priests and Pharisees (in whose neighborhood he was now dining) in precaution of his life, and this was not the time to be seen, even by a stray servant running an errand in the streets at night. The time to draw the fullest attention to himself was not yet come, and with the relatively quiet, wide-paved streets in this part of the city, it did not pay to have three poorly dressed Jews found out alone in this part of town at night, for that in itself could lead to arrest. And, if the daggers were found, it could mean arrest for sedition – and death.

When he felt that the street was again empty, Jesus hurriedly led Peter and Judas out of the house. Speaking softly, and with some urgency, he said, "Now, let's walk. Draw your cloak about you. Come, don't tarry." Then they hastened past my own home, down the steps of upper Jerusalem, along the wall, then through the poor section where the common tradesmen and workers lived.

The last sounds and smells of the day were comforting, as the moon first showed itself over the houses above the narrow streets ahead. These men of Galilee, used to the open country of the north, could never totally relax within the confines of any city's walls. They turned south for a moment at the bottom of the gully of Tyropoean, past the Pool of Siloam and out the gate on the road to Bethany and Jericho. Here, the slow cool breezes coming up the open Kidron valley refreshed them for the long walk ahead. All this while, no one said a word, but as they passed above the olive press of Gethsemane, Jesus began to speak. And speak he did, with a tone as hard and cold as ice. For time was becoming so very precious, and lessons had to be learned, and they had to be learned now. The time was soon coming when he would be gone, then there would be none to offer-up what had to be done.

"Now, you see my, `dark ones,' all the while we were in that room tonight, you kept your hoods on, and laid your hands upon your hilts. It wasn't necessary. Do you see? Do you understand? *You* can be the master of the situation. I take you along to show you these things. Do you see? They invited us to make sport; and do you understand yet, that you can even teach the Greeks. Do you see that? Keep your wits about you, know that your Father will help you – he is *always* with you!

"When I send you out to do His bidding, do you think you can *carve* your way through every situation? Do you think you can *carve* your way with your daggers into men's hearts? Do you see, my dark ones, standing in the corner with your hoods on, all night in the shadows? Do you see that every guard you sized up, was also sizing you? Do you see that you wouldn't have lasted two steps before being cut down, and me along with you?

"Do you not see that I can walk among any of them? I can be with them, and never be touched by them (in *any* way), until I choose. Learn this lesson this *one* time. I have no time to repeat it! I walk among them, among your enemies, to teach *you*, that *you* can walk there too.

Judas, wanting to speak, to tell of his anger, grasped the hilt of his dagger.

"Judas, when will you ever learn? The sword is not why I come! You can carve out a niche with a sword, and the animal will devour you; or, you can give our people a living spring – with your tongue, and your heart. When will you throw away your sword? It will destroy you!"

Peter said that his ears began to burn again, as Jesus now turned his attention to him.

"And, Peter, you big animal! With your great strength, you could have broken two or three men before they took you. Don't you see either? I don't want you to. Don't you see, you have a golden tongue. Don't you see, it is with your soul that you carve your way into men's hearts. You big dumb fisherman, use your eyes, and your heart, and you will capture the world!

"Now, go before me, I want to be alone with my Father."

Peter began to protest. He felt that he had been unjustly accused, and he wanted to defend himself in his Master's eyes; and he was also uneasy about leaving his Master alone in a, now hostile land. "No, do not argue, Peter, I'll be fine. Our Father is with me, I need nothing else. He is with you, too, Peter, if you would just open yourself to him, and *see*."

This time it was Judas who protested, as he reached for Jesus' arm to urge him on with them. Trying a tentative grin in the darkened silver light of a thin moon, Judas started to speak. He was still stinging from the rebuke he had received, and sought to change Jesus' menacing mood. He didn't understand Jesus when he was like this; he liked the Roman pigs even less than Peter, but now was not the time to argue, he would leave that for tomorrow. He felt wronged, hurt, and angry, but that too would have to wait – his only desire now was to be gone from this place with Jesus safely in tow.

Jesus' look, without a word, was enough to freeze Judas' hand in midair, as Jesus hissed, "Go! You make me angry. You still don't *see*. Think on your blindness today. I will find you on the morrow. Go!"

Judas was stung by his Master's harsh words, and thus was planted the seed of evil in Judas' heart. A seed that was to fall upon fertile soil, and in the next few months, become an all consuming monster in Judas' heart.

Chapter 14

*I am leaving you with a gift -- peace of mind and
heart! And the peace I give isn't fragile like the
peace the world gives. So don't be troubled or
afraid. Remember what I told you. I am going
away, but I will come back to you again. If you
really love me, you will be very happy for me, for
now I can go to the Father, who is greater than I
am. I have told you these things before they
happen so that when they do, you will believe in
me.*

John 14:27-29

We reached Jericho just before the sun broke above the
hills beyond the Jordan. Behind us the sky was still
a royal purple in which the last stars of the evening were
rapidly fading from sight. Before us, the lightening sky
silhouetted the mountain steeps into great pools of mysterious
blackness, broken only here and there by torches lit earlier to
start the work of the day for those who plied their living from
this dry but fertile land. The smell of the desert air rising to
the nostrils in the early morning is something I have always
cherished, and is as impossible to describe as the total and
absolute unbroken silence that can also be found only in this

place called "the wilderness" by people who have come here for centuries to hide – and HELL by those who come here to die.

The clopping of the hooves echoed against the mud houses and walls that lined the way, and my excitement grew as we neared the house which gave me such fond memories of my last visit here. As soon as we reined the animals to a stop at the gate, two men followed us into the stable area next to the house. There they took our tired and dusty steeds to brush, water and feed. Meanwhile, Peter and I were led, each of us in turn, to bathe and change before taking a light meal of fruits and dates.

Looking around, I could stand the suspense no longer, and inquired about our hosts, and Jesus, of course. Peter said that our hosts had been with Jesus, but had left on an extended trip earlier this week, leaving their home and servants at our service, to use as we saw fit. I was very anxious to see Jesus again, especially since, upon this occasion, he was the one to send for me. In addition, what with all the trouble of late, my mind was in a foreboding state most of the time now anyway.

"We must wait," Peter volunteered in his usual un-meaning, authoritative fashion.

"But, for how long?" I asked, with a shortness brought on by a long ride and no rest at all for the past twenty-four hours.

"Until he sends for us," was all that he said. So, with my body still aching in every joint, but relaxed from the bath and being fed, I accepted the bedroom offered by one of Ruth's handmaidens, and like a child, I fell instantly asleep.

I slept most of that day, and a good part of the next, still without a word from Jesus. During my waking hours I paced nervously back and forth through the house, in the garden, to the stables to check on the horses, and back again. I didn't dare to leave the confines of the grounds for fear that the minute I did, a messenger would come, and I wouldn't be there. All during this time Peter seemed totally unconcerned and at ease. I noticed that there were always people coming to the house, one or two at a time, and Peter seemed always willing to sit with them and talk with them about the problems of the day.

On the second day I begin to watch Peter very carefully. At first I didn't know why, then suddenly it hit me – this man had changed. This was not the same man I had seen just a few months ago in Galilee. Yes, he still had his blustery ways, but there was something different about him now that I had not seen before. As I watched him with poor and rich alike who came to seek his strength and advice, I noticed that his voice now mellowed to a whisper at times. There too, was a gentleness about him (and in his eyes), that I had never seen before; perhaps a mellowing would be the best way to tell you of the change.

As people came to him, he would take them into the garden, apart from everyone else (as I had seen Jesus do before him), and listen to them with a new earnestness and caring, both for them, and for their needs, that I had not recognized as being there before. I listened to him encourage them, in the most eloquent of ways; cajole them, with a pleading in his voice; and inspire them in the ways of the Lord. In so doing, he elicited a response that I had only seen in our Master before him.

I thought back on the conversation Peter and I had had

two nights before, as we rode together to Jericho from Jerusalem, and I reflected on the way that Jesus had chastised him for not learning his lessons well enough. With these things in mind, I began to look at Peter with new eyes, and with a new respect born in my heart. For this had been a rough and ready fisherman, and now he was a wise and gentle soul. How far Jesus had brought him in the last two short years. I also wondered within myself, if I, too, had been changed, in ways as yet I was totally unaware.

As I thus pondered within the depths of my soul, and sought answers to questions untold, the waiting ended. It ended as quickly as it had the night Peter had come to my door. Without warning, there was John standing in the entrance-way holding out his hand. It startled me, and I gasped as he said, "Come Asher ben Ammi, give me your things, I will carry them for you." That was all he said as I hurriedly gathered up my few belongings to go. Peter was already waiting for us at the courtyard gate, and following John, we silently left on foot and headed for the desert floor that lay in the valley below. We were heading for the village of Bethabara, when John said, "That is where Jesus is quietly seeing people, teaching, and healing." How appropriate, I thought, for this is where Jesus first met John, and was baptized, and found his beloved Abba, before retreating to the mountain top, where he and his Father became totally and irrevocably One.

We walked at a good pace for about two hours, then slipped into the village unnoticed, except for a mangy dog who came snarling out of the darkness and into the middle of our group before any of us could react to stop him. He went right for me, and tried to take my old leg for his evening meal. A whack from John's staff sent the cur whimpering and yelping away, but not before he had done considerable damage. It's a good thing we were close at hand to our destination, for I had to be helped as I limped the rest of the way to the house in which we were to stay.

They sat me in the courtyard, and the mistress of the house went to fetch water, ointments and rags to wash and bind my wound. I was inspecting my torn and bruised leg under the light of the lamp when suddenly I became aware of a robe, and sandaled feet before me. Slowly, I raised my head to find in the flickering lamp, my Master standing in front of me, with the gentlest of smiles etched upon his face. I tried to rise, but was restrained by his powerful hand upon my shoulder. Then, as I sat there, my heart coming to my throat with the pain and exertion of the trip, and all the worry and frustration and sickness of the month gone by, he slowly bent down to look at my wound. He didn't have to say anything, he didn't have to hold the bruised and battered flesh of my weary old limb, for just being in his presence again, was more than my emotions could bear. I tried to hold back the tears that were rushing to my stinging eyes, but it was useless, they broke as if from a dam, down my worn and dusty cheeks. "Oh, Lord. Oh, Lord." was all I could say, as two dear friends held each other in the sheer joy of just knowing each other, and knowing that the other was still alive.

Finally, my sobbing ceased, and a new and wonderful calmness descended upon me, as if I had been anointed by a balm. My Lord bent down, and looking into my eyes again, took his hands away from my wound and placed them on both sides of my face. Jesus knelt in front of me. We were all alone, with only a flickering lamp, the muffled sounds from the house, and a silent desert darkness all about. "Asher," he started, "I need your help." There were wrinkles and deep furrows in his sun- baked brow, and for the first time since I had known him, there was a sense of urgency and pleading in his eyes.

Here was my beloved Master, whom I would have followed unto the ends of the earth, my teacher who opened the heavens unto me and gave me everlasting life, now bent at my feet asking me for help. I answered the best way I knew. "My dear Jesus, you have been like a son, and father to me, at the same time – no – you have been so much more. Master, you have been my teacher and given me life. Without you I would die. Will I help you? Lord, but say the word, and I will give you everything that I have."

"I know you will, dear friend, and that is why I have called you to me this night. Tomorrow, I want you to come with me to a place east of here. It is a humble farming home, but filled with love. Here the crowds will not find us, and I will tell you what you have sought from me... and so very much more."

With that, Jesus rose to his feet, and I rose to mine, and together we embraced each other, sharing a love that to this day I cannot describe. And in so doing, it happened again, as if by magic; he held me, gave me his love, and no fear, no anger, no doubts in him could I find. He was my teacher, and as I watched him retreat into the flickering light of the house beyond, I knew I would live as long as he would – and that like him, my days grew short.

When the woman returned to bathe my leg, I was

already gathering my things to retire for the night. It was only when she insisted on seeing my wound, that I sat again, pulling up my robe for her to inspect. "Where is the wound, sir? Perhaps, it is the other leg." I looked down. She was right, there was no trace of a wound. Although I knew it was my left leg that had been mauled, I couldn't help looking at my other leg just to be sure, but it was fine, as I suspected. The leg had been healed. Quietly, lovingly, without special notice, or request for any thanks, he had healed my leg. He had completely healed my leg!

The tears glistened in my eyes, as I rose from my seat and headed to the room set aside for me to sleep. I tried, but I couldn't talk, nor could I even thank the kind woman at my feet, my emotions were too strong, and too deep. I just picked up my things and silently padded to my room and fell asleep.

Sleep was indeed an easy blessing that night, for which I was thankful; for knowing my Master's habits, I judged waking would come well before dawn, so that we could be on our way without notice. My prediction proved right. Before the first hour of the morning there was a tiny tap on the door. I was ready, and silently my Lord and I slipped out the door. We headed east, out of the town, toward the mountains. Our destination was but an easy walk, for the house we sought was not too distant from the town of Abila, which lay directly east of us in the foothills along the road north to Philadelphia, and Syria further still.

Abila, like Bethabara in the valley below, depended for a great deal of its existence on travelers that constantly come and go. Abila lay as the last village before starting the long climb up the hills of the Perea, and furnished forgotten items, such as refreshments, various sundry provisions, and necessary water from their wells. As the first village upon coming out of the hills, the town also had its share of travelers staying the night before crossing the desert that lay spread out before them to the west, and Jerusalem beyond. Our destination was the home of a disciple, who had the most lovely date farm I had ever seen, slightly above, and just south of the town.

The edge of the orchard looked over a magnificent view of the desert plain below. From this vantage point, one could see the land dip and roll its way down from the high hills on both sides of the river, which lay at its center. The River Jordan wound its way from the lush and beautiful Galilee in the north, down the steamy Valley of Aulon, ending in the waste of the long Dead Sea, which memory records, covered the evil cities of Sodom and Gomorrah to the south.

As we sat that evening on the wall surrounding the grove of trees, and there looked across the valley, I could envision so much of my people's history. Looking back on our trail, I could see the white walls and roof-tops of the few houses that made up the village Bethabara, now looking as if it were afire in the last rays of the afternoon sun. Bethabara lay close-in to the patch of green that marked the ford across the River Jordan where our people first entered into the *promised land*, and twelve hundred years later, where Jesus had found the harbinger John, and had been baptized, and been spiritually born.

Looking across to the other side of the valley, I could just see Jericho in the gathering shadows of the wilderness hills. Jericho, the oldest living city in the world, they say. For thousands of years it has seen every king and would-be king that has come this way. Its irrigated trees and gardens are famous far beyond our lands, and the balsam plantations produce the rarest essence in all the world. The palm and date trees produce abundant crops and shade, and banks of flowers and beautiful gardens adorn this favorite city of our past-dead tyrant king – Herod, who used the people's money to build himself a lovely palace, theater, amphitheater, and circus, all with the finest of imported marbles and tiles, from the sweat of our people's brow.

To the south, the barren hills rise steeply on both sides, from the Dead Sea far below. Nothing grows in this sun-baked earth, nor in the water that lies below, but in the mellow colors of the dying sun, sinking low beyond the hills, everything seemed to be at peace, and rightly in its place.

I turned to look at Jesus, whose face was now a golden brown in the late afternoon sun. He, too, had been looking out across the valley with a far-off look of an eternal dream deep in his soft blue-gray eyes. He didn't turn to me immediately, but continued to stare out across the ages, past or future I was not sure, and spoke in a voice, that was at the same time, both sad, and yet filled with resolve and hope.

"Asher, I think you know my time is coming to a close. Only a few months remain before they hammer me to a cross, and there is so much that still remains to be done. Our Father has set the stage, my beloved disciple, and now, at long last, he beckons me home."

He said this while he still stared out across the void. His voice was not grieved. Perhaps there was a note of resignation, or finality, but not grief. He spoke as if he had carried a terrible load for many years, and at long last, the end was in sight. People hounded this beloved soul day and night. I worried so at times that he was being pushed beyond all human endurance, and so one part of me could understand the need for the eternal rest. Because of this, I cannot say I had not expected that the end was coming near, but just the hearing of the words, made a great, empty sadness appear in my heart – a kind of dread. It was as if I had just heard of the loss of a loved one, one perhaps who had lingered long and was expected to go, but nevertheless, the leaving is still a shock and leaves a hole in one's soul.

"I have given my people all that I can give," Jesus said, "and they have absorbed all that they will. Now, it is time to complete the act as it has been foretold. Someday, dear Asher, my people will have grown, and time it will be for them to know much that will be lost through the ages, or never told. Listen very carefully to what I tell you, for in my words now, I will give you the kernel of truth to all who I have come to know.

"My kingdom is not of this earth, Asher. I think you have lived long enough in years to also realize this, long enough to know of what I speak. It hurts my heart though, to sometimes see those closest to me still clinging to this thought, of kingdoms and courts, and princes and generals, and armies, and who knows what, for ultimately they all will fall. For all of what *man* builds, I tell you, must surely come to an end.

"Of all my disciples, Asher, you are the only one I was to take beyond these earthly bonds, into the world of our Father. After you, only Peter was able to see a part of me, and thus it is to him that I turn over my reins. It will be to him that I will invest my trust in the future that my Father has foretold. And, for two millennium it will be his church that will endure and grow. Then, that too, will pass from this earth, as the religion of our forefathers has during our lifetime come to its pinnacle and past. For I bring the new covenant of our Father's hope, a covenant that some will be able to accept, and others will not. I tell you also, that in time, even *this* Law of our Father will have become so twisted as to be lost for the common man, and then the time will come to pass when my spirit must walk upon this earth again.

"I ask you to seal all these things in your heart so that when the time is ripe, I may call upon you to give my love to those who wait. Tell my people, that wherever they find cruelty, or hate, wherever they find sadness and hurt, anguish or fright, wherever they find a soul in search, that is where I ask them to be. I am not different, Asher. I am no different than you, or your son, or that woman whore you once saw me save at the Temple door. I am in each of them, I am One with them. And if you wish to follow me, you must be One with them, too. For the people of this world are my Father's creation, as surely as am I, and He lives and dreams and suffers in the lowest of them, too.

"I become so furious at the priests who prescribe a rule for every imagined sin or social ill. Tell my people that if they could truly see within their brothers, they would know, that he or she is doing the very best they know. There are evil ones around, but they only have a longer road to travel before they too, come around. Even the hated Herod suffered more than you realize, and I pity the hell that man must suffer before he finally comes to know, there is only one true Law in the universe, and that Law pervades all that we know, and that is the almighty Law of His unending Love.

"Wrap yourself in Light, the Light you saw upon that mountain top. Wrap it about you, and make it you, in all you say or do – and someday it *will* become you, and in that instant, you will know without question, what I am saying when I tell you that, I and my Father are *One*.

"Perhaps it will be a million years before our souls find perfection, I don't know, but surely we will try over and over and over again, for it is in our nature that we all shall grow. I only lead the way, as others have before me, and as others will who follow. I show you that to gain everything in this world, you must also give everything you have or know. For those who give everything, unto them my Father bestows the most. Until one day, of this I give my solemn word, they will awaken and find themselves at last in the arms of our beloved God, and no more shall they be made to go out.

"When I picked my disciples, Asher, you chose *me* as much as I *you*. For each of you was required for a specific task, and each of you vowed your life to me long, long ago. Whether I found you as merchant or a priest, as tax collector, rebel, fisherman, Roman or saint, I knew you from the past, and you knew me, and willingly you took up your appointed task. I say this to you so that you will know too, that when the time comes, even poor Judas will fall to his fate, as surely as the last leaf falls in the bitterness of the winter-coming wind.

"And now, with mention of the one who will betray me, I will tell you of what is to come, and what services I need of you, my dear beloved friend, to insure my Father's plan unto fruition."

I pause, even now, as I write, for the impact of what my

Lord Jesus gave me was more than I could then (or can even now) imbibe. My head was whirling until I felt as if I would faint. My mouth had long ago dropped open, and shut again without a sound, and within me, I was beginning to feel a funny, strange, kind of light, almost as if I was about to lose my senses, almost as if I were about to float silently out of my mortal body. I was changing. Something inside knew of what he spoke, and with that part of me, I *knew* I had to unite.

Suddenly, I grabbed him, to steady my balance, and keep from falling off the wall. As my senses struggled, and my vision blurred, I thought, "Indeed, this is death!" I felt myself slumping against his shoulder and arm. I knew he grabbed me; I know it now, intellectually, but then it was different, for I was lifting away, and into a Light that was brighter than the day. And the Light and I merged, and I heard a voice, and I saw the Path; and finally, within me, I knew with the knowledge of self, that his Father and mine, and I, had truly merged. And His love flooded me until I could hold no more, and then in peace, I gratefully slept the silent sleep of ages past, and ages yet to come.

Of the experience I had that afternoon, I can speak no further. Not that it is not my wish, nor am I unwilling, but I simply cannot. The memory of this time is beyond words to express, and any attempt I might make, would only defile something that belongs between my God and me in sacredness. It will never leave me, and yet, strangely enough, it is also beyond my understanding. I tell you though, that no one can come back from an experience like that without his life being inexorably changed. As Jesus said before me, and as now I finally understood, my Father, my Master, our people, and I, were finally and truly *One!*

I opened my eyes. I could hear the tiny twittering birds outside the window, as the first rays of sun streamed through the opening, in one brilliant beam. The morning was cool, and I could smell fresh turned earth somewhere close, as I moved my head to orient myself to where I was. I was in a small room; all the walls were immaculately white and clean. The floor was of an earthen tile, the door of dark worn wood. Along the wall by the door I saw a plain undecorated cabinet within which to store one's clothes, and upon the top stood a pottery vase, with water I would guess. The bed upon which I lay was simple enough, made of scraped barkless tree, with a rope support between, and over me was a thin, down-filled coverlet. The vision of the night before had left, and in its place there was a beautiful peace. I felt wonderful! I reached up and stretched as far as I could, while filling my lungs to bursting with the crisp, cool, dry desert air.

My robe hung on one of three pegs on the back of the door, and my sandals were neatly placed at the foot of the bed. What a beautiful way to wake, I thought, as I poured the water into a bowl and washed my face. Hurriedly, I dressed and mused over the night before, and what had happened, sitting there on the garden wall with my Lord. Then opening the door, I strode down the covered walk toward the heart of the home – the kitchen. I entered the open door to find Jesus sitting comfortably at the table talking to the woman of the house, Debbra by name, who like the rest of us loved this man named Jesus with all her heart. Having Jesus alone without the crowd, was indeed a delight for her husband (long out in his fields), and for her, as well.

Jesus had his hands around a steaming drink made from barley and herbs, and the aroma was wonderfully enticing. The smell had awakened the hunger within me, and I suddenly remembered that I had not eaten last evening, and was famished. Actually, my stomach was first to notify me, and the others, by growling in anticipatory delight. It was so loud, both Jesus and Debbra stopped their conversation and turned to face the source of the strange gurgling sound. Jesus threw up his hands in mocked surprise, and pretended fear, saying; "Asher, you're alive!" Debbra couldn't maintain her composure, and holding her apron up to her face, turned away and began to laugh. For myself, I played along with the happiness of this bright morning, by feigning a look of horror too, and I started feeling all about my body to see if I were really there. Then, shouting with glee, I whooped, "Your greatest miracle, Lord — you raised me from the dead!"

I thought I saw a strange tremor sweep over Jesus as I said those words – just a flicker of surprise – then something of a glazed look came over his eyes. It lasted only the barest fraction of a second, and then it was gone. He gave a little shudder, and shook his head as if to clear a thought that wanted to hold him sway, then his face changed as the dreadful mood passed, and he was happy again.

A grin caught him mid-stream, he winked at Debbra, then grabbed his sides and doubled over with glee, as did Debbra. I added to the merriment by continuing my charade, but inside I catalogued the startled look upon Jesus' face, and the fraction of an instant when I saw him shudder, and the distant look upon his face, when I joked that he had raised me from the dead.

When Debbra finally regained her composure, she set before me bread and drink, which I ate ravenously. Talk was light during the meal, Debbra wanting to know the latest from Jerusalem, of people and events, and most importantly about my Miriamme, and other friends she had met who were followers of Jesus. Then, time came, and Jesus took the bundle of fruit, goat cheese, and a sealed jar of local wine that was already prepared, shoved back his stool and looking at me with a wink, said, "Well, young man, do you think you are ready for a walk?" Not waiting for an unneeded reply, he approached Debbra and gave her a friendly hug, squeeze, and grateful thanks for the meal she had prepared that morning, and thanked her too, for the one he carried for us to eat later in the day.

The climb was often steep, and Jesus had to wait several times for me to catch up as we made our way up the barren mountainside. We said little to each other, which was all the better for me, for I needed all the strength I had to make the climb up the well-traveled trail of the holy mountain called, Nebo. It was on the desolate plateau atop this mountain, more than a thousand years ago, that Moses stood and looked out upon the Promised Land of our people before he gave up his staff to Joshua, and finally let his massive burden slide. And it was here that Jesus was taking me, for what, I could only guess.

The location Jesus had in mind was well short of the top, and at a point that could be discerned only by his senses, not mine, he left the beaten trail, and headed down a little incline that showed no sign of any prior human passing. The grassy slope turned around the face of the hill several times before ending on a flat outcrop of rock where Jesus now indicated that we were to take our rest. After setting the food upon a stone, he turned and motioned me to climb upon the rock and make myself at ease. He held out his hand to help me up the waist-high rock. Once safely balanced, I dropped to the hard surface, grateful for an ending to this difficult climb. From here I surveyed the view; this lofty perch suddenly making me feel a bit giddy. Looking out for miles, I had the strange feeling that somehow it was all mine.

The silence of the spot was broken only by the breeze rising up the hill, as it rustled through the dry golden grasses, caressed its way across our faces, then cascaded into the sky, where a hawk screeched its defiance high over our heads. The graceful hunter rode the endless rising currents of air higher and higher, gliding noiselessly out over the great active fault in the earth to the Dead Sea valley below. I followed Jesus' look, and his outstretched hand, pointing to the west. There, in the harsh early afternoon sun, I could just see the white jewel of Jerusalem, a mere speck in the Judean hills, sparkling and shimmering in the waves of heat rising from the barren desert floor.

"It was here that Moses died, Asher. He died with contentment in his heart, as he saw this view of `The Promised Land.' His God, and the God of our fathers, was a harsh God Asher, for a harsh time, and an unruly people. But now it is different, everything has changed. It is a different time, and we are different people. We are all *one people* in Him, and now that we have conquered ourselves, we must dare to help *all* peoples know Him, too."

I looked at him in surprise, for I had not heard him speak

as such before, and in fact, he assiduously kept his disciples away from the Gentiles, of whom I assumed he now spoke. He read me clearly, and continued. "Yes Asher, even the Gentiles. For you believe that there is but one God do you not?"

"Yes, Lord, but..."

"Yes, and so it is," he interrupted. "We have always believed that we were his chosen, haven't we? And indeed we were, for He needed a people to show the way, to remain faithful, to die for Him if need be – to be an example to all nations in the One living God. But now is the time for the new covenant, a covenant for *all* people and *all* lands. He loves them not less because they were born outside his `chosen'. He loves them more. For, just as I have come, not so much for those who already know Him, but more for those who do not, so too our Father has determined that now is the time for His Light to flood the world, so that all may see. If you look within you, Asher, you will know that they are His children, too. It is time for humanity to take an unfathomed leap outside our narrow land, and it is in so doing that I am about to die.

"There is only one way this can be accomplished, Asher, and it is a bitter cup indeed that is forced upon my lips, but one that I willingly and lovingly take; for in so doing, *all His people* will have an opportunity to find Him, not just the elect, not just the few."

"You speak of your death, Lord, but why? Why must it be? Isn't there any other way?" The fears were rising again, I could feel them wind themselves around me, as if I were being slowly encircled by a terrible poisonous snake. Yet, as I now looked at Jesus with searching eyes, I could see no fear, no pain, no questioning at all. He looked at me with his gentling eyes, and the peace I had known the night before once again settled about my being, and fright took its leave. His smile spread to my lips too, as I reached within to a Source, a great quiescent pool, that I had not known existed before the happenings of the day before. In the calm, I also *knew* that his death was a *joy*, and not a thing of dread.

Jesus handed me cheese, and bread, and passed the sealed jar filled with wine, as he continued to explain why it was that he had taken me apart. I put the food and drink down upon the stone, and continued to listen.

"Asher, I am not looking forward to my death, for I have found more love here among our people in the past two years than I could have ever imagined. But now, you, too, have felt His calling, and you know that all life is in Him anyway – it matters little whether I am here of this earth or beyond. For this life on earth is but a passing dream, reenacted time after time after time, and it is only in finally *knowing from within* that we are special, that we are truly born again.

"And now that you have experienced death, Asher, in its truest sense, and know yourself from within that there is no such thing, but in its stead, *eternal life*, you alone among my people know for certain that I *can* go to a Roman cross in absolute peace. My beloved one, there will come a time for you to help His people just as I have done, by giving freely of what I have taught you, sharing the knowledge that all peace lies within. For this is where our Father resides, and it is here within you that all mystery lies.

"You do not need me, only what I teach you; and you do not need the priests to intercede for you, for peace will come only when you take responsibility for yourself. His grace can take you only to the edge of His kingdom, but there is more. *You* must make the effort if you are to *see*, as you have seen. To find Him, and merge with Him in bliss, you must work very hard.

"For those who tell you that I will save them with no effort at all, ask them what I required of those who were closest to me. From them I have required much more, more than they will ever know. Yet, it was not difficult for them, and that is really the highest mystery of all. For when you truly give *all* you have to give, *without any reservation*, you will find that you have had the secret peace within your grasp all along. And this, all men must ultimately find – all by themselves.

"I have called you apart to *see*, Asher, and now that you have seen, I need your help. I need your help desperately, because you are a man of power in the court, and your money finds answers where there were none before. Everything is coming to a fixed point now, Asher, and there is no room for error; every action I now take, every word from my mouth must be calculated to find its mark. If you see or hear something that would ordinarily cause you to wonder, or bring you to doubt or pain, ignore it, and follow precisely the plan we will lay out together. I tell you that the time has come for a preciseness of action that will allow no error, a plan that will bring me to the culmination of my life on an exact day, and even at an exact hour! There is no room for an uncalculated delay, once we set the play in motion it must be without error. Asher ben Ammi, will you help me to die?"

My God! Will I help him die? The very sound of the word made me turn cold, and tremble involuntarily.

Then, strangely, for it seemed but a moment later, the feeling passed, and in its place a strange peace fell about me, and I knew that it was God's plan for Jesus to hang upon a cross, and that I could do nothing less than help him when he needed me most. He was waiting for my answer, his attention held closely upon my face. He saw the moment's hesitation, then finally the blissful peace descend, and a small smile formed at the corner of his lips, and I needed say nothing more, for in my eyes he saw that the answer was – yes.

Have you ever been at a place in time when a moment of monumental decision has come upon you, and a choice has to be made? You are not sure what to do, but you can no longer delay the inevitable. The time leading up to that moment is fraught with anxiety and unbearable tension; then, when the decision is finally made, for better or worse, it is over. You sigh, and it feels as though a tremendous weight has just lifted. Well, that was what it was like. Once he saw in my face, and in my nod that I had agreed, he changed. He seemed to soften, and release the tension that must have gripped his body, too. It was as if there was at last a "friend" he knew he could trust implicitly, and now he could relax, and know that everything would come to pass as he had seen.

Suddenly, he took the goblet that was sitting next to me, broke the seal on the clay jar, and slowly filled the goblet until it overflowed symbolically upon the stone beneath. Then slowly again, he picked up the cup, closed his eyes, offered it up to the Father, then brought it to his chest as he recited from the Psalms: "Thou preparest a table before me in the presence of mine enemies; thou hast anointed my head with oil; my cup runneth over." Then, with his eyes still held shut, he lifted the cup to his lips and seemed to be quoting an ancient source of which I knew not. His last words spoke of the mystery "...revealed to us while we are in the cave," as he took the small cup and drank from it until it was but half full.

I cannot explain the radiance that seemed to surround him as I watched in awe. Then, as I sat in reverie, the strange floating sensation started within me again, but this time I seemed to be able to control it and remain in full awareness, yet somehow my senses became heightened to a wondrous degree. All of a sudden I was watching that mysterious Light I had seen around Jesus in Galilee, and not only in him, but also in the cup, I now saw it shimmering with a radiance all to its own. This ordinary wine had somehow been transformed into the living waters of which the mysteries spoke – and it was beautiful beyond understanding.

After taking the cup from his lips, he opened his eyes, and I saw the God within him, all in a moment's time. As I took the cup now offered to me, and in my turn held it up to drink, Jesus said with a softness that took my breath away, "This cup I give to you surrounded by a brilliant golden light. This light of love of every Master past and every Master soon to be. Take and drink, feel the light in you, of you, around you, and with you, in God's own peace."

I tipped the cup and drank it to its end, wherein he asked me to, "Give this overflowing love you have been given to a thousand others in turn, for no end there lies to His love, His peace, His bliss."

Chapter 15

As Jesus and the disciples approached Jerusalem, and were near the town of Bethphage on the Mount of Olives, Jesus sent two of them into the village ahead.

"Just as you enter," he said, "you will see a donkey tied there, with its colt beside it. Untie them and bring them here. If anyone asks you what you are doing, just say, `The Master needs them,' and there will be no trouble."

Matthew 21:1-3

A s the two of us sat together on this lonely mountainside, neither of us said a word, for words would have invaded the sanctity of the moment, and neither of us had any desire to speak. So we, each to ourselves, sat silently and partook of the meal that had been prepared for us to eat.

I ate absentmindedly, for I had little appetite now as my mind continued to go over and over the events of the last few days, and my last trip to Galilee. Almost an hour passed before I noticed the gathering clouds coming at us from across the valley. It was a beautiful sight, as we sat high up on the mountainside, and watched the gray-black shower of water drop from under the ominous clouds. Slowly the clouds worked their way across the clear blue sky, inching closer and closer to our side of the valley. Then I noticed something that can only be seen in a place such as this. By watching very carefully, you could see that the water, which fell in torrents from the clouds above, never touched the ground below. The rain evaporated in mid-air, and disappeared into the warm dry air as if consumed by an invisible source.

The rolling and boiling clouds rushed north toward Galilee, and the now rapidly moving wind smelled wonderfully of the wetness of rain. Our side of the valley remained in the bright afternoon sun, accompanied only by God's own sign, His brilliant multicolored arch across the world. His rainbow. I was divinely full, in both body and spirit, and watched in staggering amazement at God's beautiful play being acted out in all its majesty in front of our very eyes. It made my spirit light and happy. I looked over to Jesus, whose eyes were twinkling with delight. "What are you thinking, Asher?" he asked, with a grin coming across his face.

"I was remembering a story about you, Lord, that John, the son of Zebedee, told me whilst I whiled away an afternoon with him waiting for you on the shores of the sea of Galilee."

"Well, it must have delighted you! Tell me the story, Asher." Jesus urged. "From the smile on your face, it must have delighted you no end!"

"It did, Lord, it did." I said, and then proceeded to tell him the story as John told it to me.

"As he told the story, Lord, it seemed that you and

several of your disciples had gotten a late start one morning, and had walked all the rest of the day with little or no rest at all. He said that you pushed them hard to reach your destination before dark. However, at the close of the evening it was clear that you were not going to reach any village or town in time to spend the night, and that you would just have to make do with what you had – which was precisely nothing. `There were no miracles that evening,' John told me. You all wrapped your robes around you, and tried not to think of food as you drifted off to sleep. That was a night that John was not to forget, I guess, for he was cold, tired, hungry, and most of all, mad – at you!

"John did make an admission though, for he said, `Of course, I didn't think of anyone else there that night. As usual, I was only thinking of my own miserable self.' He just couldn't understand how you could have allowed them to have gotten in such terrible straits." I related all this to Jesus, who seemed to be enjoying the story quite a bit.

"`About midnight,'" I continued for John, "`I was awakened by the rumbling sound of thunder in the distance. As usual, fear gripped my loins, for as I lay there, now wide awake, I could hear it come closer and closer. Then suddenly, there was a clap of thunder right over my head, and a bolt of lightning shot out of the dark, and nearly scared me to death!'

"`Then it started, first one, then another – splot, splot – rain! I lay quietly, and heard the popping and sizzling sounds as the rain began to put out what was left of the fire, and slowly drench the others, and me. There was nothing I could do but lie awake, cold and wet to the bone, and stare into the pitch blackness of the endless night. As the rain turned into a torrent, it soaked me to the bone. All I could hear was the splattering, now coming in a deluge. The once firm ground became a mire of ooze and slime, as I lay in the mud and contemplated my pathetic state of affairs.'"

The more of the story I told, the more I could see that Jesus was enjoying it. By the time I reached this point in the story, he was laughing uproariously, wiping the tears from his eyes. "Stop, Asher, for heavens sake stop! I can't take anymore." I don't know why I continued, but I did. Perhaps it had been the heaviness of the trip, or perhaps it had been so long since I had heard him laugh from the depths of his being that I wanted it to continue. I don't know, perhaps it was just the devil in me. All I do know is, the more he laughed, the more animated I became in the telling, and the more I exaggerated poor John's manner of speech.

"'Ever see drowned rats?'" I mimicked John's telling, as I stood up, pretending to scrape the mud from my face, arms and hands, as he had shown me they had done in the morning gloom. He told me that his wet clothes were clogged with layers of muck from tossing and turning all night in the mud. He must have been a sight. But, John's story was not finished...

"'Jesus is sitting there in the slop, just sitting there looking at us – and grinning! Yep. This sure is fun! You tell them that it wasn't all sunshine... you tell them that!'" John had been really worked up by this time in the story, and was gesticulating all over the place – which, of course, I dutifully mimicked.

By now I was afraid Jesus was going to fall off the rock; he was doubled over with laughter, begging me to stop. I finally did pause long enough for Jesus to wheeze, "Asher, you can't imagine it. John pointed his finger at me that morning and said, `You promised *this* did you? You didn't tell us about *this*! Said all sunshine, all light... Where in the hell is the light? This is a mess, you know that?' He fumed and ranted with rage, his face turning a brilliant purple, I thought he would stroke for sure. Judas said, `I saw you rolling around in it last night, John. You looked so comfortable, I thought for sure you must have once been a pig.' Just then one of the others said, `Just tuck it up John, it will be all right.' That was all poor John could take." Jesus smiled with delight in remembering the scene. "He headed out for the next town without us. We didn't see him all day. When we did, he had washed and cleaned himself, and pretended, with an air of haughtiness that nothing that concerned him had ever happened. Poor, poor, John, I will have to try and spend more time with him before it is time to go."

The mention of him going, brought back the reality of this world, my own precious teacher's coming end, and sobering thoughts for me to contemplate from within. Not Jesus, however, for he continued to chuckle every now and again all the way down the hill, as the thought of the muddy scene would once again flash into his mind.

As Jesus started to gather up the things that were left, I stood to move and stretch my weary legs. Then we started the long trek back down the hill. We hurried, for the sky was getting darker and darker and more ominous by the moment, as the lead edge of the storm hurtled across the sky, spilling over the lip of the mountains to the east, which usually meant that the rain would be coming down in sheets, soon. My feet were killing me as we reached the short path to the house, for we had kept up a mean gait down the steep hill, and my toes had been forced down into my closed toe sandals until they crumpled and complained of undue pain. I silently thanked our Father, as He held the rain until we were but a few short running steps away from the warmth of Debbra's kitchen. She had seen us coming, and had the door standing ajar as we burst into the heaven-sent sights and smells of her culinary delights.

We stayed in the kitchen well after the evening meal, as the warm and friendly oven was kept well stoked, and much to everyone's delight, Jesus told stories until it was far past time to go to bed.

It rained off and on most of the following day, so Jesus put off our return, and used the time to brief me of what was expected of me, and what he felt was about to be. I could see that my role was going to be pivotal if everything he had laid out was to succeed. Three powerful forces had to be played against each other – Herod, the Romans, and the Temple priests (especially the power of the High Priest Caiaphas) – if we were to see him through to Passover. Jesus told me that powerful events were about to happen that would show the world in a very real way the powers that are available to anyone who would follow his way. He said that it would quicken the end, but at that time I had no idea it was already starting in Bethany as we spoke.

A thousand thoughts seemed to be going through my head as we left early the next morning to walk back to Bethabara, where the disciples waited. My quiet mood agreed with Jesus, for he too seemed to be preoccupied, and we walked most of the way in silence.

As soon as we entered the courtyard of the home in which we were staying, we were greeted by all the disciples at once. Each had something to say, and none of them could be understood. Jesus held up his hand for quiet, and gradually the turmoil died down. "Now," he said, "there is a guest among us. Please let him be properly greeted and let him speak his mind." With that, the stranger stepped forward, saying that he was a messenger sent by Lazarus' sisters, and that Lazarus was very sick. He said that the sisters needed him, and asked, would he come without delay, to save their brother. Jesus nodded his head yes, and bade the messenger return immediately to tell Martha and Mary that he would be along presently.

The messenger left at once to prepare for his immediate return with the message that Jesus was sure to come. The man was no more out of the courtyard, when bedlam broke out. Again everyone was speaking at once. Jesus sat down quietly upon the bench where he had healed my leg, and again held up his hand for silence. Peter stepped forward to speak of what was on all of their minds. "Sir, it was only a few weeks ago that we barely escaped from the Temple alive. The Pharisees will surely kill you if you return!" There was general agreement with what was said. Jesus, with his head down, waited until they quieted down again.

"I go not only for the obvious reason that my dear friend Lazarus lies sick unto death, but also because in his rest, I will be brought one step closer to the glory of my Father. The authorities will not dare to take me in the daylight hours, for the people whom they fear will not allow that – nor will you. Therefore, we need only watch during the hours of darkness, that our position is not revealed." Then Jesus looked up at me standing in the crowd, and asked, "What do you think, Asher? Do you feel that it is still safe so close to Jerusalem?"

I chanced an answer, although I was not at all as sure of myself as I sounded. "Yes, Master, I think if care is taken by those who love you, you will still be safe."

"See!" Jesus said, slapping his leg. Pausing, he looked from man to man for any objections, then, finding none, he gave a shrug of finality, rose, and left the group standing where they were, and went inside.

Even though they would not challenge Jesus to his face, I don't think all the disciples were yet convinced of his safety (or for their own for that matter), for as Jesus left, Thomas said, "Come, let us get ready to go too, all of us, and die with him if that is what is needed of us."

I left the group, still in the midst of a heated debate as to the wisdom of the trip so near to those who would have him, and bade my Lord goodbye. There was much for me to do, and I was useless here in this little out of the way village near the bottom of the world. My place was back in the council halls where my Father's plan needed to be set in motion.

My leaving was made easy, for my things were yet unpacked, so I left Jesus and the other disciples within the hour, and headed west in the company of the messenger. It was a fortunate turn of events, for both the messenger and me, as I had no desire to travel these roads unaccompanied, and the messenger, having come on foot, could certainly use a ride to ease and speed his journey back. During my journey here with Peter a few days earlier, I had left two fine horses in Jericho, which would now serve us both well on the journey back up the steep road that leads to Bethany, and Jerusalem, a short space beyond.

I wondered at Jesus' farewell words to me as I walked along toward the cool springs of Jericho. He told me to have my son, John, meet him in Bethany in three days time, there to report to him of my activities, and John in return, to report back to me of the coming "miracle". Of what he spoke, at that time, I could not have known. I thought perhaps he spoke of healing his friend Lazarus; but to bring a body back from the grave, of that I could not have guessed. My quizzical look to Jesus when he mentioned the "miracle", was met with no reply. He just held me closer than I ever remembered, and with a look of peace upon his face, bid me farewell. Of course, now I know, save his own reported rising, this was to be the culmination of his ministry here, and was to set the stage that would cause the wheels of darkness to begin their move toward the final blow - the taking of his life.

What happened next, I am sure you have heard. Jesus came to Bethany after tarrying two more days, and there he raised his friend, in front of many witnesses, from the grip of death itself. When word got to me that night from my son that Jesus had raised a body from a rock-hewn grave, it brought back to me the words spoken to me by the Master, almost a year ago, when I had asked him about death and dying. He looked at me, then hesitated for a second, measuring me I think, to see how much he could trust with me, how much I could understand. Then he responded with a great softness, using gentle words that seemed to caress me with their touch.

"My beloved one, no matter what I or anyone else tells you of the mystery of death, the simple fact is that the *truth* lies within. No religion, neither the Greek, Roman, Hindu, or even our own, can tell you differently; for there is no religion higher than truth – and that truth you can find for yourself, by merging in Him.

"I have shown you how to go within, to touch the ultimate truth, to become One with your Father, to *know* with certainty that you do not die. Life is a continuum, it does not end for any of us in the brief span of forty or fifty years. Open your eyes, Asher! Your Father gave you eyes to see. Can you make any sense out of the injustice of this world, if there are but forty or fifty years to spend? You have lived sixty years and two, Asher, have you seen justice prevail? Have you yourself found perfection in those things you do? Do you have perfect love for your brother, as yet? How about your beloved wife, Miriamme? Do you have perfect love for her? How about me? Do you even have perfect love for me?

"In truth, we both know that you do not, and that is not a sin! The sin we commit upon ourselves is the sin of not trying, for it is in trying that we learn and grow. And, it is in experiencing and growing that we are most dear to Him. He does not fault us for trying to find Him, and failing. He loves us all the more for it. For it is in the trying, that ultimately *we will succeed!* We are all His sons or daughters, Asher, and if we open our eyes, we all see the same Light. That Light calls both Jew and Gentile alike.

"Why am I here, dear brother, tell me that? I am no different from you. I am trying... and yes, failing too... but I will never give up my efforts to come just one step closer to Him. For it is in Him that our ultimate happiness lies. It is as easy, and as hard, as totally letting go. Give up unto Him *totally*, Asher, and your life shall be everlasting more."

He said these things not just to me, but to others too, and of this the priests (through their spies) surely knew. And so it was, when he conquered death for them all to see, he struck the final blow, and this too he knew would be. I cannot tell you what turmoil that caused among my peers, so much so, that a special session of the Sanhedrim was called within the Temple to deal with just this situation, this Jesus of Galilee. For the High Priest, and other leaders among the Pharisees, knew his timing was the worst it could be for all of them. The word of this miracle was just six weeks before the highest of all the holy days, just time enough for all of Israel to hear of it and come to see this man of miracles – and perhaps demand of them to declare him *King!* He had to be dealt with, and soon, otherwise the crowd could get out of their control, and into the hands of the Romans it would surely go. And if it were determined by the hated Pilate that Caiaphas could no longer govern and control, then unto another would go the dubious honor (and the incredible wealth attached thereto).

My first concern was for Jesus' immediate safety, for his ending time, as he shared it with me, called for Passover, which was yet well over a month away, and the priests meant to hear him scream well before then, if they could. Thus, I sent that very night, under cover of darkness, my trusted servant to warn him of the situation as it was developing. And so, it was because he had been forewarned, that he and his followers disappeared into the darkness well before dawn, to the edge of the wilderness, to the village of Ephraim, where he stayed with his disciples and taught no one, until he knew his time had come.

A week before Passover, word came to me secretly that Jesus was on his way to Jerusalem again, and that I should make ready. To be sure, the next night found him in Bethany with Lazarus, where he planned to stay until the end. For in this village he was surrounded by friends, and those who knew him to be the Messiah, and here he felt safe, even though he was but a short walk from the city, itself. From here, too, the road to Jerusalem could be watched by night, to insure he would not be taken by stealth. And so it was here that a dinner was prepared by Lazarus for Jesus and his disciples, for no greater love was there for him than that held by Lazarus and his sisters. I stayed completely away from Jesus at this time, for if I were to serve him well, then I had to appear to have nothing to do with him now.

Word of Jesus' arrival spread from Bethany to Jerusalem like a wildfire before the raging desert wind. From all parts of the city people by the thousands flocked to the road as it entered the city gates to the east. That morning before dawn, as Jesus had asked, I sent two of my servants from my stable to the village of Bethphage, near the Mount of Olives, with a donkey and her colt. There they were to wait with the animals until one of Jesus' disciples identified himself as needing them for our Master, then they were to give them willingly to him.

Early in the morning I made sure that the donkey and her colt were on their way, then proceeded to the Temple, telling my family only that I was going to the morning service, which began shortly after dawn each day. It was a beautiful service to watch, especially during the holidays, when even the morning service was crowded beyond the Temple courts themselves. The service began with the proclamation by one of the priests atop the Temple walls, "Priests to their service, Levites to their stand, and Israelites to their post." The priests entered the court in two groups, each carrying a burning torch. One group went around the covered porch to the east, and one to the west, meeting back at the entry gate, declaring that all was in order. Then the priests removed the ashes from the altar, and arranged it again for the new day. From this point, the priests who were now sanctified, waited for the announcement that the horizon had become light, even unto Hebron.

Then the trumpets sounded as the gates opened to the sanctuary. It was now that all activity everywhere on the mount stopped for the service, for it was now that the lamb was slaughtered, and its limbs were offered upon the altar. As many people as could, now crowded into the Chamber of Hewn Stone, and with the priests, read the Ten Commandments and part of the Shema. Then they left the Chamber, once again to offer up prayers, as the priests entered the sanctuary to prostrate themselves following the offering of the incense. At this time of year the curtain which normally blocked the view into the sanctuary itself was rolled up so that all that assembled could see the Holy of Holies, the ceiling joists of cedar, the hanging crowns, walls, and service vessels, all of pure gold. The crowds were so heavy though, that few could actually enter the Court of the Israelites or the Court of the Women and see; yet even unto a man, they all joined in the morning prayers with the priests with a dedication found nowhere else in the world in those days.

When the priests finished their prostrations within the sanctuary, they stood outside, raised their arms, and pronounced the sacred name of God, whereupon all the people fell to their faces. After the benediction, the priests offered up the animal limbs for sacrifice on the altar, then they offered up the meal. At this time the trumpets sounded, then the cymbals, and then the Levites began to sing. Because of the holidays, young boys were added to the choir to increase the melody. Then the wine was poured upon the altar, and the service was complete. For those who had never seen, it was an incredible sight, and for a moment that morning, I stood transfixed, thinking of how all this must have looked to a young boy of twelve, here for the first time from a little town in Galilee so many years before. I reflected on how this beautiful service, dedicated to the Lord our God, would now, in its most human form, kill the most holy son it had ever produced.

I left the service with tears running down my face, as I realized with clear brutality what was about to take place. I proceeded out of the Court of the Israelites, through the Court of the Women, out through the Beautiful Gates that had meant so much to our people, and then on past the lattice fence that separated Temple Mount from the Court of the Gentiles beyond. I climbed the stairs that led to the Royal Portico at the south end of the Temple's outer court, where I could see over the Valley of the Kidron to the east, and the Mount of Olives where I should first see him come toward the city walls.

Jesus had planned his entry to the city well, for he had allowed just enough time for those who had attended the morning service to finish their obligation before they heard the crier who had been sent ahead to announce that he was on his way along the road from Bethany. I had not heard the crier, but the excitement spread through the courts like a wave. "He is coming! He is coming! Come see!" People began running for the gates and high places to get a better view of this wonder worker who could raise the dead.

I marveled at his planning and knowledge of the psyche of our people. His timing was absolutely perfect. The city in general was now teeming in preparation for Passover, and the largest concentration, by far, of pilgrims was in the open area just north of the Temple by the Pool of Bethesda. Here, in the ramshackle congregation of tents and shelters of the poor, he would find those who cared least for the pomp and high-handed authority wielded with scorn by the priestly Judean casts since the time of Herod. These were the very ones who would support him now when he needed numbers most. Here, too, he would find the largest grouping of his own people from Galilee, who would find pride in one of their own kind, and erupt with rage if a Judean laid a hand on him.

Yes, his plans had been thought out with infinite care. I had felt they would work when he first laid them before me in the desert, but now, now that I saw them becoming a reality, I knew that they were nothing less than brilliant.

It was through the middle of this mass of people that he now would walk. He had chosen this, the only entry to the city that passed not only through the city of tents (the same place he had himself slept with his mother and father when he first trod these stones), but in addition, passed right under the noses of the Romans in the fortress Antonia, whose presence included Pilate during the holidays to insure against rebellion. Thus with thousands gathering to welcome him into the city, he chose the one entry to the city that would most arouse the ire of those with the powers to decide his fate. There was no doubt in my mind that this man could have been King, if that is what he had set out to be. But, this king was of a different sort, and that was to be so hard for the people to understand. Even Judas, who should have understood, gave him up as a "pretender king" when he came this day on the back of an ass, instead of a mighty steed. For Judas, within the Zealot's cause, had pleaded with Jesus to declare himself King of the Jews when his brethren attacked the Romans this week of the holidays. Romans and Jews alike had died in what Jesus thought was a ridiculously futile attempt to conquer an unconquerable foe. Judas was outraged that Jesus would hear nothing of the plan, and had lifted not one finger to help. He had told his brothers of stealth that with Jesus the people would rally, and the holy city would be theirs. Jesus had berated Judas, and sent him away with his plan of death. This, too, was in preparation for the end.

The people met Jesus on the far side of the Kidron valley, on top of the hill where the sacrifice of the red heifer is held. They came in numbers hard to believe! They heard he had risen Lazarus from the tomb, and came to welcome him, and see him for themselves. I could not pick him out from among the crowd at this distance, but I could mark his progress from the swelling of the human tide down the side of the hill. His path was strewn with palm branches, and the very cloaks off of their backs. They sang his welcome and praises so loudly that it could be heard clear across the valley. Those who had known him not, were soon staring with wonder at this man whom this tumultuous crowd had brought.

As he neared the entrance to the Temple, the roar of greeting drowned out all else that was going on within. I could see the Romans atop their ramparts coming from all parts of the wall to see what the gathering commotion was all about. They were very watchful of trouble that might spill unchecked into the streets and be directed against them, especially after the events of earlier in the week. And, I could be sure (as I had confided in a message sent the night before to Jesus in Bethany) that any entry such as he had planned, would be met with affirmative action, if not by the Romans, then by the Temple powers to assure that the Romans did not think that they had become involved in anything such as this.

Unlike Jesus, the crowd surged into the Temple courts, without ever stopping to observe the proper cleansing rites. But so many were they, and in such a frenzied state, that the Levites, whose job it was to insure that the ritually impure were not allowed entry, ran in fear of their lives. From my place above the court, I watched those gathered within the court splinter and run as, like a maddened bull, he strode right through them with a raging gait, fire flashing in his eyes. He headed straight for the place below me where the money changers and merchants held court. He never saw me, as he disappeared out of sight under the floor below my feet. I stepped to the stairs to watch my gentle Master throw over tables and people alike as he rampaged the length of the colonnaded court, upturning the startled merchants and moneychangers alike, to the exalted cheers of those who watched, and the excited joy of the poor who rushed for the coins clattering about in profusion upon the floor. The animal cages spilled upon the ground, and birds and lambs among them, set off in a frenzy of fear and noise. The sound of man, beast and bird alike was deafening!

The poor Temple guards didn't know what had come amongst them. A military assault they could understand, but this... They knew not what to do. I watched as this gentle loving soul, who taught only love, began his quest for the end that he alone now sought. His Father had set the timing and the stage, now it was up to him to play the part that would insure his teaching throughout all eternity. The stakes were no higher than the minds and souls of men. And the master of the playing board was in front of me, railing at the very men whom he now dared to do him in.

Even Jesus did not know, that at that very moment the pieces of this terrible puzzle were one by one, falling into place. As he stood now in the Temple court far below, lecturing the crowds and showing them the evil ways of the Temple casts, Pontius Pilate, with short cropped hair and striped cardinal tunic, was pacing back and forth in fury on one of the roof-top patios of the Antonia that lay outside his administrative office. His young assistant took the brunt of this cruel man's anger, as my informer, Placidus, sat quietly on the edge of the roof-top balustrade outside, and watched the man with the strange eyes, whom he had met in Galilee, excite the ragged mob below. He told me later in the Baths, that the scene had an unreality about it that troubled him a great deal. Not knowing why, he felt that for some strange reason, he was watching history being made, as he sat there in opulence high above the Temple grounds, watching the effect of Jesus' silent words far below, upon the crowd.

Jesus' entry had not been missed, for Pilate had been

summoned to the fortress walls, as the teeming noisy mob approached, and it was then and there, watching the mob stream past at his very feet, yelling "Savior... Messiah... King!" to a "dirty beggar on an ass," that he had decided that these demonstrations were going to be stopped, *"By any means necessary!"*

"I will not tolerate another demonstration like this one today," Pilate screamed, purple with rage. "I want to make an example out of someone. I want an example now, before the start of the Passover. That will dampen their fervor. These Jews must be taught another lesson in humility. We, the Romans, are the Masters here! I want a leader whom they all know. I want someone who will make them quake until their bowels turn to water. Find someone, then hang him with the rabble we took this week. That will quiet them down."

With that, Placidus told us, Pilate stormed from the sun-bright patio, through the darkness of his office and out of the room, knocking over a wine pitcher on his way, sending it crashing and clanking across the marble floor. An uneasy silence followed, as the more experienced Placidus quietly waited for Pilate's junior to react. He didn't have to wait long, for the young man came quickly up to the unmoving Placidus, wringing his hands in indecision, and talking all the while. Placidus' face wrinkled with disgust as he related the incident to me. For he considered the young man offensive and weak, yet typical of so many sons of rich and powerful men that now inhabited the senate and secured positions of power for their progeny. Placidus, unlike many, was not of wealthy stock, but had been chosen for his honesty and bravery to represent the common man in this august assemblage, and as such, despised the wealthy inept he found throughout the empire.

"The young man's thoughts were rambling," Placidus told me, "but deadly in the conclusion that they reached. `Placidus, I don't know quite how to go about this. How do I find a leader, a rebel at that? If we had one, he would already be hung. How do I find some poor devil?'

"He looked at me, expecting me to answer. Can you believe that?" Placidus said. "Then the idiot lit up like a lamp. `I have it!' he cried. `I'll let the priestly peacocks do the dirty work for me. I'll call for the High Priest, Caiaphas, it's time he earned his keep. I'll tell him what the Procurator wants, just maybe we can work this out together. That's it, I'll let *them* find one of their own; they know their people better than I. It's perfect! They want no trouble, and they don't want us to choose from among them either, so this task they will perform to my satisfaction with glee. They disdain their own people as much as we.'"

The last statement, given with no offense by Placidus, hurt me from within. For I, too, had judged my people for so many years, and to see this Roman point the finger of justice my way, was more than I cared to bear. But, now I couldn't afford the luxury of letting my mind wander, because I needed to hear everything Placidus had to say.

I picked up on the conversation as he was quoting Pilate's assistant again. "`... stupid habits. You can't just invite them to supper with you, because they won't come. I would much prefer to do business like this over a fine meal and wine – but not with the Jews. They say we can't keep our food *clean*, whatever that means. Oh well, it would probably drive our cooks crazy anyway.'"

One thing we had in common with the Romans, was that we both talked as much with our hands, as with our mouths. Placidus was mimicking all the gestures, as this young man paced back and forth like his master Pilate, from whom he had learned. The statements about my race didn't bother me, I had become numb to it through contact with them throughout the years. Now, the conversation got back to the points I needed to hear – how this man would be chosen.

The young man stated, "'It's very easy now. I'll send for the High Priest's emissary. Caiaphas is too haughty to talk to me personally. I'm not *clean* he says! I will tell them the predicament I am in. I will tell them that if they do not pick one, then we will go among them and pick our own. Instead of this, I will say, why not work together. Surely there is one among you whom you would rather see out of the way. Just give me someone you want to get rid of.'

"'The plan is perfect in its simplicity,'" the young man continued. "'The priests can choose whom they like, the people won't know anything about it until it's too late, and the man will be crucified just on the approach of Passover eve. Seeing their people on the crosses will surely sober any hopes they might have had for a savior on this holiday. Most importantly, however, Pilate will get off my back, and the people will be quieted for another six months, at least. That will take care of all the politics, and this mess can be neatly wrapped up. They will all have just what they want.'

"'Just two more of these horrid holidays to go, then my tour is over, and I can go back to Rome,'" he added exuberantly. "'I'm not suited for this work anyway, eh, Placidus.?'" I will delete Placidus' response to the young official's remarks as being unprintable. I cared little for the remainder of his story anyway, for it spoke only of the man's connections and wealthy ties in a Roman city I could never bring myself to care about, nor even comprehend.

Thus, as I watched Jesus leave from the Temple that fateful night, with cheering throngs following him around the Temple wall prostrating themselves thirteen times, as was the custom when leaving, his fate had already been sealed in the wax of a Procurator's order. An order that Pilate himself would never see. The decision of a minor functionary had sealed my Master's fate, a fate that was but three days away.

Chapter 16

And he replied, "As soon as you enter Jerusalem, you will see a man walking along carrying a pitcher of water. Follow him into the house he enters, and say to the man who lives there, 'Our Teacher says for you to show us the guest room where he can eat the Passover meal with his disciples.' He will take you upstairs to a large room all ready for us. That is the place. Go ahead and prepare the meal there."

Luke 22:10-13

Jesus came each day into the city to teach in the Temple. Each day his manner of speech became more caustic for those in power to hear; yet, each day, his teaching to the common and poor about him became more loving and sure. Each day those in power sought new ways to trap him, and show him up as a traitor, a blasphemer, or fool in front of the crowd, but nothing worked. Each day those cocky and arrogant ones who went into the courts to try their hand at tripping him up came back empty of hand and red of face. And as a consequence of the presence of this man, the members of the Sanhedrim would informally gather in the Court of the Israelites, in the Chamber of the Hewn Stone which was located at the southern end of the court. Here, each day, Jesus was the sole topic of conversation.

There were many supporters now within the council, who in private conversations honored him with beautiful words and praises, but in public, few there were that spoke openly for fear of the wrath of Caiaphas. Caiaphas' position was clear, for he had the most to lose, if indeed this was the Messiah. And, if he truly was the Messiah, what then? So, the conversation and arguments went on and on.

In actual fact, it mattered not at all what went on in the Council that met within the Chamber of Stone, for as has always been the case with governments, it is the Throne alone that makes the real decisions, and the rest is all for show. As a result, while those who were yet foolish enough to think that they had a hand in his fate, endlessly argued and debated, the fact was, the agreement had already been struck. Caiaphas had his man to sacrifice to meet both his, and Rome's needs.

My job was clear. I had to know what was going on, and of this I had to be sure, for as Jesus told me, "The history of the world will turn on what just a handful of men do this week, Asher, let us all make sure we do our parts flawlessly."

It is interesting to learn exactly how much guards can see and hear when they are paid enough. This week, I guarantee, they made a year's worth of salary to have eyes and ears for me. There was not one moment of the day that I did not know exactly what went on behind the closed doors of Caiaphas' private chambers, as well as at his residence, and that of his father-in-law, Annas, the High Priest before him.

And so it was, that through the eyes of the unblinking watchmen, Jesus observed his disciple Judas deliver him up for silver to the merciless Caiaphas. Little did they know, that for all their planning, they were but puppets and pawns in a force whose time had come.

This was a difficult time for me, for I knew of the horrible end that awaited my beloved Teacher, for crucifixion was a far more cruel way to die than even I could contemplate. For a man who gave so much, it seemed more than I could endure to know beforehand the suffering that he would soon have to bear. If it had not been for that time alone with him in the desert, I would not have been able to carry out my task successfully; and, I am sure that is exactly why he devoted over two precious days alone with me so close to the end. He told me that our Father had need of me, and in that I would not fail him. But, even as I carried out my appointed tasks, I knew, as Jesus himself had alluded, that my life too, was soon to end.

Because it was of vital importance that I remain completely away from him during this week, I watched him only from afar. I entrusted the carrying of messages by stealth each eve to a man who owed Jesus his life, and thus was more than willing to give it again, if need be, for the man who gave him sight. I entrusted the messages to none other than Maston, who had, sure to his word, returned with his family to serve me (and, as an embarrassing aside, had returned my fine black steed).

Jesus did make one promise to me. Knowing that I yearned to be with him just one more time before the end, he agreed to eat his last meal at Miriamme's and my home. He looked at me with total love, as we remembered all the wonderful times we had shared together in front of the fire, as we talked and told stories far into the night. Those were beautiful, easier times.

It was then that he gave me the following instructions: "Go on the day before Passover eve, at the exact time you hear the trumpets from the Temple walls sound the sacrifice over the city, and have your man-servant dip his water jar into the well by the lower pool; Peter and John will be there, and will follow him home. Make sure that whomever you send, he is not known to Peter or John, for I do not want them to know in whose house it is that we will eat, in case they are intercepted. Also, make sure that your man does not go directly to your house, for the faces of Peter and John are well known, and they may be followed closely. I will set the time of my arrest, not the Temple whores, and the having of the last meal with my twelve is more important to my Father, than any of those at the table will know."

That day and the next are etched in my memory like no others. At the morning service, I watched carefully for signs of nervousness in the High Priest or in any of those closest to him, and there was plenty to see. They knew that their time was running out, for Passover eve was but one night away, and they had as yet failed to deliver up their "scapegoat" to the Romans, who grew more impatient as each day passed. I took pleasure in their anxiety, yet I knew that, as far as they were concerned, they would still have their victory; and, unbeknownst to them, their "victory" lay only hours away.

As for myself, I was nervous as I waited for the start of the Temple day. Maston was well on his way by now to the well that lay at the lowest end of the city in the Tyropoean Valley, which in turn led into the Valley of the Kidron and the road to Bethany beyond. Although both Peter and John had seen the raggedly dressed Maston when he had been healed long before, I knew they would not recognize this handsome, wealthy dressed man, as the same beggar Jesus had healed almost a half year before. As it turns out, I was right, and the three of them made it to the house quite easily, apparently, at least to their knowledge, without ever being followed.

Even to this detail Jesus had thought of everything. For up to now, he and his disciples had entered the city each day by the road north of the Heifer Causeway that spanned the Kidron valley from the Mount of Olives to the City, not once did they enter from the south. Therefore, there was no reason for the authorities, who now had spies out everywhere, to ensnare Jesus by any possible means, including stealth, to suspect this entrance through the southern gate.

Maston had been easy to find, as Jesus had undoubtedly known, for I would bet that at no time had a Jew ever seen a man carry a water jar anywhere – especially dressed as he. That is strictly a woman's job, and certainly not for a man of means. When Maston had Peter and John in tow, he set aside the jug, and walked with them up through the poorer part of town where streets and houses are tightly packed, to the market place, now swollen enormously by the influx of the holiday crowd. It was here, we thought, that any who followed, would soon be lost. From there they followed the aqueduct back to the upper part of the city, then through broadened streets and well-kept homes to their destination.

By the time they reached my house, I had also returned home, having received the report I had awaited for during the prayers of the morning service. I did not see Jesus, because of the tremendous crowd, but I know he was there to worship for the last time in this, the house of his Father.

When Maston flung the door open, Peter and John knew, of course, whose house they were at, and Peter threw his big arms about me and gave me a death-threatening hug. "I am glad to see you too, Peter," I wheezed, "but please, leave enough for Miriamme, or she will never forgive you." We all laughed, and Miriamme and Peter and John left to inspect our large upper room, and then the kitchen, to insure all would be in readiness for the evening meal. As they cheerfully left, I slumped against the courtyard wall and grieved, "Poor Peter and John, they have no idea. They will be so all alone... so will I."

The guard had told me that, as yet Judas did not know where they were to gather for supper, but he had told the High Priest that he was sure that they would eat together. Once he was sure of where Jesus could be found, he would slip away, and meet the authorities at the house of Annas. Little did Judas know at that time that he would be eating his last meal with Jesus at my house, and that the house of Annas was but a short walk from my door.

Judas told Caiaphas' men that once he knew where Jesus would be, and when he would be most vulnerable, he would come with the information, and arrest could follow. As the day passed, I paced like a caged animal. I couldn't stay in the house and wait, nor strangely, did I want to return to the Temple to see Caiaphas (in his golden robes) defile that shrine I held so holy. So I did the only other thing that I enjoyed, I went to the Baths to wile away the day. Although

I stayed until the afternoon, and made small talk with several there, my heart had no place in it, and I sought to stay alone.

At the ninth hour I returned home to find everything in readiness. Now we missed only our Master, who wouldn't be coming until his path was covered by darkness. "For heavens sake, come into the other room and sit down. You have been standing by the door all evening. He will be here soon," Miriamme chided me, as she put her arm around my waist and prepared to guide me to the living area of the house. I had given in, and was starting to follow her when the knock came in three hurried raps. I turned and ran to the door as Jesus, and the remaining ten, walked in. Jesus greeted Miriamme, John, and his wife warmly as they all converged upon the door. Jesus shot a glance my way, and I nodded to let him know that I had news. Jesus started to walk my way, when Miriamme took his hand and pulled him to the bench along the wall to the side of the door. There Miriamme bowed down upon her knees, and taking the bowl of water and clean towels brought to her by her maid, carefully removed Jesus' sandals and washed his feet. As she washed, Jesus looked up at me with wetness in his eyes. Then, bending low, he held her head to his lap for the longest time... then kissed my sweet Miriamme, good-by.

In the excitement of the holiday mood, the meaning of the moment was missed by all but the three of us, who for the barest moment of time, shared a love that would last throughout eternity.

The mood was finally broken as Peter came from out of the kitchen where he had been sampling the fare, and shouted his usual greetings to the gathered crowd.

"Get down here on the bench, Peter!" Miriamme

mimicked, "You're next to have your feet washed. I'll have no one in my house with dirty feet." With that Miriamme insisted on washing each disciple's feet in turn, to show them the love she had for them, and how our house was honored by their presence. As Peter took his turn, Jesus and I slipped out the other end of the patio into my private rooms.

It was here that I told Jesus in great detail of the murder that the High Priest and Pilate had planned. Although he knew from my messages, I wanted to fill him in on all the subtleties he might have missed. Lastly, I told him of what was to transpire tonight, once Judas found an opportunity to leave. Jesus was quiet for awhile, as he absorbed what I had to say, and I am certain, to ponder his moves for this night ahead. When finally he spoke, he was deadly serious, and new lines in his once smooth forehead showed the strain that he had been under, as he put his hand to my arm and gave it a squeeze. "The last thing I want is for us to be found here. I will make sure Judas knows that we will be found alone at the olive press in the garden of Gethsemane. There I will await them. From there I will be able to see my Father's beloved Temple once more. I think it will help give me courage, Asher. Will you pray for me?"

Hearing Jesus say these words, I was struck by a knot in my stomach, for I realized that he knew what horrible death awaited him in just a few short hours, and yet he gave himself up to it willingly. There was still time to save him; a swift horse, and soldiers at the gates whom I could bribe. He could be gone in an hour, safely on his way to the protection of Galilee. But the thought passed as rapidly as it came, for he had willed himself here this night, and thus fulfilled the prophecies to see God's dream survive throughout eternity. With nothing else to say, we embraced, and headed for the door. Just before going out, Jesus turned, and with compassion flowing from him like the Light that he was, said, "Asher ben Ammi, I will find you again someday. Remember well this time together, keep it safe within your soul, and when it is needed, I will call you, as I did with the overflowing cup, and ask you to give the light to a thousand others, so that they too will know our Father is within their hearts."

He turned and left. When I could regain my composure, I came out to find that he had already taken my son, and his disciples up the stairs near the front door to the room prepared on the second floor. Only Miriamme, John's wife, and I, were left. I tried to tell them what was about to happen, now that the mold was cast, but I could not. So we ate a quiet meal, with my dear sweet Miriamme intuitive enough to honor my silence, and wait until I could feel free enough to communicate. She spoke softly to her daughter-in-law, who was almost her own age.

Once, well before the end of the meal, I heard the sound of rough hinges grate as the door quietly opened to the upstairs room. I silently moved into the shadows of the patio and watched as Judas silently slipped his sandals on and disappeared into the dark. There was no turning back now. What was to be, had begun.

The meal lasted quite a long time, or so it seemed to me, not being a part of it. But, finally we heard the upstairs door open and the latch bang against the rough plaster wall, and this time it was accompanied by the sound of the muffled speech of many men, and scraping of feet on wooden stairs.

We all got up and hurried to the entry, where the stair they now descended terminated. The covered portal opened directly onto the street outside, and its rough-sawn wooden doors served as the main entrance to our home.

It was a different group that descended the stairs than had gone up, that was evident immediately. The happy group of men which had arrived a few hours ago to celebrate the coming of the Passover holiday, was now somber and intro-spective, each unto himself. At my insistence, the whole household gathered to wish them good-by. Jesus went up to each of them in turn, and holding their hands, or giving them a hug, whispered into their ears something personal, some-thing to remember him by. Maston, more sensitive than the rest, sensed that something was amiss, and grabbed Jesus as he came to him, not letting him go for the longest time. Even with all that bore down upon him now, Jesus rushed him not, but rather held Maston in return.

When my Lord came to me, he held me close, then whispered in my ear, "Asher, my people will be criminals and lost sheep in a few hours. Please take them in and hide them if you can. And, Asher, please take my mother as your own for as long as she has need." I nodded to him in the dim light of the oil lamp along the wall, and with that, the double doors closed, and they were gone.

After Jesus and the eleven disciples left, my son John along with them, Miriamme and I started to retire as the servants cleaned up the room. As we were walking toward the stairs leading up to our quarters, Miriamme stopped as if an idea had just come into her head. "Do you mind, sweet one; let's go up to the the room where they ate." "Why?" I asked.

"Never mind, just come along." I was deeply in love with my young beautiful wife, and she knew I would go anywhere with her, all she had to do was ask.

We went back towards the front of the house and up the narrow stairs into the room where the girls were busy picking up dishes of leftover food. Miriamme walked to the opposite end of the low table where Jesus had been sitting, and bending over, picked up the silver goblet that was standing there. I was not present when the table had been set, and was surprised to see the single silver goblet, when all the rest were of common brass. As if reading my mind, Miriamme said, as she returned down the length of the room, "It was a special night, and this cup was for him."

As she stopped in front of me, I looked down into the shining vessel with just a touch of red wine still swirling in the bottom, and thought of Jesus' words to me in the desert: "Take and drink, feel the light in you, of you, around you, and with you in God's own peace. Then give this love you have found to a thousand others, for no end there lies to His love, His peace, His bliss." Remembering his words put me at ease as I put my arm around Miriamme and started for the stairs.

"What was that you mumbled, dear?"

"Oh, nothing, Miriamme, just something Jesus said to me in the desert." Together, arm in arm, we climbed the stairs to bed.

I didn't think that I had fallen asleep, but I must have, for all of a sudden I woke with a start. My mind began to work. The banging was on our bedroom door. It was Maston shouting, "Come quick, master, there are police at the door!"

"Tell them I will be right there," I answered, while I tried to find my clothes in the dark. "Don't be frightened, Miriamme," I said, with a conviction I didn't feel myself, and rushed out the door and down the stairs into the black unlit court below.

My mind was racing, what was happening? Did someone report us as harborers of Jesus? What else could it be? Wait... Caiaphas wouldn't dare do this to me, not with my wealth and power. I would have heard of this from my high-priced ears among the court. Could it be the trial of Jesus, then? No, it can't be the trial, not until after day-break, that's the Law.

Then it hit me. Caiaphas (or more probably the crafty old Annas to be more exact) had found a way to hurry the trial of Jesus, to finish in time for Pilate to hang him by sabbath eve – desperate solution.

The answer was there before me, I just hadn't seen. Because of the tremendous crowds present for Passover, and their need to offer sacrifices, the Temple was opened at midnight and services began at the first watch, therefore it *was* legal to convene the Sanhedrim at this early hour. Maston had said that the police had come for me, not soldiers, which also reinforced my belief that this was exactly what had happened. For I, as a member of the high council, had to be called if Caiaphas were to follow every jot of the Law – and I knew he would. What right did they have to do this? Others would be asking that question right now as they were being awakened in the middle of the night. The answer was, of course, that they had every right. For, as the cart follows the ass, so does "right" follow power, just as surely as life itself will someday end.

I asked about John, but was told that he had never

returned. Maston had roused the stable, and two horses were waiting. I looked at Maston, and he said, "Sorry, master, I must go with you, I must know!" I nodded my head in agreement, and as the yard gate swung open, we rode off at a gallop.

I found out later from John that he had been with Jesus when Judas had approached with some of Caiaphas' men, Temple police, and even a squad of Roman soldiers to insure the results of the arrest. Apparently my son, John, not an unimportant man in his own right, demanded of the officer in charge to go with him, and demanded to know the charges. The officer, knowing that John was a member of the ruling Court, allowed him to accompany him, and together they took Jesus to Annas' house. This reinforced my thought that the powerful Annas' hand had set the planning for this miserable deed. Apparently Jesus gave Annas nothing that would serve his needs, and thus, after being beaten by a snarling guard for insubordination, he was next sent to the Temple, which was the only place an official seal could be placed upon his fate.

When I arrived at the Chamber of Stone, Jesus was already there, his hands bound behind him, his face red and swollen from the beating he had been made to endure. In front of him, in the first row was my son, who acknowledged me, but didn't want to break into his argument being waged in front of six or seven priests listening to what he had to say about this man – who, in fact, had already been condemned. The whole room was filling with noisy, arguing, shouting, and angry people. These were important and illustrious men here, used to being treated with deference, and they were not taking it lightly that they had been dragged here in the middle of the night.

Looking around, I saw others too, for I had developed a shrewd political eye after this many years, and I could spot those with the satisfied and "all knowing" smugness about them which said to me that they were of the elect who had known beforehand what the results of this night would be. Those names and faces I cataloged by habit, for future use, should the knowledge be needed.

Jesus had his back to me as I entered. His presence before me was a shock for which I couldn't have adequately prepared. When you love someone as I loved him, I... I just couldn't explain the feelings I had. I put my hands to my mouth so as not to cry out in grief at the abject sight of him. The utter emptiness that gripped me was beyond anything I had ever experienced, even at my first wife's passing, my son stillborn and left within her womb. Then, suddenly, as if I had actually uttered a cry, Jesus straightened up, and slowly turned to look my way. In his peaceful eyes, already swollen from a blow, I found my courage again, and my voice, and was able to return his look, and let him know that I would not fail him. The words that needed to be said, would be said with clarity and force, and in the end, everything he had wanted of this meeting would come to pass.

I found a place high in the back, out of my usual order, just as a hush came over the assemblage and the High Priest, adorned in all his golden robes, entered the chamber. "Pompous ass!" I thought, as he took his seat, and the highest court of the land was convened to "officially" decide Jesus' fate.

My son and I, as well as others in the court, argued and used every legal trick we knew to point out that Jesus was innocent of any provable charge that they might level. Then, as prearranged, when Jesus knew his time had come to end, and this nightmare game had come to a close, he slowly lifted his head, and looked straight into my eyes. Even from a distance, there was no mistake. Within my head my name sounded (it imploded!) and I stood dumbly silent, stunned by the sound still reverberating within my mind. I sat strangely transfixed by his face and those incredible eyes. The arguments within me slowly died, one after another – it was finished.

John, just to the right, below me, was desperately arguing now, but losing the battle to the gathering silence of those still opposed to the High Priest's will. He looked back, seeking my support for some point he had just concluded, when he saw my face. His mouth fell open as I stared, transfixed, at my beloved Master. He was like no other I knew upon the earth. He was the Messiah – and they knew him not.

John's eyes pleaded in vain for my help, but I held my silence as I had promised. Although the argument raged on for a short time still, and John carried on the best he knew how, it was over, and the verdict was in. Finally, when Caiaphas' menacing looks had silenced all but a few, he finished the show. Slowly he stood, and respectful silence fell like a leaden curtain about the Council. Then in a deep clear voice he looked directly at Jesus and roared:

"I demand, in the name of the living God, that you tell us whether you claim to be the Messiah, the Son of God!"

Jesus answered simply... "I am."

With that, the High Priest tore his vestments and shouted, "Blasphemy! What need have we for other witnesses? You have all heard him say it! What is your verdict?"

"*Death! - Death! - Death!*" was the chant that rang spontaneously throughout the Chamber, as the guards grabbed Jesus under his arms and dragged him away through the Council that I once thought distributed the fairest justice of any land. Caiaphas looked my way for an instant before pushing his way through the crowd to lead the procession across the Temple grounds to the fortress of Antonia. A smile was now openly displayed upon his cunning face, thinking he had beaten me, that he had won. "Oh, woe unto you, Caiaphas," I thought. "You think you have saved yourself and your nation, but alas, truly it is you who has lost—*everything!*"

I sat back down on the cold stone bench. All of a sudden, I was a very tired, weary old man.

Chapter 17

I have loved you even as the Father has loved me. Live within my love. When you obey me you are living in my love, just as I obey my Father and live in his love. I have told you this so that you will be filled with my joy. Yes, your cup of joy will overflow! I demand that you love each other as much as I love you. And here is how to measure it – the greatest love is shown when a person lays down his life for his friends...

John 15:9-13

T he barest hint of light was to be seen in the cold eastern sky, and there was a smell of moisture in the morning breeze as it drifted in from the west. John and I joined Maston in the Court of the Gentiles where he had been confined. Maston, however, already knew the outcome of the trial, for he had seen the High Priest lead the parade to the gate of the Antonia, and had seen Jesus with Temple guards immediately behind.

Maston said that even as we debated Jesus' fate, there had been priests out in every court quizzing people as to their feelings about him. If they professed a belief in him, he noted, the priests said nothing to raise suspicion, but let them on their way with a blessing. If they were against him, or seemed to enjoy the questions and favors of the priest, then they were gradually herded close to an angry group that was gathering near the northwestern gate, that led to fortress Antonia.

Maston pretended to be a pious Jew working his way around the Temple wall, praying and prostrating as he went. As he came within earshot of the now *righteous* throng, he could hear the priests taunting them, goading them into a religious frenzy. The priests called on all their loyalties, and *prejudices*, until they felt confident that the mob would do anything they wished. It was then Maston knew, that even if Caiaphas lost in the Court, the carefully chosen mob would insure Jesus' fate anyway. The High Priest was not a fool. He gained and held his position with deftness in his craft and thoroughness in his planning, that even my well paid "*ears*" could not penetrate. As Caiaphas led the Sanhedrim, who now followed dutifully in his tracks, and his priestly caste, the rabble also did its job in screaming for his death. When they reached the confines of the Temple grounds, Caiaphas would go no further, for Passover was coming that night, and he didn't want to be defiled. So he sent the others on into the stone paved court of the Governor, and with an evil grin spreading across his face for having successfully delivered up a "leader" to Pilate as promised, turned with his two chief priests, and quickly returned to the confines of his own "sacred" palace.

"What do we do now, father?" John asked limply, as if his feelings had all been drained from his body.

"Now comes the hardest task of all son – we must watch

him die.

"There could now also be much danger for his disciples, John, maybe even for us – but I doubt if Caiaphas is that bold – or dumb. Do you know where the rest of his disciples are now?"

"No, father. When they came to arrest Jesus everyone except Peter left at a dead run down the hill through the olive trees and into the darkness of the valley. They are probably hiding somewhere in the city to be close to Jesus. They might even be hiding among this crowd, or in the city of tents just north of here.

"When they arrested Jesus," John continued, "the officer of the guards knew me personally, and didn't dare tell me what I could or could not do. I could tell that he was considering arresting and holding Peter, however, for Peter seemed to care little for his life at that moment, and roared his insults at Judas and the rest of them, while taking a swing at one of them with his sword. But, thinking better of it, the officer of the guards turned and left, satisfied that he had his quarry. I imagine that he thought twice when he saw the look I gave him, which made him act more cautiously than he otherwise would. "That officer's time will come, mark my words, he will know my wrath when this is over!"

"John," I cautioned," have you forgotten already what our Lord taught us, why he came, why he is about to die?"

John blanched, and lowered his eyes, then continued his story anew. "When we got to Annas' house the guards stopped Peter at the outer entry to the court. It took but a simple coin and my name to change his mind. When last I saw Peter, he was going over to the fire with the servants and guards to await the news. When we finished, which didn't take long, he was already gone. I have no idea where he went."

"Then go, both of you," I said to Maston and my son, "find them and gather them up. They will need a place to hide. Put them in the room over the stables, behind the room where we have the grain. There are no windows, and but one door that's almost impossible to find. Even if the idiot Caiaphas is so bold as to search our home, they won't find them there. Now go, find them, they will be like frightened sheep in the city. I have other work to do. This task is just for me."

As Maston headed off for the horses, and John began to search the Temple courts, I set my feet for the Fort of Antonia. Taking a deep breath, I thought, "All right, lions den, here I come!"

The mention of Placidus' name, and also my position, sent the Roman guard off to find his Captain. His name was Caius, and I knew his reputation well. I saw the guard approach him in the stone paved court of the barracks where he had his men lined in files. The guard saluted him as he approached, then spoke of me and pointed in my direction with his spear. I saw Caius nod, then bark an order to another who took charge, and head my way with a soldier's stiff gait.

I strained to look about, to see if I could find Jesus somewhere in the court. It was then that I caught sight of them; three of them there were, all tied to the whipping stakes, their backs bloody from the scourge. I couldn't see their faces, as their backs were to me in the darkness of the early dawn, but none of them looked like Jesus in body, or shape. Even their hair was different, for Jesus wore part of his cut and bound in the back with a thong. Of course, that could have been removed by the guards, but still, none of them looked like him at all.

"What do you want?" was the rude, brusque greeting I received from Caius, a soldier, not a statesman, through and through.

"I have to see Placidus, I have reason to believe he is with Pilate now."

"You can't see him now, there is a trial going on. Besides, you can see I'm too busy to be your guide. Today these men will be crucified. It's the first hour now, by your time, and I have orders to have them up by the third, or they will have my hide. Go back to your temple, see him tomorrow."

"I know very well there is a trial going on, Caius," I spit with icy precision in my words, letting him know I would not hesitate in making my position good. "The trial is for Jesus of Galilee. And, you are right, Placidus is with Pilate at the trial this very moment. Now, take me to him, Caius, or I swear by nightfall you will be the lowliest foot soldier in this garrison!"

There was a frigid silence, as a Caius, now crimson with rage, sized up my threat. For him to take an order from a Jew, any Jew, was more than he could abide. As he hesitated a fateful moment to decide, I felt that I needed one more weight to tip the scales in my favour. I played my last game piece, and added with venom spitting from my mouth, "Need I ask you, Caius, how is Pilate's wife?" Caius exploded with all the rage of a wounded bull, but I moved not a muscle, nor did my eyes waver for an instant from their glare. Beaten, Caius turned and stormed off down the column-lined hall, with me closely behind. The original guard stared after us in disbelief.

Placidus was standing off to the side, as Pilate was already questioning Jesus when I arrived. I waved Caius off as he was about to step to Placidus' side and announce my presence in his ear, and instead quietly walked up to my Roman friend without saying a word. Caius was glad not to have to enter the judgment hall, and retreated down the gilded corridor, the heels of his military sandals echoing as he went, anger adding to their impact on the marble floor.

Placidus was so engrossed with the spectacle before him that at first he didn't notice me slip up beside him. When he did, the muscles of his massive shoulders flinched in startled surprise. My worried look said everything this man needed to know. He gave me a little resigned smile, and shared a *knowing* in his eyes, then once again he turned his attention back to this most amazing trial in progress. I knew that I would be "defiled" by my presence in this hall, but I no longer cared what ridiculous rules governed me. I had seen his *light*, and knew that it could not be defiled by anything as petty as whom I saw, or what I ate.

Pilate's questions were aimed at finding a rebel guilty of sedition, plotting a rebellion, a crime against the emperor punishable by death. He was instead being treated to a lecture by Jesus on the world of his Father God in heaven. Outside the open window the Jews who had been carefully selected by the priests were chanting, *"Death! Death! Death!"* just as had happened before in the Council Chambers. Pilate's temper was naturally short, and the noise outside was making him furious. Here was not a rebel whom he could show to the people and say, "See, here is what happens when Rome is defied!" Rather, he had before him a preposterous Jew, who thought he was the Jewish Messiah, come to "save" his people with LOVE! Ridiculous! He shot a dangerous look at the young functionary who had brought about this mess, but the young man had shifted his position nervously away from Pilate's gaze, pretending to be engrossed with what was going on outside.

Pilate had told him to bring a zealot, not a religious fanatic! I knew he couldn't care about this Jesus, pretender to a heaven-made throne. As far as he knew, *all* Jews were religious fanatics. Pilate couldn't tell one from another when it came to religious ranting. He wanted someone who had drawn his sword against imperial Rome, a local hero to be sacrificed as an example, a warning, for all that would defy the State. There were plenty of them out there, robbing and pillaging, and killing Romans whenever they could. And here before him stood a poor, dumb carpenter who was guilty of nothing – except *blasphemy*. Who cared?

Pilate, wanting no part of this trial, annoyed beyond his normal tolerance by the rabble yelling outside his room, and his own people too, sat slouched in his chair, brooding, tapping his fingers on the arm of the chair as his face grew darker and more menacing with every moment of the trial.

Then, with suddenness that startled everyone in the room, he bolted from his seat and walked rapidly to the balcony above the court. There he held up his arms for silence and shouted, "You brought this man to me, accusing him of leading a revolt against the government. I have examined him thoroughly, and find him *innocent!*"

He couldn't have spoken with more force or venom in his voice. He fairly hissed the words, but I had participated so many times before in the ways of controlling others, I knew what was to come next in exploiting Pilate for Caiaphas' own desires, and was treated to my own just desserts. Priests on the pay roll, and those loyal to Caiaphas, were placed uniformly throughout the crowd, and as Pilate finished I heard their individual voices clearly an instant before the chant was picked up by the throng. "Crucify him! Crucify him!" Once again, I saw Pilate hold up his hands to gain silence.

"I will have him scourged for you, but that is all I can do."

Now a mighty roar rose from the mob, and Pilate tried for the third time to reason with them. "Why? What crime has he committed? I find no reason to sentence him to death." But, it was all over. The multitude drowned out his words, and started to surge against the guards. I saw Pilate's shoulders droop, as he held up his hands for the last time, appearing to wash them of the condemned man's blood. I heard him say softly as he turned to go down to the Judgment Seat on the raised platform below... *"It is done."*

My eyes betrayed my stony face, as the stinging sensation once again came. Placidus kindly grabbed me by the arm, and led me away, saying, "Come, we will watch from a distance. What they are about to do to him, you do not want to see."

Placidus guided me out of the room, down some stairs, and into very opulent quarters, where he said that he was staying. Once inside, he poured me wine, which I gratefully took, and there we sat in silence for the longest time. Placidus was again the first to move. He quietly said, "Come, we will watch from a distance." I rose, my old body feeling very heavy now, and went out into the streets where he took me to a mercantile building. There, he guided me through bags piled high of what smelled like grain, then up the back stairs to the roof overlooking the street below, the city's wall beyond, and then the *Skull* past that.

We didn't have to wait long, for the noise of confusion, wailing cries, and screams of grief were growing louder in the street below, telling us that my Master and the three others were coming this way. I grabbed Placidus and thanked him, and told him that I just couldn't watch.

"You'll be back, friend, you'll be back, and when you do I will still be here – until they take him down." I turned to leave just as I saw the first of the soldiers round the turn below. I pulled up the door in the rooftop floor, and as I descended the stairs I heard Placidus yell at Caius marching past in the street below, "Where's the fourth? You should have been more careful, your men are too harsh. It shouldn't have happened. See that it doesn't happen again!"

Why did Placidus worry? What difference did it make whether the poor soul died at the whipping pole or on the cross? For a moment I wondered whether it was Jesus who had already met his end. Then from the darkness of the room of grain, I heard the women who followed the procession wail his name. I hid my eyes and sobbed until I could cry no more. Then, empty, I headed back to our home to see if I could help any of the disciples that might be there.

At the house I had found no one there, neither Miriamme, nor John nor his wife. The servants were gone, too. It was like a morbid tomb. Later I was to find, to my humiliation, that each of them who had been at the house had followed John up to the hill to keep watch.

Placidus was right, I couldn't stay away, I had to see the

end. I felt that I was a coward. Even though I wasn't at the foot of the cross, I made myself head back to watch from the rooftop with Placidus.

I returned back through the city the long way round, an aimless path that took me by the Baths, the Hasmonean palace (where Herod Antipas was in residence), the market full of noise, and then along the Temple wall north to the Fortress where I had started. I ended up there because I was not sure I could find the little storeroom if I did not take exactly the same route I had taken that morning with Placidus.

I watched the sky as I walked, for it had become dark and foreboding, and the wind had become a gale. I wrapped my cloak about me, as the dust and dirt from the streets began to swirl about everywhere. A shutter to a window high above my head broke loose in the wind and came sailing at me, narrowly missing my head. I heard people screaming over the wailing wind, and watched ahead as three stones fell from a roof top, narrowly missing a handful of hurrying people in the street below. I looked up just in time to see a bolt of lightning rip across the ominous black sky.

Then, as the ninth hour approached, the earth began to tremble. I grabbed hold of the Temple wall, as a rumbling deep within the earth began to grow. "It's Jesus, I know it, he's dead! He's dead!" My mind shrieked as I struggled to keep from falling sideways onto the ground.

I pushed away from the wall, and started to run, then I heard the sound. It was like a crack! Involuntarily, I stopped, and reeled back as if the very stones of the Temple were poison to touch. And then it came, a great cry of lament from behind the Temple wall that told me something awful had just happened inside.

I turned again and headed west up the street as the shaking began to subside. People were still running every which way as I turned the first corner – and ran straight into Nicodemus, and Joseph of Arimathea (whom I didn't know had supported Jesus until that morning during the meeting of the Sanhedrim). They didn't see me either, until we bumped headlong into each other, three old men almost knocking each other flat. "Where are you going?" I stammered, as we struggled to hold each other up.

"He's dead, Asher, he's dead!" Joseph cried. "We are on our way to get permission from Pilate to let us have his body, so that we can bury him as he should. I have a tomb not far from here that has never been used. It was going to be for my family and me, but now it will give me honor to prepare it for our Lord."

I had been running in panic, yet here were two men who had never been as close to Jesus as I, yet in this dire moment they were thinking of their Master; and I, oh God, I was thinking of *me*. Thus started a conflict that raged within me until my end. I found that I was either thinking of myself when I should have been thinking of his flock, or flailing myself for just that cause. Not a pretty picture I paint of myself, nor one of which I am proud, but a true one just the same.

It was a miserable man who climbed the stairs to the rooftop where I left Placidus just a few hours past, but Joseph and Nicodemus had sobered me, and my mind was once again beginning to clear. Placidus, his hands together behind his back, was staring silently at the billowing black clouds, and out across the city wall to the hill called the Skull that lay beyond. I followed his gaze to see that they were just now taking Jesus from the cross and letting him to the ground. They must have been some of his followers, for he was being lowered carefully, whereas the Romans would just have let him fall.

I hadn't realized that Placidus was speaking, for my attention was on the cross, but then turning my attention his way to listen to him, I realized that he wasn't speaking to me at all, but to himself, and I think, to all of history.

"Here comes Caius. Yes, Caius, you did the job for which you're paid, but this one was different wasn't he – not like the rest of them up there. Something strange about him. Something inside you changes, doesn't it? Yes, great strong hard Caius, I can even see it in you. Something is different. You can fool the others, but I know you too well. I see it in you (and in me too). God protect us now. God protect us — for today is the first day of the fall of the empire. Stupid Jews, you don't even know what you have done. You have conquered us without lifting a sword. Damn you! Damn all of you!"

He turned to me, but I'm not sure he knew who I was, for he continued as if I were a disembodied spirit, somewhere listening to his hidden thoughts. "That man up there is not a man like us. You saw him, didn't you?" I nodded my head, but I don't think he was looking for an answer. "Mark these words, his legions will conquer Rome, like none of these rabble will. We'll eat these people alive someday. They can't stand against our armies, but in the end we – we won't be able to stand against the likes of him!" He turned and pointed at the now empty cross silhouetted against the ominous sky.

"He'll sweep through the armies into the Senate itself. Even the emperor someday will fall!

"All his people deserted him, didn't they. But they'll be back. The next time we won't be able to stop them. There's no winning this one for Pilate." Placidus laughed an eerie laugh that made my skin crawl. "The fool wrung his hands like a woman. He didn't know what to do. Kill him? Leave him alive? By Zeus, he didn't know what to do, and I enjoyed seeing him squirm. I guess I shouldn't be so hard on him, he's doing the best he can, probably the best any one could do. Who would want to stay here anyway. I'm glad I am going back – the sooner the better."

I'm sure my face reflected a look of utter disbelief. I couldn't believe what was happening. When I left him just a few short hours ago, he was quiet, but normal. Now he was different, he had changed. He was seeing a future I could not imagine, and I thought he must have gone mad. Had Jesus done this to him? I could not imagine, but I had the greatest desire to get away from him, for truly, my instincts told me, this man could be dangerous if I but tipped him just a little off the middle of the scale.

"They took him down," Placidus said, his mouth tight. "At least somebody has some courage. What do I care, it's done. Let's go back."

He started to turn, looking for the stair, but his eyes were still glassy, far from normal, and their look was far away. As I helped him down the stairs, through the room, and out onto the street, he looked up at the sky with gravity and said, "It's strange. It's so quiet. I wish I'd have kept back some soldiers, plenty of these people would slit my throat."

Not knowing what else to do, I started to walk him back. Then, without warning, he pulled his arm away from me, and looked at me as if I were a total stranger. He shook his head as if to clear it, then turned to go, as the thunder crashed, and the rain came in a torrent. I never saw him again.

Chapter 18

You may find him anywhere, and everywhere, for truly he lies within your heart. Go within the silence as he taught you, and find him there – he waits for you even now.

Asher ben Ammi

By the next morning, all the disciples had gathered at our home. Most had arrived under the cover of darkness the night before. As soon as I had returned home from my experience with Placidus, I set about having the room over the stable readied for the men, and the storeroom in front rearranged so as to show no sign of anything but staples. Finally, when I could see that John had things well under control, I let myself slip into a fitful sleep, broken every hour or so by a newcomer who needed protection and a place to rest. The next morning, I felt like I had been drugged, from lack of sleep for two nights straight, and all of the emotion of the previous day had sapped my strength.

The next day was Passover, and it was spent at our house with all of the disciples save Judas, whom none of us had seen. In addition, Mary (Jesus' mother) now joined us too, and several others who sought protection because they followed in his name. Because it was Passover I had no fear that Caiaphas would send anyone to search the house, and so we quietly celebrated our first holiday without Jesus, each afraid of what the night might bring. For I reasoned that if Caiaphas were to move on us, it would come soon, and what better time than by the darkness of the shadowless moon.

During the day each of us was lost in his or her own world, and if the others were like me, they were reliving their lives with him, those special precious moments he had with each of us, wherein we found our God through him. So preoccupied was I in my own thoughts, I hadn't noticed John, son of Zebedee, when first he had come. Now, I saw him in the corner of the courtyard all curled up like a ball. There was fear in him, of that I could tell, and my heart went out to him. He had been kind to me while I was in his home land of Galilee, and suddenly I realized what this loss of his teacher must mean to him. I remembered that he was much afraid, and never quite understood those things that were going on around him, so I sought him out to help if I could.

I sat down beside him, not saying a word. After a moment, still holding his arms around his knees, he lifted his face, tears streaming silently down his sunburned cheeks, and he spoke into the bright blue sky, anguish in his voice. "I ran, Asher, I ran! I never ran so fast or hard in my life. I didn't know where I was going. I was just running, running. I was so afraid. I've never known such panic and fear. Ohhh..." he moaned, "I left him, I deserted him. I didn't even know what happened to him. I was so afraid of the soldiers. I'm sorry, Jesus, *I'm so sorry.*" he intoned, overcome by wracking sobs now. I could do nothing but let him cry it out.

Through his sobs he said, "At least Peter stayed with him. He's the only one of the twelve – then even *he* ran! Oh, God, I'm always so afraid! Why, Asher... Why?"

I didn't pause to think, I only reacted with the loving pity I felt for John at this moment. "John, look at me." I softly reached out and turned his face to me so that I could look into the depth of his eyes, and have him know that I was speaking to him from the deepest part of my being. "Listen to me, John, for I tell you, *he is not gone.* You may find him anywhere, and everywhere, for truly he lies within your heart. Go within the silence as he taught you, and find him there — he waits for you even now, John."

I could see the change. I could see it in his eyes. Somewhere, somehow, I had touched a responsive chord, and slowly, ever so slowly, before my very eyes, I watched a boy die, and a man being born. Now, as he nervously wiped his tear-stained face, a smile worked its way across his face. I asked him to please tell me of the supper in the upper room two nights ago, if he wouldn't mind. "Of course, Asher, of course – and thank you." His eyes said everything. I dismissed his thanks with an embarrassed wave of my hand, and settled down to hear the story of what went on in the room two nights prior. I realized then that I could have asked my son, but with all that had happened, it hadn't occurred to me, until then.

"How did you know I was thinking of that night?" John asked. I just shrugged my shoulders. I really didn't know why I asked then, except to divert his attention, and too, I wanted to hear. "When you looked at me just now," he said, "it reminded me of how Jesus looked at me night before last. When he looked at me, I saw all my fears... whew! You know what I mean? I don't know how, but I saw all those failings, all those things that I didn't do for him when I could have — all the things I messed up. I should have done better for him. I'm such a weak man, but I loved him."

I put my hand on his arm, and invited him to look around the court at all the others, each to a man brooding and glumly introspective. "See, you are not alone. I, too, yesterday went through this, for I could not bring myself to go to the cross and see him die. John, you know better than I, that Jesus would be the first to forgive you and me for any weaknesses we have, and ask us only to build on them, not to sit and cry. Now, continue, please, with what happened that very special night upstairs."

Watching John now was wonderful, and filled me with awe. For when he first began to speak, he was like a lamp with but little oil left, and the barest flicker of life yet to burn. Then, as he began to recount the tale of that night, it was as if suddenly the lamp had been filled, and the wick was now soaking up the fuel. Brighter and brighter he became as he now recounted the experience of this amazing dinner to me.

"He will look at you sometimes and it's like he'll look right through you. I mean, he knows what we think. I've seen him do that before lots of times, but night before last was different. When he looked at us, he stopped with each of us. He looked at us like always, but that night his eyes were ever so sad. And, he was quiet. The reason I noticed was that it was the celebration of the Passover, and everyone felt good, and we were talking and happy, but by the end of the evening everybody was quiet, too.

"Jesus was silent for a very long time," John continued.

"He was holding a piece of bread, just looking quietly at it. Slowly, one by one, we all noticed, and each in turn stopped to stare at him, and an absolute quiet descended on the room. Then, while holding the bread, he broke off pieces and handed them all around. We were all sort of looking at each other, because we didn't know what to do with it. I mean, it wasn't enough to eat, but just a little piece. Then he said, 'Eat this... this is my body... and in this you will remember me.' He looked around, and there wasn't a sound anywhere, no one even breathed. Then he kind of sighed, as if he were in some terrible pain. 'Tomorrow, you won't find me here... you'll find me taken to the tree.' We were all wide-eyed by now, not knowing what he was talking about. He shook his head, as if throwing away a thought, then said softly, 'Eat – Eat.' We did, but still no one said a word. As we ate, I watched him. He had picked up the silver goblet of wine that lay in front of him, and he was swirling it about, and staring into the bottom of the cup, kind of transfixed. Then all of a sudden he held it up in the air with both hands and in a strange and wonderful voice that seemed to come from the depths of his being, and heaven itself, said; 'Yahweh... Yahweh, hear me now.'

"I looked at his face, and it began to *shine*, I mean actually shine as if it had a light all its own. And then right before my eyes, his face changed; it became soft and peaceful and all the worry lines I had seen just vanished, and in their place was a radiance about him that I had never seen. It was almost like God was right there with us all! I felt beautiful, like the Light was in me too. 'Yahweh!' we whispered once more, as we all lifted our wine, and together we drank. We drank and felt Him in us. It was like no other time I can remember. You are right, Asher. He is here, he is in me, he will always be, won't he?"

All I could manage, was a small smile, while saying; "Yes, John, he surely is."

As the Sabbath was ending, Miriamme came to me and said, "Husband dear, please let me talk to them, for this sadness must end. Never once did Master mourn the things he could not change, nor shrink from trials that were about to be upon him. In the worst of times, he found reason to gladden our hearts. The Father has not left him just because he is gone — nor has he departed from any of us."

Oh, how I rejoiced in her. I held her close, feeling her long silky black hair against my rough skin, smelling the bitter-sweet perfume that she wore only for me, knowing that in all the world I could never have found another as sweet as she was to me. I revered and treasured her above all others for her equal veneration and sustenance. She blessed me with her light, lively, young, blooming youth, both day and night, in the most caring of ways. And, in those ways of her caressing love, she led me in the most soft and gentle way to the highest and closest moments of ecstasy.

In her, I knew what God desired when he gave man and woman the gift of loving one another, truly sharing and trusting in each other's arms at night. In a bond of faith, we handed each other our souls to keep, to hold them dear, in a sensitive loving trust, so that each unto the other might know the beauty of belief in someone else. Most of all, it was in the little things that proved her love to me each day. No man could have cherished her more, and I silently swore a oath within me, that if God granted me the opportunity, I would seek her out and find her again, but this time I would have a young and healthy body.

"My sweet blessed Miriamme, what would my life have been these past few years without you? Of course, you may speak to us all." It was just what we needed.

She spoke to us of the love and joy that Jesus had brought to our lives. Then she began to admonish them all by saying, "He did not die a traitor's death by hanging on that cross. Ask Asher here," she turned and pointed toward me, "Jesus left nothing to chance, he even planned his death!

"Did he ever fail you? Did he? Even once?" Her dark-brown eyes flashed back and forth, daring any to challenge her. "No, he never did. Then why do you sit around here with faces of gloom and death? I tell you, he promised that he would be with us again, and I, for one, am going to believe it."

The disciple's mood lightened noticeably. We continued to talk of him, of course, but the lighter moments were the ones now being remembered, and even his mother joined in with stories I had never heard.

That night, as the men filed up to the room over the stable, I heard Peter's booming voice say, "It all began in the stable, why not end it here, too." Everyone laughed, and for the first time in days, they fell into a dreamless sleep. For there, on a distant mountain in the land of Judaea, in the ancient city of Jerusalem, the time of the old covenant passed out of memory, and by dawn of the new day, a new life would be born.

In our bed, my Miriamme wrapped herself around me, and in a sweet and dreamy voice pleaded, "Tell me more about our Master, please."

Staring up at the blackness of the ceiling I answered, "I will tell you about him by telling you what he said about you, but only if you are good."

Her interest was piqued, as I knew it would be, and placing her icy feet upon my leg she said, "Tell me now, old man, or it will go higher!" We both laughed, for the pretended outcome of this little charade was known to us both. I got up and out of bed, lighting the lamp as I went.

"I almost forgot," I said, as she watched me fumble through my private case, "he gave me this the last time I saw him, in the desert, and asked that I give it to you when he was gone." From under a stack of documents came a torn piece of parchment with his writing thereon. Miriamme sat up in bed as I handed her the note and the lamp, and I climbed back into bed as she read.

"And the soul found certain smugness and comfort in its holiness. In its aloofness blindness fell, and could feel not the pain of its people.

So God reached down in love to touch His handmaiden, and the greatest He made small.

And from the ashes rose the phoenix of love, as understanding tempered pride. And like her Master before her, she could walk among the least of them, and cry."

Miriamme blew out the lamp, and in the darkness I could hear her soft aching cry. I reached out to her, and wrapped myself about her, and together, in oneness, we fell sweetly asleep.

✽✽✽✽✽✽✽✽✽

I lived but another month or so, long enough to find that as he had promised, Jesus tarried not long in his rock hewn-tomb. But my job was done. There were others now to carry on. My son, John, became a leader among the flock that grew now daily in our home. Mighty wonders were occurring, but my skill at politics was no longer needed as it became apparent that Caiaphas no longer found our motley group a threat once our leader was gone. And Miriamme too had found her niche. She now spent all her time counseling, and tending to the homeless, and the sick.

As time went on, I felt his pull stronger and stronger each day. I was just an old man now, my time having gone its way. My home had become a center of his love, and for that I was glad, but increasingly I knew this was a new world, a world in which I played no part.

And so, one beautiful morning as I stood at the top of the stairs, with my Miriamme beckoning me lovingly below, I felt the sudden surge of pain race up my arm and into my heart. I reached out for just a second to the woman I loved so much, who had given me more love than I had ever known... and then it was over.

There, in the light that flooded my being, I found my Master Jesus, with gentle eyes, waiting for me, as he had always done.

✽✽✽✽✽✽✽✽✽

The Memory Ends

And I suppose that if all the other events in Jesus'
life were written, the whole world could hardly
contain the books!

John 21:25

Asher ben Ammi's story was complete.

I sat there, my fingers on the computer keyboard, tears washing down my face. My wife, Trudy, came in and saw me across the room, shoulders shaking as I sobbed uncontrollably. She touched me and I rose from the chair and we walked slowly to the edge of the lake. There, I told her how painful those last few moments had been.

"Asher died," I cried, "and *I felt like it was happening to me.* The pain was excruciating – it crawled up my arm and into my chest – then it was over. It was dark for a moment – then the light came. And there was Jesus. He waited for *me*! He still loved me. I was so relieved that I hadn't disappointed him when I couldn't go to him on the cross. I thought I was a terrible man who hadn't the courage to be with him at the end." I shook my head, and once again was overwhelmed by deep, wracking sobs.

We sat for some time, neither of us said a word. We stared across the placid lake with only the soft hoot of the loon occasionally breaking the quiet that seemed to calm me. Then Trudy touched my face softly. "There's more, isn't there?"

"Yes. There was something I saw in that last moment before the memory faded..." I paused, a bit embarrassed to relate what I had seen. "I know this sounds corny," I apologized, "but the scene was like the classical vision of Jesus in the clouds, a painting by Raphael or some other Renaissance master. Everything went black, then out of nowhere there was the light, a pastel light, and the clouds. He was there Trudy, he was there waiting for me."

I cried again unashamed, while Trudy waited for me to continue. "I went toward Jesus – I couldn't tell if I was walking or floating – and all of a sudden the memory was over. It was as if I had been swallowed in the mist."

I sat down on the grassy hill leading to our little dock, Trudy close to me, and continued. "I have this feeling that Asher really killed himself, not with a knife, of course, but with guilt. Once Jesus was gone, he no longer wanted to live. That's the way it came to me in those last few mental fragments of Asher's life."

Trudy put her arms around me. "That's when I found you."

"Yes, but it's okay," I said, a smile on my face. "You see, Jesus loves me." When I said *me*, I knew that once again, for one last moment, I was *Asher ben Ammi*.

✤✤✤✤✤✤✤✤

Afterword

So many things in the book puzzled me, not the least was the name of Asher ben Ammi. I had no idea what it meant, if anything. In hopes of discovering the truth, Trudy and I went to the Museum of Judaica in Chicago, which contained a library of historical papers dealing with Judaism. The manuscripts and research materials are kept in a low ceilinged room down darkly lit stairs under the museum proper. The place smelled of musty books and crumbling parchment.

A very old Jew sat hunched over a desk littered with books and old papers stacked high all about him. So totally engrossed in his work, he was oblivious to our arrival in his basement tomb. Trudy and I walked up to him, and I cleared my throat to get his attention, saying, "Pardon me, but we would like to find out more about what we saw and heard on a recent visit to Israel, some things we don't understand."

Pleased to be of some assistance, he looked up and said, "I would be happy to help," and with great effort he started to rise from his chair.

"No, please don't get up," I said quickly. "The first question I have only requires you to translate the meaning of a name." I nodded toward Trudy. "My wife and I heard it in Israel and it stuck in our minds. Perhaps you could help us with its significance, if any."

The old man slowly sat again, as if age made the whole world move very slow. He nodded his head wearily. "What is the name?" he asked.

"Asher ben Ammi."

His eyes instantly flashed, and in his voice I heard disbelief and challenge, as if I was purposefully toying or deceiving him. *"You didn't hear that in Israel,"* he snapped.

I stepped back, thinking I might have uttered some obscene word of which I had no knowledge. "Yes we did," I said defensively.

"No you didn't!" His eyes were ignited by the light from the desk lamp. "No! You did not hear that name in Israel."

Now I *had* to know where the name came from. I leaned forward and asked once again. "What does it mean?"

"I'm going to tell you" – he shook his head at us – "but you didn't hear it in Israel, of that I am sure. You wouldn't have heard that name since the time of the second temple. We were defeated by Rome in A.D. 70. That was the end of the Jewish revolt against Rome. The second temple that had been built by Herod was destroyed. The very stones of the temple were hurled down the mountain so that Jews could never again rebuild their hopes for a Messiah."

He looked at us intensely. "Asher was one of the twelve tribes of Israel. The name would have meant, 'Son of the tribe of Asher.' A name of great honor."

He sat down in his chair again, fingers pressed against his eyelids, adding, *"Asher ben Ammi is a very special name."*

Trudy and I left the museum hours later feeling a new sense of identity with this man whose story had been my greatest joy to write. Asher ben Ammi was a man who walked with Jesus 2,000 years ago, a man who loved his teacher more than his own life on earth. A man who offered this final testament to his Master, which now I lovingly give to you:

> *"You may find him anywhere, and everywhere, for truly He lives within your heart. Go within the silence as He has taught you, and find Him there — He waits for you even now.*

✸✸✸✸✸✸✸✸

For those of you that wondered about the letter signed with the symbol **ᎩᏐᏉᎧ** at the beginning of the book, I share with you this last experience.

An unusual thing occurred toward the end of the memory. Shortly before I experienced Asher's death, I rose one morning as always to continue the story as it unfolded, but this morning was to be different.

Instead of the feeling of falling, I was immediately surrounded by a rush of light. There in the light, without form, was his voice — the voice I knew from the beach two years before — it was my teacher and lord, Jesus. His words started tumbling into my mind. This was different, this wasn't Asher experiencing life as I had become accustomed, it was the voice of my original vision, the voice that asked me to give up everything, and sent me to the Holy Land in search of an ancient memory.

I can only tell you my heart sang when I heard it. My spirit leapt with joy. Jesus was once again speaking to me.

Perhaps it is only now that you have read the book, and have a feeling for the truth contained herein, can you accept that perhaps this is truly a very special gift indeed.

These words from my Master were the last he spoke to me.